CW00524941

Edited by: Steve Hendrickson

ISBN-13 978-1-61325-078-5

Printed in USA

Back Cover:
Top:
Adding some cubic inches with a stroker crankshaft has
become a very affordable way to make more horsepower and
torque. Custom stroker crankshafts are available in forged or
more affordable cast iron.

Middle:
Working on a budget means doing a lot of the work yourself.
Iron heads in a performance book? Of course. Many factory
castings work great for budget performance buildups.

Bottom:
It's surprising how much power you can pick up from a simple camshaft upgrade. Chapter 6 is exclusively devoted to
helping you understand camshaft specs and choose the best
cam for your application.

CarTech ®

39966 Grand Avenue
North Branch, MN 55056
Telephone (651) 277-1200 • (800) 551-4754 • Fax: (651) 277-1203
www.cartechbooks.com

Acknowledgments

A book of this magnitude could not be completed without the help of a lot of special friends in the industry. It is with gratitude that I thank Larry and Kim Ofria of Valley Head Service in Northridge, California; Marcie Innes and Rick Mix of Fastline Performance in Simi Valley, California; Mark Jeffrey of Trans Am Racing in Gardena, California; Chris Huff of Coast High Performance in Torrance, California; Bill Sneathen of Sneathen Enterprises in Cape Girardeau, Missouri; John Da Luz of John's Mustangs & Classics in San Diego, California; and John Baechtel of Westech Performance in Mira Loma, California. Each of these people went to bat for this book effort again and again, asking nothing in return except for a chance to be a part of it all.

To all of you, and CarTech President Dave Arnold for asking me to do this book, many thanks.

George Reid
Los Angeles, CA
July 2001

CONTENTS

INTRODUCTION

Enthusiasm for Ford V-8 engines has been high among hotrodders since the 1930s. From those early days and throughout the years following World War II, enthusiasts had a limited choice of flathead V-8s. In 1954, enthusiasts witnessed the dawning of Ford overhead valve V-8 power with Ford's introduction of the "Y-block" family of engines. These engines displaced 239, 272, 292, and 312 cubic inches (ci) over their production life. Though these engines were impressive for their time, a generation of engines to follow in the late 1950s and 1960s would overshadow the Y-block, rendering it obsolete in the performance arena. Lincolns of the period also had a separate Y-block never perceived as a performance engine despite the "Hot Rod Lincoln" image.

FE-SERIES BIG BLOCK

Late in 1957, Ford introduced the FE series of big-block V-8s, which displaced 332, 352, and 361 cubic inches. At the time, few thought of the FE as a big-block engine, simply because there was no Ford small block with which to compare. The great potential of the FE would be realized at race places like Sebring, Riverside, and LeMans, against heavyweight competition from around the world. Ultimately, the FE would be bored and stroked to 427 cubic inches for a whopping 425 factory horsepower at 6000 rpm. This engine would clean Ferrari's clock at LeMans, eclipsing all European egos in the process. Later, in 1968, the 428ci Cobra Jet big block would stand NHRA Super Stock competition on its ear at Pomona, California.

We're convinced the FE-series big block is under-utilized today. Those of you with 1967-69 Mustangs, Cougars, Fairlanes, and Comets with the 390 High-Performance engine may be disappointed at its lackluster performance. However, this author has never forgotten the 1961-62 High Performance with an aggressive solid-lifter camshaft and three Holley carburetors on top. You can wake up that sleeping hydraulic-liftered 390 Hi-Po with some vintage off-the-shelf parts from Ford. With the right parts inside your 335-horse 390, you can spank a 396 Camaro. We point a finger at the 1967-69 390 Hi-Po because it's an engine that never realized its potential from the factory. This book is written to ensure yours does.

SMALL BLOCK

In 1962, Ford introduced the lightweight, graywall iron 90-degree Fairlane V-8, displacing 221 and 260ci. A Texas chicken farmer turned respected racer, Mr. Carroll Shelby, would capitalize on this small block's potential in competition from coast to coast and hemisphere to hemisphere. The name "Cobra" and Ford's nimble small block would travel hand-in-hand for years to come, embarrassing the competition with lightning speed. The rest, as they say, is well-documented history. The Fairlane V-8 would grow to 289ci in 1963, 302ci in 1968, and a raised-deck 351ci Windsor (351W) in 1969, becoming one of the most successful engines ever produced.

Later on, the 302ci small block would evolve into the 5.0L High Output V-8 with roller tappet camming and sequential electronic-fuel injection. In many respects, the 5.0L H.O. has been more trend setting than the old 260 and 289 because it has created a huge following of drag racers bent on winning. The 1979-01 Mustang has been coined the 1955-57 Chevrolet of the new age. Despite any loyalty to Fords, one can't

underestimate the success of the classic Chevrolets. To compare late-model 5.0L Mustangs to such a great classic should tell you something about fuel-injected Mustang power. It's legendary.

335-SERIES SMALL BLOCK

Ford introduced the 351ci Cleveland (351C) small block in 1970, and produced it through 1974. Although the 351C has the same displacement as the 351W, it has little in common with the 351W aside from similar head gasket patterns and a four-inch bore with the same spacing. The 351C sports a heavier block with an entirely different oiling system, cooling system, and timing cover design. Its short production life span of four years makes it less popular today due to the limited availabil-

ity of usable castings. Built correctly, it makes unwieldy amounts of power.

Two spin-offs of the 351C — the 351M (introduced in 1975) and the 400M (introduced in 1972) — offer enthusiasts an abundance of usable cylinder head castings, but their heavy block weight and big-block bellhousing bolt pattern make them less desirable to build.

385-SERIES BIG BLOCK

The 385-series big blocks — those heavyweight 429ci and 460ci luxury car muscle mills of 1968 and beyond — have proven themselves in drag racing competition around the world. In stock form, they remain solid sources of low-end torque. Modified correctly, these engines can spin to 6000 rpm and make more torque than they ever produced in a Lincoln

Ford introduced the FE-series big block late in 1957 as a 1958 model-year engine option. In the beginning, the FE was available in displacements of 332 and 352 cubic inches in Fords and Mercurys. In the Edsel, it was available as a 361. Later Ford would pump the displacement to 390 cubic inches in 1961, 406 in 1962, 427 in 1963, and to 428 cubic inches in 1966. The 428ci Cobra Jet would appear in 1968 as a mid-year surprise.

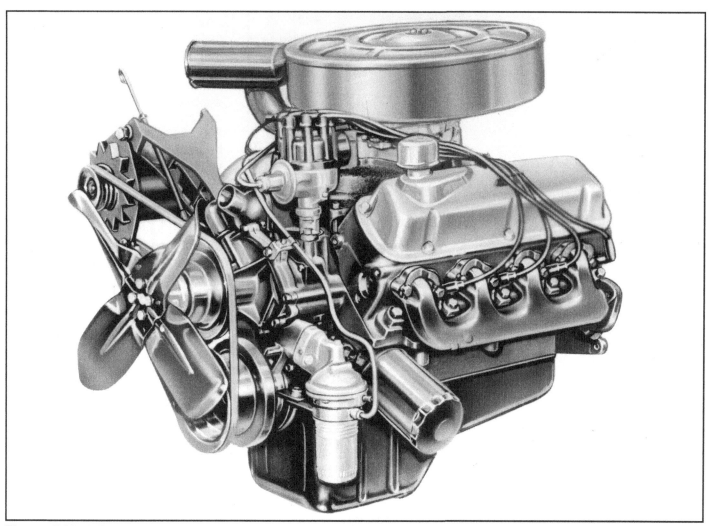

The small-block Ford first appeared in 1962 as the Fairlane V-8, displacing 221 and 260 cubic inches, respectively. This super lightweight V-8 engine evolved to 289 cubic inches in 1963, and to 302 cubic inches in 1968. In 1969, Ford gave the small block four-bolt mains and large-port heads to conceive the Boss 302.

sedan. Because Ford has produced so many 385-series engines over the past 33 years, you can count on plenty of buildable cores for your Ford big-block engine project.

The nice thing about the 429/460 big block is the amount of power you can draw on from these engines without spending a lot of money. They have a super strong bottom end that will tolerate great increases in power without failure, making them one of the best budget engines to build.

We've given you a quick rundown on modern Ford V-8s. The engine you choose depends on budget, vehicle type, and how the vehicle will be used. Bigger isn't always better. Small-block V-8s offer simplicity and lighter weight. Big blocks can give you abundant torque and horsepower, but with the weight penalty.

The 351W small block, introduced for 1969, was a raised-deck version of the popular 221/260/289/302ci V-8. With more stroke came displacement, giving buyers more torque from a lightweight small-block engine.

The 351C, offered from 1970-74, might easily be called a middle block because it is a small block that acts like a big block. It is not a lightweight casting, either. Displacing 351 cubic inches, the Cleveland small block, named for its manufacturing plant, was conceived to accommodate large-port heads that would generate greater power from 351ci. Although the 351C has the same displacement as its sibling the 351W, these engines have little in common from an interchangeability standpoint. You can install Cleveland heads on a 351W block, however.

The 429/460 385-series big block didn't have a performance image when it was introduced in 1968. Today it serves as a Ford performance powerhouse. You can build one of these on a limited budget.

Which small block should you choose? Our natural inclination as performance enthusiasts is to go for displacement in our pursuit of power. However, that's not always the best solution. Ford and Mercury compacts do best with the 221, 260, 289, 302ci family of engines because these engines are the ideal weight for a Falcon, Comet, Mustang, or Cougar. Some of us like the 351W or 351C, but these engines consume too much engine compartment space in Ford and Mercury compacts. It also makes them nose heavy, which adversely affects handling.

The 351W is best for 1969-73 Mustangs and Cougars, and 1966-up Ford and Mercury intermediates because it is weighted and sized for these vehicles. The 351C is ideal for applications where it was installed originally — 1970-74 intermediate and full-sized Fords and Mercurys.

Both FE and 385-series engines enjoy the respect of Ford buffs everywhere. Because FE engines tend to be pricey in terms of parts and services, the 385-series 429 and 460 big blocks make excellent replacements for FE engines. The only hang up is bellhousing and engine mount dimensions, which are different between these big-block families. Displacement tends to be limited to roughly 454ci for the FE big block. This is what gives the 385-series engine family the edge because it can be bored and stroked upwards of 550ci. Knowing as much as you can about your favorite Ford engine family gives you the advantage of knowing which engine to choose, and then how to approach the build up.

This book was conceived and written to help you make the most of your Ford V-8 engine project. We'll show you how to build a powerful Ford V-8 engine on a limited budget. We'll also show you how to build a high-end mill for that more liberal budget, too. Then we're going to share dyno results from ten different engine builds to show you what is possible for your Ford V-8 on a budget.

Thanks for adding this book to your Ford reference library.

CHAPTER 1

ENGINE BUILDING BASICS

While there have been some considerable advances in engine-building technology over the past 30 years, one of the most important lessons we can learn is that it's the small details that can make or break an engine-building project. The two most important details are checking clearances and triple-checking your work. Far too many of us are not attentive enough to detail, and we learn some hard and expensive lessons — when an overlooked rod bolt fails half way down the track, or when a carelessly seated valve keeper escapes at high revs, destroying the piston and cylinder wall below in less than a second. These are the kinds of important details we don't want you to miss during your budget engine build.

Lack of proper planning is another reason for the demise of many an engine project. Wise planning is the most important tool you should use in your project. Before heading off to the speed shop, ask yourself the all-important question, "What do I want from this engine?", then do the plan.

Part of doing the plan is knowing exactly what you can afford, then not giving in to ego and the temptation to spend more than you have. That's the mistake many of us make along the way. We tend to want to impress our peers, the machine shop, and especially the significant other, but these are the wrong reasons to build an engine. Don't build an engine to impress anyone besides yourself because you're the one who has to live with the result. If you've overspent, then you can count on grief when it's time to pay the monthly bills. This is why we stress staying within your budget.

Most of us overbuild our engines. We build more engine than our Ford needs, which costs unnecessary time and money. For example, if you're building a 1965 Mustang and you want it to be the fastest thing around, your first thought might be to build a 351W stroker that displaces 427ci. Future plans include

fuel injection and a supercharger. Just imagine, the power of a big block in a lightweight stallion, but is it more than your Mustang (and your driving skills) can handle? You don't have to worry about impressing us. We've been there, too, and we understand the drawbacks of overbuilding. This is why we're sharing the cold, hard facts of engine building with you — so you don't make the same mistakes.

Too many enthusiasts build more engine than a car can safely handle. When we infuse big-block displacement power into a lightweight Mustang, Falcon, or Fairlane, we're not thinking about the engine and vehicle as a package. Most of us get it backwards. We build a powerful engine, then we wonder how to manage all that power safely. It is better to build the car first, then the engine, because too much power in an unprepared platform can get you maimed or killed. A well-thought-out platform will have good brakes, a handling package, traction enhancement, the right tires and wheels, a rear axle that can take the punishment, and a mature driver who understands all of this.

The goal of this book is to teach you how to build a reliable, affordable engine that will make the power you need. No matter the formula, one basic principle is constant: Performance level is tied directly to budget. The greater the budget and know-how, the faster you will go. You are not going to make a 600-horsepower small block for $2,500. However, you can build a healthy 350-horsepower small block for approximately $2,500 to $3,000 that will serve you reliably. Keep your expectations and planning realistic. Then go work your plan with perseverance.

PLANNING YOUR BUILD

Before you even start to plan, you must decide what you can reasonably spend on your build. Believe it or not, if you do your homework and learn how to do much of the work yourself, you can get into a fresh engine for approximately $2,500. Even if you have never done it before, building an engine is not difficult if you pay close attention to detail. Engine assembly is costly if you farm it out. Machine work is also expensive, but most of us don't have the necessary equipment or the know-how to do it ourselves. Engine assembly boils down to having the right tools and a super clean shop environment. Certain tools, like the torque wrench, piston ring compressor, micrometer, and dial indicator, can be rented locally. You will only need these items for a weekend, which makes them affordable.

TOOLS OF THE TRADE

When you're new to the world of engines, it is easy to get carried away in the tool department. After all, we need all those things to get the job done, right? That first trip to Sears is often like a first trip to the speed shop. You lay down the credit card and come home with a wealth of goodies, but they don't always apply to building an effective engine.

We suggest Sears Craftsman tools because they have a lifetime warranty,

great reputation, and there's a Sears store in nearly every area of the world. The Craftsman warranty is written with no nonsense and no fine print. Bust a socket and Sears will replace it with no questions asked. Strip out a ratchet and Sears will hand you a new one or rebuild your old one. Sears Craftsman tools are the best tool value going. The next best tool value is Husky in the "bang for the buck" department. You can find Husky tools at many home improvement or hardware stores for even less than Craftsman, yet with the same no nonsense lifetime warranty.

Our Beginner's Tool Shopping List is intended to get you started and will last you the rest of your life with care. It is even something you can pass along because, with proper care, it will last several lifetimes. Most of us buy socket sets, but we forget to go for the deep-well sockets, which you will need in the course of an engine build. One other thing to keep in mind, opt for 6-point sockets, not 12-point. A 6-point socket won't strip a bolt head and provides a firm grip. Make sure your socket sets have at least two extensions — one 3-inch and one 7-inch. Spring for the universal adapter as well for easy access. If you can afford it, buy a matching set of 12-point shallow and deep-well sockets because they do have a purpose with some engine applications.

When you're shopping for screwdrivers, hold one in your hand first. You want a screwdriver that feels good in your hand and offers adequate grip comfort and mechanical advantage. If your hand slips around the handle, then it is a poor design. The tip should be super tough steel that will not strip out or break. Go the extra mile and invest wisely now in a screwdriver that will last you a lifetime. Another idea is to buy screwdrivers with bright orange handles for visibility and safety. This lessens the chance of leaving tools where they don't belong.

We push the idea of quality tools because there really is a difference. Inexpensive wrench sets you can buy for around $10 won't get the job done effectively. A low-quality forged or casting will strip out and leave you hanging on a Sunday afternoon when you need it most. With Sears Craftsman (and this

is not a commercial endorsement), Husky, MAC, or Snap-On tools, you get a lifetime warranty that's good for as long as the tool exists — for you, your child, your grandchild, great grandchild, and more. MAC and Snap-On tools tend to be very expensive and available only off a truck at better garages everywhere, which makes Craftsman and Husky a better value and easier to find.

Proper tool care once you've made the investment is what assures you

Beginner's Tools Shopping List

- Set of common- and Phillips-head Screwdrivers

- Set of open/box-end wrenches (1/4", 5/16", 11/32", 3/8", 7/16", 1/2", 9/16", 5/8", 11/16", 3/4", 7/8", 15/16", 1")

- 3/8" drive socket set (3/8", 7/16", 1/2", 9/16", 5/8", 11/16", 3/4")

- 3/8" deep well sockets (3/8", 7/16", 1/2", 9/16", 5/8", 11/16", 3/4")

- 1/2" drive socket set (7/16", 1/2", 9/16", 5/8", 11/16", 3/4", 7/8", 15/16", 1", 1 1/16", 1 1/8", 1 1/4")

- 1/2" drive deep well sockets (7/16", 1/2", 9/16", 5/8", 11/16", 3/4", 7/8", 15/16", 1", 1 1/16", 1 1/8", 1 1/4")

- 1/2" drive breaker bar

- Pliers

- Needle nose pliers

- Diagonal cutting pliers

- C-clip pliers

- Set of Vice Grips (and we mean Vice Grip brand only!)

- Set of punches

- Small and large hammers

- Five-pound sledge hammer

- Torque wrench (optional, but a great investment)

- Drill and bits (spend the money and opt for high-quality bits)

- Putty knife or gasket scraper

- Hack saw (use 24 teeth-inch for best results with metal)

- Magnetic bolt tray

- Large top chest or heavy-duty tool box with drawers

Tools to Rent

These are the tools you're going to use only during an engine build and probably won't need again until the next build.

- Torque wrench
- Piston ring compressor
- Harmonic balancer and puller
- Valve spring compressor
- Freeze lug driver
- Seal driver
- Thread chaser
- Small grinder (if you port your own heads)
- Easy Outs (for broken bolts in blocks and heads)
- Engine hoist
- Engine stand
- Dial indicator

reliability in the future. Keep your tools clean and serviceable. Lubricate ratchets periodically with engine oil or white grease for best results. Drill bits should be sharpened periodically. When you're using a drill, run the bit slow and keep it wet with lubrication while drilling. Drill bits begin to squeak whenever they're dull. Invest in a drill-bit sharpener or find a reliable shop that sharpens drill bits. Most shops that sharpen lawnmower blades and chain saws can sharpen your bits.

It's also important to know when it's time to retire tools. Tools that are not serviceable can be dangerous. A loose hammer head, for example, could rearrange yours or someone else's dental work — or break a window. Cracked sockets, worn wrenches, busted screwdriver handles, stripped ratchets, and other forms of serious tool deterioration are reasons to invest in fresh equipment. It is about your safety and the integrity of your work.

RENTING TOOLS

There are many tools you will only use during an engine build that are expen-

sive. It may be more cost-efficient for you to rent these items. Most shops make rental tools available. Look for the "multi-purpose" in any tool you're thinking about renting. If you expect to use the tool again, it may well be worth the investment to purchase it now. When renting tools, rent only at the time you intend to use them. Don't rent every tool mentioned here at the same time because you're not going to use all of them at the same time.

When renting torque wrenches, keep in mind they are typically either beam or breakaway types. We suggest the breakaway type that "clicks" when the specified torque is reached. Be sure to learn how to properly use a breakaway torque wrench. Ask for instructions when you rent the tool. Keep in mind two things: First, never use a torque wrench to remove a bolt or nut, as you will disturb the calibration. Second, never overtorque a fastener. When you torque a fastener, you are stretching the bolt stock. Too much torque and you stress the fastener. Specified torque readings are there to ensure fastener integrity.

Piston ring compressors are available in different forms. The most common type available to rent is an adjustable type. There is also a ratcheting type that makes piston installation a snap. Custom-sized billet ring compressors are costly and not for the novice.

Harmonic balancer pullers are a borderline rental item. This is something you may use again and again. They don't cost that much to buy, which is what makes them a borderline item. Balancer pullers also make great steering wheel pullers.

There are two basic types of valve spring compressors -- one you use in the shop on a head in the raw (looks like a huge C-clamp) and one you use with the head installed (more like a pry bar used only for ball/stud fulcrum rocker arm applications). For engine rebuilding, you're going to need the C-clamp type. You can sometimes pick these up at a discount house for less than it would cost to rent one for several days.

Freeze plug and seal drivers are one of those borderline items you could use again and again. You an also use a like-sized socket as a driver on the end of an extension. This

saves money, but could damage the socket. Don't be a tool abuser.

Thread chasers are a vital part of any engine build because you want clean threads. Clean threads yield an accurate torque reading when it's time to reassemble the engine. Thread chasing should be performed when the block returns from the machine shop clean, machined, and ready for assembly. Machine shops that are on the ball will have already chased your threads. However, thread chasing is time consuming and machine shops don't generally do this unless asked and paid for the service. If you do it yourself, it's a good idea to chase every bolt hole. When a thread chaser is outside of your budget, use Grade 8 bolts and other fasteners with WD-40 to chase the threads. This may sound crude, but it will save you money and get the job done.

Engine stands are one of those purchase/rent questions because renting can sometimes cost you more than simply buying. Harbor Freight Salvage has some of the best values going at $50 to $100 for a stand. If you're building a heavy big block, don't cut corners here. Invest in a four-legged engine stand for stability and safety. The low-buck $50 stand will not hold up under the weight of a 650-pound big block. You don't even want to think about what happens when an engine stand fails — it's sudden, noisy, and destructive.

The decision to rent or buy tools boils down to how often you will use the tool and how long you will need the tool during your engine build. Any time you're going to need the tool longer than 1 - 3 days, you're probably better off buying. If you have to buy, look on the bright side. You can always loan it to friends or sell it after your engine is finished. Keeping it makes it a useful piece of community property among friends.

KEEP A CLEAN SHOP

We cannot stress enough the importance of keeping a clean, organized shop. Do your engine teardown work where you can catalog everything and keep it in its rightful place. Keep engine parts and fasteners in jars or plastic containers that are labeled. Haul the block, heads, crankshaft, and connecting rods to a machine shop immediately upon disassembly. This avoids any confusion and keeps you rolling. If you cannot afford the machine shop at the time, leave the engine assembled until you are ready. We speak from experience on this one because too much is lost both mentally and physically once the engine is disassembled. Keep disassembling, cleaning, machine work, and assembly as cohesive as possible.

It is always a good idea to keep an engine project organized from planning to completion. Know what you're going to do and when you're going to do it. Then get busy and see your engine project through to completion. Nothing is more discouraging than a disassembled engine that's going nowhere because you didn't have a plan.

PARTS AND SERVICE SOURCES

We live in a day and age when there are more sources for parts and services than ever before. You can order engine kits, cylinder heads, camshaft kits, accessories, ignition and induction systems, etc. and have them on your doorstep within a week in most parts of the country. If time is vital and money is no object, you can have your engine parts within 24 hours.

The objective is to shop wisely and determine which mail order house has earned your business. Don't just shop price, shop service and quality. Price means nothing if you receive poor service or a critical part you found "cheap" fails. Make no mistake, to most companies in the performance parts industry, you're just another "customer number" buying speed equipment. They're all too happy to sell you something even if it's something you don't need and have to return. (Check on restocking fees, which makes every return experience profitable for them and costly for you.) You must be educated about performance parts, who makes them and markets them, and what you can expect once you put down the money.

Being "educated" is knowing all about the company and the components you're ordering. For example, you need a camshaft kit. You need to know who makes the kit, what the specs are (lift, duration, etc.), and how your engine will perform with this camshaft. Vague answers won't help

you. If you cannot get a definitive answer from the mail order house or speed shop about the product, then look elsewhere because they haven't earned your business. It is a competitive marketplace and someone is genuinely interested in your business.

Compatibility is also important to your engine project. You're going to want parts that work well together. Like the camshaft kit we mentioned earlier, matched components are important. Camlobe profile and valve spring pressure must be compatible or you could experience engine damage. Spring pressure that is too great will wipe the camlobe. By the same token, too little valve spring pressure could cause catastrophic failure at high revs because it cannot keep up with an aggressive camshaft profile. This is what we mean by matched components.

Other examples of this concept are manifolds, carburetors, and cylinder heads. If you're installing a set of Edelbrock Victor Jr. race heads (not exactly budget-priced pieces) and you have a Performer RPM intake manifold, the ports will not match because the Victor Jr. heads sport huge ports. The Performer RPM manifold does not.

One other thing to keep in mind is vehicle compatibility when you're ordering parts. If you're ordering a used set of 427 Low-Riser heads from Perogie Enterprises in New Jersey and you're building a '67 Fairlane, you're in for a rude awakening when it's time to install the exhaust headers or manifolds. The 427 Low Riser head will not work on the Fairlane due to exhaust manifold/header clearance issues. You're going to need 1966-69 390, 427, 428 Cobra Jet heads that have four bolt holes around the exhaust ports. This is what we mean by vehicle compatibility.

Reputation is also an important issue when ordering parts. Some of the national mail order speed/performance warehouses have spotty reputations despite their grand size. This is something you have to check out before ordering. Consult with some of the machine shops and engine builders in your area and see what their experiences are with mail order businesses. This is where you will likely get an unbiased answer. As much as we want to trust car magazines, they aren't always

going to give you a straight answer because these mail order houses do a lot of advertising that keeps magazines in business. They're going to refer you to their advertisers regardless of the advertiser's reputation.

One other way of determining reputation is to check out the names of sponsors on the race cars and which cars are coming in as winners. Legitimate, successful racers don't have time for a sponsor who's going to waste their time. Watch successful, long-time racers and see with whom they have long-standing business relationships. This becomes a good indication of who you should be doing business with.

Another source for parts is the beloved salvage yard. Ideally, you will find a local salvage yard that will allow you to look around and scout amidst the rubble. This is important when you're looking for castings and need to inspect numbers and date codes. Yards that don't allow you to look around aren't going to invest the time you would looking for a specific piece. You're going to ask for a specific piece and they're going to bring you something that fits and that's about it. You need a good level of cooperation from a salvage yard or used parts business if you're ever going to be successful.

The important thing to remember about salvage yards is you must get a written guarantee that a part is serviceable. When buying parts like cylinder heads and other engine castings, you want a guarantee that a part is not cracked, warped, or damaged. If the yard isn't willing to give you a guarantee, then move on and find one that will. Reputable yards want your future business and will offer a guarantee.

If you're building a vintage Ford V-8 like the FE big block, 351 Cleveland, or early small block, you'll want to visit a salvage yard that specializes in older Fords. There are few things more frustrating than driving the distance to a modern salvage yard, only to be told they don't have anything "that old". Knowing exactly what you need helps when making a phone call, which can result in solid answers on what's available at a given yard. Because some local jurisdictions penalize and tax salvage yards for keeping older vehicles and parts, finding a specialized yard isn't always easy. Check your yellow pages.

Swap meets are yet another valuable source for parts, but beware. Parts aren't always what they seem at a swap meet. Sometimes illegitimate parts wind up on the vender's tables either knowingly or unknowingly. Pieces like run-of-the-mill nodular iron 289 crankshafts with bogus markings that would lead you to believe they were 289 High Performance crankshafts. Another example would be modified 351C heads being passed off as Boss 302 or Boss 351 heads. An education is your greatest companion when it's time to go shopping the swap meets. Don't be ashamed to take a battery of Ford parts identification books with you to the swap meet, then go shopping. Take plenty of sunscreen, a 360-degree brimmed hat, a note pad, a child's wagon, cash, a camera, and your enthusiasm. Then walk the show and enjoy. Walking a swap meet can be a lot of fun because you never know what you're going to find or who you're going to meet. It's a terrific way to bond with fellow enthusiasts and share stories. You might even learn a new rebuilding trick.

Swap meets can be found in all corners of the United States. The most recognized swap meet is the Carlisle All-Ford Nationals at the Carlisle Fairgrounds in Carlisle, Pennsylvania every June. This show yields a wealth of Ford parts and beautifully restored examples from all over the Eastern United States. California has the Long Beach and Pomona Swap Meets in Los Angeles several times a year. This list of swap meets across the country is vast. Check out local and regional newspapers and auto traders for swap meets in your area.

Another great place to find the parts you need is in the local auto traders and classified ads. Think of the classifieds as a swap meet on paper. Ads can also be found on the internet with a wide variety of potential finds. Like the humble swap meet, the classifieds must be approached carefully and with sound logic. We say this because it is so easy to get excited by a potential find in the classifieds, plunk down the cash, and find out you've been duped by the seller. Sometimes those 427 Low Riser heads wind up being 390-4V heads because we didn't do our homework on

casting numbers. Be careful, do your homework and make a sound decision.

A BUDGET'S SAVING GRACE: ENGINE KITS

Performance Automotive Warehouse (PAW) offers some of the best engine kit packages in the business because they ship you a complete package, including machined components, for as low as $1500 - $2000 depending on the kit (not including shipping). You provide the assembly labor.

PAW engine kits are available as short blocks (without the heads) or long blocks (with the heads). A basic engine kit includes a machined block and components ready for assembly. This means forged pistons with rings, high-quality bearings (cam bearings already installed), nodular iron crankshaft, reconditioned stock connecting rods with new bolts, mild hydraulic flat tappet camshaft (except 5.0L and 5.8L engines with stock roller tappets), a dynamic balanced bottom end, gasket set, and all block plugs installed. PAW long-block kits include reworked heads that get a valve job, new valves, hardened exhaust valve seats, screw-in rocker arm studs, and guide plates (where applicable).

The nice thing about PAW is that you can custom tailor your engine kit. If you want a more aggressive camshaft, look it up and specify the cam when ordering (it typically costs extra to do this). If you want a more ironclad bottom end, you can specify heavy-duty connecting rods or even a steel crankshaft (depending on the engine type). Maybe you're looking to save a few bucks and would like cast or hypereutectic pistons. You can specify these too for a mild street application.

One of the most expensive aspects of any engine build is machine work and balancing. Where you save big with PAW is machine work because it's a mass production thing with them. Because PAW does hundreds of engines every year, you save money on machine work, balancing, and parts. This concept gets you into an engine for less money than if you did it yourself locally.

We suggest the same thing with a PAW engine that we would with an

engine you have machined locally. Check all of the tolerances and thoroughly clean components before assembly. If you must have a local machine shop check the tolerances, then go that extra mile. We stress this because mistakes do get make even with the best shops. Because PAW does produce hundreds of engines annually, there's always the risk of error. Check the cylinder bores, crankshaft journals, line bore, cylinder wall dimensions, decks, and even compression height before following through with final assembly. Before doing any of this, and after, wash the components to remove any stray metal shavings, iron grit, and dirt. All it takes is one stray microscopic piece of debris to ruin an engine. Remember to keep your engine covered, always. Dust in the air settles on vulnerable engine parts no matter how clean your shop is. Dust will score bearings, journals, and cylinder walls.

More upscale to the PAW engine kit is Coast High Performance. This company specializes in Ford V-8 engines, and you can expect personalized service and the very best quality. In the many years that Coast High Performance has been in business, it has never experienced an engine failure due to quality issues. Now that's integrity. Coast High Performance offers the Street Fighter series of stroker engines. These engines bring you greater displacement from the same sized block. The 347 Street Fighter, for example, is a 302 stroked to 347ci. Certainly this stroker package costs more than something you would receive from PAW, but you're getting more -- greater displacement, forged custom pistons, heavy-duty connecting rods, custom crankshaft, precision balancing, special block treatment, roller camshaft, and more.

Coast High Performance prides itself on offering the best engines and kits in the marketplace. A very consistent track record makes a Coast High Performance engine something you can count on. If you're building a late-model 4.6L or 5.4L SOHC or DOHC V-8, Coast now specializes in these Ford engines, too.

One alternative to the engine kits is the crate engine. These are available from Ford Racing Technology and Summit Racing Equipment. Crate engines range from completely rebuilt assemblies to all-new engine packages. Ford Racing Technology offers a wide variety of complete crate engine assemblies. One example is a complete, all-new 5.0L or 5.8L High Output engine assembly ready for installation for under $3000. This is not a bad price when you consider the time and money you save, and the engine arrives with a warranty. How can Ford Racing Technology do this? Mass production overflow. These small-block engine packages are simply excess from new vehicle production.

Crate engines don't always arrive ready for installation, however. If you have an early Ford, those double-sump FOX-body oil pans we find on most Ford crate engines may not always fit your vehicle's crossmember. This means you'll have to source a single front or rear sump oil pan and pick-up when you order the engine. Whenever you go from a late-model double sump to an early-model single pump, you will have to change the dipstick location as well. This means removal and modification of the timing cover to accept the dipstick tube. Then you're going to need to plug the original dipstick tube location.

Accessory mounting can sometimes be an issue as well. Late-model 5.0L and 5.8L crate engines arrive on your doorstep designed for a late-model serpentine belt drive. If you're ordering the engine for your '65 Mustang, you're going to need to swap the timing cover and water pump for those designed for the early 289/302, unless you want a serpentine belt drive. Your early Ford alternator will fit the late-model serpentine belt drive with a simple pulley swap. It's easier than it appears.

A late-model Ford small block (mid-1970s up) does not have the provision for a clutch equalizer shaft. However, your Ford dealer or local salvage yard can help. Bolt-on clutch equalizer shaft brackets are widely available for small-block Fords. Inserts are available for the smog pump injection ports in the cylinder heads. Without these inserts, you get exhaust noise and it becomes impossible to install accessories. The inserts provide a threaded hole for the accessory brackets.

One more issue with crate engines and engine kits, is dynamic balancing. Late-model small blocks have a 50-ounce balance offset which means you will need to use a late-model flywheel or flexplate. The same is true for the harmonic balancer. Earlier 289/302 engines (prior to 1982) have a 28-ounce offset. Use a 28-ounce flywheel or flexplate on a late-model 5.0L V-8 and you will experience extraordinary vibration. Likewise, a late-model flywheel or flexplate on your 289 will have the same effect. Compatibility must always be considered when mixing early and late. This includes radiators and water pumps. Keep in mind where cooling system inlets and outlets are if you're swapping in a late-model engine.

LOW BUCK, NOT CHEAP

If you've picked up this book seeking the super low-buck, $500 engine build up, this book isn't for you because we're not about to recommend foolish judgment. Some of the automotive buff magazines have published articles on how to build an engine for $500. While we hold great respect for the special interest automotive magazines, we cannot recommend the low-buck, $500 engine because those are not built to be long living and reliable. For $500 you'll have to reuse the old pistons with a fresh set of rings and bearings. In the old days we called a low-buck rebuild that included the old pistons an "overhaul" with new rings, bearings, and gaskets. An overhaul was good for the short haul, but not the long haul. We want you to build a budget V-8 for the long haul.

Your objective, even though it will cost more, is to build a budget performance engine designed to last 100,000 to 200,000 miles depending on how you take care of it. To achieve a solid budget performance engine, you're going to need new parts and precision machining where it counts. Machine work on the block, worst case scenario, can cost upwards of $800. What is a worst case scenario? Main bearing saddles must be align bored and honed (quite rare, actually), and block decks that have to be milled (likely). A good block will have a true align bore (main bearing saddles that are straight) and decks that won't have to be milled flush. Your foundation needs to be right from the start.

If you're shopping for an engine, it is wise to source one that hasn't overheated or failed in a serious way (oil starvation, thrown rod, spun bearings, dropped valve). Engines that have overheated can have warped or cracked castings that will be of no value. You

Leave the machine work to professionals with experience. Save money by disassembling and reassembling the engine yourself.

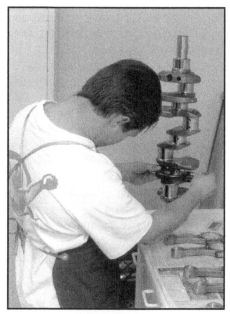

Save money by learning how to do much of an engine build yourself. Even if you have never built an engine before, you can learn how by reading this book. Then apply what you have learned to your engine build. Good advice is also available from your local machine shop.

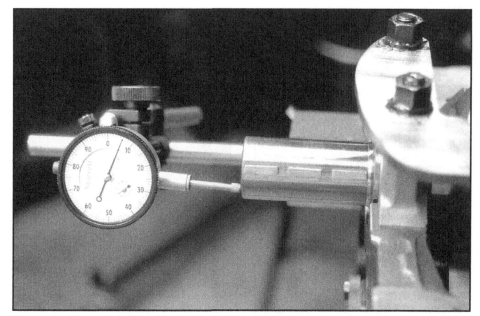

You can rent special tools, like dial indicators and micrometers, from a rental store or a machine shop. Availability varies from area to area.

want an engine that was worn out, but running fine when it was removed from the vehicle. This ensures you have a solid foundation.

A SMART ENGINE

If you are on an entry level budget, you will be spending roughly $1,000 to $2,500 on an engine. In that case you will have to be both thrifty and smart. Spend wisely and get the most for your money. Put emotion and ego on the shelf, and build a smart engine that will not only make adequate power, but will serve you well for thousands of miles. The smartest budget engine is built with the idea that it's going to last 100,000 to 200,000 miles. How do we do this? We do it by planning and building a smart engine. What is a "smart" engine?

To build a smart engine, you must put your money where it matters most. First, spend your money on a healthy bottom end that will stay together for the long haul and through a lot of performance upgrades like a hotter camshaft or deep breathing heads. Resist the temptation to focus your investment on top, at the heads and induction system, when you can always upgrade later. Smart engines are born with strong bottom ends ready for substantial mods. We invest in healthy reconditioned stock

rods or beefy aftermarket I-beam rods like Crower Sportsmans, and we use forged pistons instead of cast. A "smart" engine is ready for superior performance even if our budget isn't.

Begin your plan with a workable block. A small block that has already been bored .030 in. or .040 in. over is a throwaway. Ford 221, 260, 289, 302, and 351W don't perform well with a .060-in. overbore. This much bore raises com-

pression and causes an engine to run hot. It also jeopardizes casting reliability, placing pistons too close to the coolant. Stick with a standard block whenever possible, overboring to the minimum oversize possible. Nearly everyone bores a block to .030-in. oversize the first time around, but did you know that you can opt for a .020-in. overbore? It all hinges on bore taper. Any time cylinder bore taper runs more than .011 in., you

Begin your project with a workable block. Check the block for cracks and irregularities in the casting. Have a machine shop check bore size, line bore, and deck dimensions before going any further.

New 5.0L blocks can be purchased from Ford Racing Technology or Summit Racing Equipment for less than $300. If you're not concerned about authenticity, a new block is your best option.

Mexican Ford blocks are typically identified this way. Instead of, for example, C8OE or C8AE, you will see C8AM. Small blocks have a higher nickel content for strength and wider main bearing caps. If the block is worn out, use the wider main caps on a workable block. Just remember to line bore and hone the mains for trueness, because the line bore changes when you change the caps.

must bore the block at least .020-in. oversize. When it falls under .011 in., you can true up the bores with a hone and run an oversize ring with a standard piston. We discourage the use of old pistons, but we do recommend the use of new standard pistons if bore taper is below .011". This means getting more life out of an old block.

Another option is a new 5.0L (302) block from Ford Racing Technology (formerly Ford Motorsport SVO). These are new machined iron castings direct from Ford's Cleveland foundry and engine plant. They are available for under $300 (shipping not included). You can also opt for a complete crate engine from Ford Racing Technology.

FE-series (352, 360, 390, 427, 428 cubic inch) big blocks can stand a .060-in. overbore, with the exception of the 427. Because budget is our focus, the 427 will not be addressed at length. The 427 sports huge 4.23-in. bores, pushing the FE block to its limits — which means it cannot be bored beyond .030-in. oversize. Some engine builders discourage boring the 427 block to any oversize, opting instead to sleeve the bores, which is costly at around $1,000.

The 429/460ci 385-series big blocks can tolerate substantial overbores

upwards of .060 in. These engines can be found in 1968-78 Lincolns, full-sized Mercurys and Fords, as well as in Ford trucks and vans through the late 1990s. All in all, there are plenty of good, inexpensive used 429/460 blocks available for the budget performance enthusiast. Also, new blocks are available from Ford Racing Technology for under $400.

Another affordable alternative is Mexican Ford blocks, which have a higher nickel content than their U.S. cast counterparts. Mexican blocks are easily identified by the "M" designation in their casting numbers (example, C8AM). Although Mexican castings are relatively inexpensive, they are not plentiful in the United States. Australian castings also have a higher nickel content, a quality which makes them stronger. However, Australian castings are more expensive to come by. Other differences in Australian castings make them less desirable for American builds. The Australian 302, for example, is a destroked 351 Cleveland, not the same 302 available in the U.S. The added weight of the Cleveland blocks makes the 302 displacement pointless for a U.S. build.

INVESTING DOWN UNDER

A healthy bottom end consists of performance-proven parts that will go the distance at work or play. A solid foundation begins with a good crankshaft and rods and pistons that are properly machined and balanced.

You don't always have to invest in expensive connecting rods to get reliability. Ford has produced outstanding stock connecting rods that will go the distance in a warmed-up street engine. We have seen 5.0L engines with stock rods that have tached 7000 rpm with stock rods and ARP bolts. We suggest reconditioning the rods with a big-end resize and new ARP bolts where applicable. If you have the budget for aftermarket rods, we suggest Crower Sportsman or Blue Thunder rods, which are heavy-duty, affordable connecting rods that can take a 6500 to 7500 rpm rev.

When it comes to pistons the budget engine builder has two basic choices: cast and hypereutectic. Cast pistons will take more abuse than they get credit for. Ford's 289 High Performance V-8, for example, was factory fitted with cast pistons and could take a 6000-rpm rev. Ford's 401-horse 390 High Performance V-8 with tri-power had cast pistons with a 6000 rpm redline. Even the legendary 428 Cobra Jet sports cast pistons, which won the NHRA Winternationals in 1968. We offer this information to instill your confidence in a cast piston. Cast pistons will take high revs and stay together depending upon how you use them. They will not tolerate supercharging nor nitrous.

The use of cast pistons should be approached with reality in mind. If you're building a warmed up street engine with a hot cam and stock heads and plan to use an aftermarket induction, cast pistons will serve you well. The budget-minded enthusiast should approach the use of cast pistons with a healthy dose of reality. If you're building a warmed-up street engine with a hot cam, stock heads, and aftermarket induction, cast pistons will serve you well. However, if you're planning an engine yielding more than one horsepower per cubic inch, hypereutectic pistons are a safer choice because they allow you room for upgrades. Hypereutectic pistons are actually silicon-impregnated cast units that are stronger and can stand more abuse than cast piston, and they are cost competitive with cast.

Forged pistons can cost considerably more than cast or hypereutectic. They

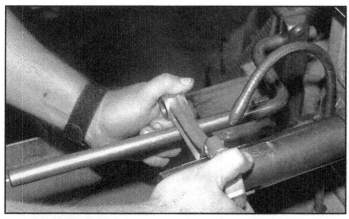 

You can save money by reconditioning a healthy set of connecting rods and installing ARP rod bolts. A set of high-performance connecting rods can cost upwards of $1,200 a set. Aftermarket rods become mandatory when power demands increase.

When you step up the power (or have plans to do so later), aftermarket rods like Blue Thunder or Crower Sportsmans make an excellent first step. These forgings can withstand 7000 rpm.

H-Beam rods (bottom) become mandatory when you are expecting an 8000-rpm engine with heated demands. These extraordinarily strong rods have cap screws and employ free-floating wrist pins.

can take the punishment of high revs and endurance, which makes them prime for high-performance engines. However, cost makes them prohibitive for the budget engine builder. For the builder who plans to upgrade his engine in the future, forged pistons are a must. For example, if you are planning to step up to nitrous oxide injection or the use of a supercharger later on, forged pistons become mandatory for an engine build.

For all the hoopla about forged pistons, they do have a downside. Forged pistons expand differently than cast or hypereutectic. This means they need greater piston-to-cylinder wall clearances to allow for that expansion, which means they're noisy in a cold engine. They "rap" (skirt noise or knock) when cold. Then they warm and expand during operation. If you can live with the cold operating noise, then the forged piston is acceptable for regular street use. Cast and hypereutectic pistons are more forgiving in terms of expansion properties. They just won't tolerate the extremes of abuse a forged piston can take.

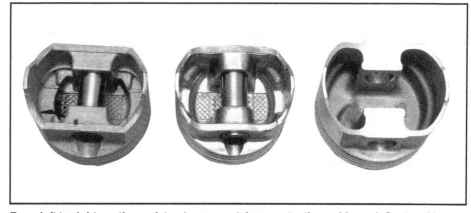

From left to right are three piston types: cast, hypereutectic, and forged. Cast and hypereutectic pistons are fine for warmed-up street engines and can take a 6000-rpm rev. Hypereutectic pistons are cast units with silicon added for strength. Forged pistons are produced by ramming molten aluminum into a die to more tightly compress the molecules for super strength. These are suggested for heavy- to severe-duty applications.

CRANKSHAFT SELECTION

This leads us to the choice of crankshaft: steel or iron. Regardless of what anyone tells you, a cast-iron crankshaft will take revs as high as 8000 rpm when properly prepared and balanced. There was a time when only cast-iron crankshafts were available for small- and big-block Fords alike. In those days, seasoned racers like Jerry Titus and Carroll Shelby spun modified 289 High Performance V-8s to 7800 rpm with cast cranks. Those cast cranks were thoroughly inspected and tested prior to use. Engine

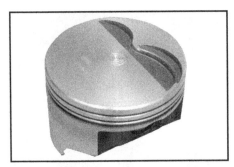

This is a forged small-block piston. Note the two-step valve relief to clear two intake valve sizes: 1.94-in. and 2.02-in.

builders chose the best of the lot when they were planning their mills. Rarely did they break a crank. Most failures were rooted in valvetrain weaknesses.

A steel or billet crank becomes necessary when major forces are exerted on the engine — circle track, drag, and other forms of off-road racing. The occasional driver and weekend play toy does not always need a steel crankshaft, even if you expect to tach seven grand.

REALISTIC EXPECTATIONS

With a healthy bottom end in tow, what about power? How much power is your Ford V-8 going to make for the

buck? You can build a healthy street engine for under $3,000 that will make anywhere from 250 to 400 horsepower, depending on the engine. We stress starting with a healthy bottom end, because making horsepower and torque is meaningless if it's all going to come apart at 6500 rpm. You must have a solid foundation first — and realistic expectations — when it comes to budget and logistics. Be realistic about your budget and capabilities, then work your plan.

When you have the rotating assembly dialed in, you then need to think about camshaft and valvetrain. Power comes from getting the right amounts of air and fuel into the chamber at precisely the right moment. You can have too much camshaft, and you can have too little. Before ordering a camshaft, think about what you have for cylinder heads and pistons. Compression height (piston travel and placement at the top of the bore) dictates cylinder head choice. Cylinder head choice dictates camshaft and valve spring choice. Our message here is simple. Think "package" whenever you're shopping for engine performance parts.

These are both steel billet crankshafts. On the left is a small-block crank; on the right is a big-block crank. The weight difference is considerable. Steel billet cranks are justifiable in severe-duty, high-performance applications. They make little sense for street applications unless you are an avid weekend racer.

A solid cast crank will take a 6000-rpm rev. Limit your machining efforts to a maximum of .020- in./.020-in. undersize rod and main journals.

CHAPTER 2

MAKING POWER

There is plenty of folklore about making power, such as the myth that it's easier to make power with a Chevrolet than with a Ford. Nonsense. The truth is, you can make just as much power with a Ford, for the same amount of money, that you can with a Chevrolet. There is no black magic here — just the simple physics of taking thermal expansion and turning it into rotary motion.

To learn how to make power with a given engine, we have to understand how power is made. How much power an engine makes depends on how much air and fuel we can pump through the engine, and on what we do with that fuel and air mixture during the split second it is in the combustion chambers.

We have to think of an internal combustion engine as an air pump. The more air and fuel we can pump through the cylinders, the more power we're going to make. This is why racers use big carburetors, manifolds, heads, superchargers, turbochargers, and nitrous oxide. Racers understand this air pump theory and

practice it with wreckless abandon, sometimes with catastrophic results. Good racers also understand the "too much of a good thing" theory. Sometimes it can cost you a race, and sometimes it can cost you an engine.

Getting power from our air pump takes getting liberal amounts of air and fuel into the chambers, then squeezing the mixture as hard as we can without damaging the engine. When we raise compression, we increase the power of our mixture yields. It is the intense heat of compression coupled with the ignition system spark that yields the energy from our mixture. The more compression we have, the greater the heat created to ignite the mixture.

However, when there's too much compression and with the resulting heat, the air/fuel mixture can ignite prematurely resulting in preignition and detonation. So we have to achieve the right compression ratio to get the most from the fuel we have. Today's street fuels won't tolerate much over 10.5:1 compression. This

means we have to look elsewhere for answers in the power equation, like more aggressive camshaft profiles, better heads, port work, hotter ignition systems, exhaust headers that breathe better, state-of-the-art intake manifolds and carburetors, even electronic-fuel injection where we never thought of using it before.

The thing to remember about gasoline engines is this: The fuel/air mixture does not explode in the combustion chambers, it "lights off" just like your gas furnace or water heater. Because the mixture is compressed and ignited, it lights off more rapidly. Combustion in a piston engine is just that, a quick fire that sends a flame front across the top of the piston. Under ideal circumstances, the flame front will travel smoothly across the piston dome, yielding heat and pressure that act on the piston and rod to yield rotary motion at the crankshaft. A bad "light off" that originates at two opposing points in the chamber is the preignition or detonation that we mentioned earlier. The opposing light offs collide creating a shock that hammers the piston dome which is the pinging or spark knock we hear under acceleration. The objective is to get a smooth, quick fire, with the flame front traveling in one, smooth direction for maximum power. Call this power management.

Power management is having the right balance of ignition timing, fuel mixture, compression ratio, valve timing events, and even external forces like blower boost or nitrous input. All of these elements have to work together if we're to make productive power. Let's talk about some of the elements we need to make power.

Nitrous oxide or "squeeze" is all the rave today for those looking for quick and easy power (50 to 150 horsepower) on demand. Nitrous makes boatloads of power at the touch of a button, but it can be very harmful to a budget engine that isn't properly prepared. Nitrous will severely damage your pistons and rings if not properly executed. It can and does hammer rod bearings resulting in severe wear. It is also hard on main bearings due to these loads. No matter what the nitrous oxide optimist club will tell you about "laughing gas", nitrous can and does shorten engine life. So don't be drawn into believing it's a magic horsepower pill without consequences. If you're going to be using nitrous oxide, be prepared for its shortcomings. Accept the fact that nitrous will shorten engine life no matter how it is used. The more aggressively you use nitrous, the shorter your engine will live.

It is easy to be lulled into believing a larger carburetor, more aggressive camshaft, and large port heads will make more power but this isn't always true, especially in budget street engines. Induction, camshaft, and heads should always jibe with your performance mission. What's more, you want your engine to survive while making all that power. Your engine build plan needs to include a common sense approach that involves the right selection and packaging of parts for best results.

If you're building a daily driver, you're going to have to compromise to some degree in terms of performance if you want reliability. We compromise because radical engines don't do well for the daily commute. They also struggle to pass a smog check, depending on where you live. Radical camshaft profiles give the engine a rough idle, which can be frustrating in traffic and make it virtually impossible to pass a smog check. Loud mufflers can cause hearing damage and make for an annoying drive. They can also get you a ticket for noise pollution in some communities. A high compression ratio can cause overheating when traffic comes to a stop. Overcarburetion fouls spark plugs and pollutes the air.

This brings us to another valid point -- air pollution. Environmentalists and performance enthusiasts don't get along, but it is our responsibility as performance buffs to build and tune our engines for cleaner emissions and better human health. This doesn't mean you have to go out and buy catalytic converters and a smog pump. It does mean you need to package your induction and ignition systems for optimum emissions performance at the tail pipe. In short, clean up your performance act.

Carburetors play a role in pollution, too. A big, fat 750 or 850cfm Holley carburetor looks good at the drag strip, cruising spot and car show, but it is not a practical carburetor for everyday street use where clean emissions are important. This isn't so much about Holley carburetors as it is about carburetor sizing in general. We want carburetor size and engine mission to be compatible for optimum performance and cleaner emissions.

If you think this clean emissions hoopla is a lot of nonsense, consider the last time you were behind a hopped up vintage musclecar in traffic that made your eyes water. Also remember that if your vehicle falls under the guidelines of state emission laws and smog checks, the law doesn't give you a choice. Clean up your exhaust emissions or face revocation of your license plates in some states.

Building an environmentally responsible engine doesn't have to be difficult either. Carbureted engines are not going to burn as clean as fuel-injected versions. If you can run electronic fuel injection, do so for cleaner air. Do so for your own health and for the sake of others who breathe. If you can't, be conservative in your performance plan and dial in the right size carburetor.

Instead of a 750 or 850cfm carburetor, opt for a 600 or 650cfm carb and see how your engine performs. A carburetor that's too small will become apparent quickly in the absence of torque as RPMs increase. Large carburetors give us more torque on the high end. Smaller carburetors do well on the low end. Choosing the right amount of carburetion is often trial and error.

Keep proper carburetor jetting in mind, too. Jets that are too large will make the engine run rich or "fat", burning the eyes of those who have to follow you. Jets that are too small can be harmful if you're leaning on it hard and lean detonation burns a hole in a piston. Again, fine tune carburetor and jet sizing for best results. Always err on the side of rich versus lean for longer engine life. If you really want to make a lasting impression on the community, go for a smog check each time you make a carb/jet change and see what it does for emissions. Cleaner air is up to all of us.

PLAN FOR POWER

The important question is, how much power do you want your engine to make and what can you afford? We're assuming you have invested wisely in your engine's bottom end with healthy parts and building procedures that will make the most of the engine's potential. For example, if your plan is 450 to 500 horsepower from a small block, stock rods and cast pistons won't cut it. Ask yourself what your engine's bottom end can withstand, and then program the power accordingly. If you are seeking 450 horsepower, then hopefully you have prepared the bottom end with heavy-duty rods and pistons, coupled with building techniques to ensure that your engine survives.

Making power in a Ford engine has everything to do with air flow. A popular misconception suggests that the larger the carburetor, intake, and cylinder head ports, the more power you are going to make. In part, this is true. However, you must ask, where do you want the engine to make power and why? If you are building a drag or circle-track racer, you are going to want the engine to behave differently than you would a street engine. Racing engines make their power in a much higher RPM range than a street engine. A circle-track racing engine is going to make power differently than a drag-racing engine. Torque needs to come on strong from part throttle to full throttle with a circle-track engine. Drag-racing engines need

Have you invested in a strong bottom end? Before you can make real power, you should have a bottom end that can handle the power. All that power is useless if you have a soft bottom end. Failure should never be an option.

to make torque at high revs. In either case, we have to design an engine that delivers power when it's needed or the whole thing is pointless.

A good street engine should make excellent low-end torque, yet be snappy when it's time to wind it tight. With that in mind, which carb, manifold, cylinder heads, and camshaft should you choose? First, you're going to want cylinder heads that are compatible with your pistons. With flat-top pistons (which most street engines should have), the field is wide open. If you're opting for stock cylinder heads, keep combustion chamber size and deck thickness in mind. Nothing beats older Ford cylinder heads for compression, thanks to smaller chambers. An early 289/302 small-block cylinder head with 57cc chambers, coupled with flat-top pistons, will yield a compression ratio of approximately 10.0:1 depending upon

Making power has everything to do with airflow. Where do you want your engine to make power? Where will your engine's power band be most of the time? Large ports, such as those found in this 351C-4V head, have little value in daily street use. Huge ports do their best work at high RPM, where we need lots of airflow. For low-end torque, we need smaller ports where air velocity increases at lower revs, giving us all-important torque where we need it most.

This is a 427 Medium Riser head. For good low-end torque on the street and acceptable high-end torque for weekend racing, your engine should have heads designed to accommodate both venues. For example, these ports provide good airflow at high revs, yet they also offer velocity down low for street use. The 427 High Riser head, for example, with larger ports, would suffer on the street.

Chamber size is also critical to power management. This is the 351C-2V head with open chambers for reduced compression. Closed-wedge chambers, like we see with the 351C-4V head (not pictured), raise the compression to 11.0:1 with flat-top pistons. With today's lower octane fuels, higher compression ratios don't make sense. Always remember the marriage between piston and chamber first, which will prevent unnecessary hardship later.

Swap meets are an excellent source for good, used head castings. Knowing what you are looking for helps. Knowing where you want your engine to make the power is important when choosing the right cylinder head.

compression height. Late-model 302 heads with 64cc chambers will yield less compression, which may mandate shaving the block and head deck surfaces to achieve the 10.0:1 ratio desired. Keep this in mind when shopping cylinder heads.

Stock Ford heads, however, are notorious for port size limitations. Small-block 289/302 heads suffer breathing limitations due to their small port size. Boss 302 or 351C-4V heads don't offer sufficient low-end torque for street use because their ports are too large. Ports that are too small yield velocity, which gives us low-end torque at throttle tip-in. However, small ports do nothing for performance when it's time to open the throttle. Engines struggle to breath through small ports when it's time to rev. This is where we need a compromise between small and large ports. The 351W head is a nice compromise between small and large ports with the 289/302 engines. So is the 351C-2V head. With the latter, we need special pistons from Bush Performance in Ft. Smith, Arkansas.

Whenever you're planning and building an engine, you are an engine designer. You have to do your homework, reaching for the most cylinder head you can find. For those building a 289/302, the best stock head is the 351W with a good port and bowl job for maximum results. The 351W head is an outstanding stock head for breathing real life into a small-block Ford. The best 351W castings to use are 1969-74 because port and chamber size are consistent. From 1975-up, the 351W used a 302 head, which defeats the purpose of a head swap.

If you are building a 351C, 351/400M, the 351C-2V head makes a great street head thanks to smaller ports and open chambers. Smaller ports give us good low-end torque. Open chambers give us improved performance with lower octane fuels. The nice thing about the 351C-2V head is its use on the more common 351 and 400M engines available for a greater number of years than the 351C. With aggressive port work, you can pull a lot of power from the 351C-2V head. A nice alternative to the 351C-2V head is the Australian 351C head, which employs the smaller 351C-2V ports with the 351C-4V closed-wedge chamber. This gives us greater compression with the small port advan-

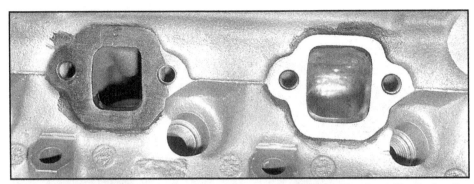

Cylinder head porting is time consuming and expensive. The best "bang for the buck" on a street cylinder head is minor port mods without polishing. Street heads do not need polish work. Open up the ports for best results, or find a good set of used aftermarket heads. Often the latter is cheaper than port work.

tage. A good source for Aussie heads Bush Performance mentioned earlier.

For FE-series 352, 360, and 390ci engines, opt for a 428 or 427 Low/Medium Riser head to improve breathing. When these heads are unavailable (or unaffordable), the early 390 High Performance or Police Interceptor head is a nice compromise over the standard vanilla 352/390. Used Edelbrock Performer 390 heads, normally available at swap meets, are another viable option if you can afford them.

The 429/460 head offers great potential given aggressive port and bowl work. The best head to seek is the 429 Cobra Jet, which can be rather pricey, or the more obscure 429/460 Police Interceptor head available through 1974. Sometimes the Police Interceptor head gets lost in the shuffle of a swap meet and a seller doesn't realize it's true value. You can get a great bargain when that happens. The Police Interceptor head has the same large 2.19" intake and 1.73" exhaust valves as the Cobra Jet head, including the 88cc chambers. Port size runs a tad smaller with the Police Interceptor head, but just imagine what you can do with some port and bowl work.

This brings us to an important point about head porting all across the board. Head porting is an art that takes years of practice and experience to refine. John Da Luz of John's Mustangs & Classics understands how to make the most of a cylinder head. He has experimented with hundreds of Ford cylinder head castings over the years. The result is 289/302 head castings that flow more than 200cfm. John performs the same kind of magic with FE- and 385-series head castings. John's porting techniques have netted flow results on a par after some of the aftermarket heads out

there. If you're building a hot 289/302 engine, John can port you a set of 351W heads that will wake up your low-cube street mill.

John tells us it is a matter of understanding port dynamics. Small-block Fords, for example, suffer not so much from small intake ports, but small exhaust ports that do not scavenge well. They're very restrictive, which hurts scavenging. John's porting technique removes the Thermactor "hump" (most small-block Ford heads have them, even 49-state heads), opens up the port, and smoothes out exhaust flow into the header. A port/gasket match porting job is economical and will yield lots of power. A full-blown porting job and larger valves will give you torque you never dreamed of from a stock head. John's Mustangs & Classics offers enthusiasts three or four basic levels of port work depending on your budget. A simple port/gasket match works wonders.

Porting that makes the most of a head's potential along with larger valves does even more for an engine's performance. Because John is a straight-up guy you can trust, he will advise you on the best course of action for your Ford V-8.

INDUCTION SYSTEM

Induction yields the single greatest potential for gains in power, given proper selection of parts. Contrary to what you may believe, larger isn't always better. A good rule of thumb when selecting a carburetor: For small blocks up to 351 cubic inches, you need no more than 650 cfm; for big blocks up to 460 cubic inches, you need a maximum of 750 cfm. What you're seeking in a street-performance engine is good low- to mid-range torque. That is what counts at the traffic light. You want an engine that pulls strong out of the hole, giving you good twist through the upshifts. An engine that makes power at 6000 rpm doesn't get the job done at street speed. This is where common sense must prevail during induction selection.

For carbureted engines, use a good dual-plane aluminum intake manifold like the Edelbrock Performer or Weiand Stealth. These manifolds offer excellent low-end torque while yielding good high-end response. They also breathe well at 6000 rpm. They do this by employing long intake runners that are also large enough for high RPM use. Long runners give us velocity and volume, which results in excellent low- to mid-range torque. Runner height helps us on the high end.

A single-plane manifold like the Edelbrock Victor Jr. doesn't perform well in street use because it is designed to help an engine gulp huge quantities of air at high RPM. A single-plane manifold doesn't afford our engine the air velocity and appropriate volume it needs at low revs. By "single-plane", we mean there's no crossover or the double-decker design we see with dual-plane manifolds. With a single-plane manifold, air and fuel gather at the plenum and go straight into the intake ports.

You can save money by searching the swap meets for a good, used intake manifold. A used manifold can be media blasted to look like new, and no one will know it's used but you. Manifolds to watch for are the older Edelbrock dual-plane manifolds like the F4B, Streetmaster, and Cobra high risers. These manifolds offer outstanding performance without the "new" price tag. Reproduction Cobra high-rise manifolds are available from Tony D. Branda Mustang & Shelby (Dept. FV8, 1434 East Pleasant Valley Blvd., Altoona, PA 16602, Tel.: 800-458-3477 or 814-942-1869).

Carburetor type and sizing boils down to mission. Street engines do well with a variety of carburetor types. Holley's tried and proven 1850-series carburetors have been in steady use for nearly four decades. Where the Holley falls short is engineering. In four decades, these carburetors haven't kept pace technologically. They're basically the same casting they were in 1965. As a result, they suffer from metering block shortcomings. The Holley is a high-maintenance atomizer, which is the downside of this carburetor for street use. Those once state-of-the-art, easy-to-access fuel bowls still leak all over the intake manifold, especially in an age of corrosive fuel additives that deteriorate cork gaskets. The Holley carburetor is most appropriate for racing applications and the occasional street driver.

Edelbrock and Carter make similar carburetors (based on the Carter AFB and AVS design) that are as time-proven as the Holley. What gives the Edelbrock and Carter carbs the edge is reliability and serviceability. Pop the top off these carburetors for easy jet, needle, and spring swaps, then go test drive. You can access the carburetor's internals without spilling fuel all over the intake manifold.

Ford's factory Autolite 4100-series four-barrel carburetor available in 480 to 600cfm sizes, is the undisputed champ for reliability and serviceability. Despite the harshness of today's gasolines, the 4100 is a stable, reliable performer. For mild to aggressive small blocks and mild big blocks, the 4100 is an outstanding carburetor. Install it, set it, forget it.

Multiple carburetion, like 6V and 8V, is terrific for weekend warriors who like to impress the masses at cruising spots. However, multiple carburetion has little advantage for the daily driver. An engine needs to have a radical attitude before multiple carburetion is of any benefit. By radical, we mean aggressive camming and heads. Mild street engines won't benefit from multiple carburetion because they won't manage the air flow successfully. Generally, they stumble on the excess, foul spark plugs, and lose precious life because oil gets washed off the cylinder walls. If you want multi-carburetion for its looks, there's nothing better for visual stimulation. With tri-power set-ups, you can shut fuel off to the secondary carburetors and enjoy 2V carburetion. The same can be said for the secondary carburetor on an 8V induction package.

CAMSHAFT & VALVETRAIN

One area we don't see addressed often enough is camshaft selection. Great power gains result from proper camshaft selection. In the old days, we opted for a radical street camshaft to get power, but then we lost driveability due to poor idle quality, high fuel consumption, overheating, and other maladies.. Today, camshaft technology has changed for the better. Roller camshafts afford us a more aggressive attitude without suffering driveability shortcomings. The roller design allows for more aggressive ramp-ups and greater lift without adversely affecting valvetrain integrity and idle quality. Dual roller timing sets and gear drives improve valve timing precision.

IGNITION

There has been plenty of black magic in ignition systems over the years and you can gain power with a hot ignition system. Generally the hotter and longer the spark, the more completely we burn the mixture. This is especially true with high compression and supercharged engines that tend to snuff out a mild-mannered spark.

Tight budgets demand simple solutions. The Pertronix Ignitor ignition retrofit is the easiest ignition upgrade there is. Pop the distributor cap, remove the points and condenser, and install the Ignitor. Because we have seen this innovative retrofit dozens of times, we know it works. The Ignitor improves idle quality and throttle response, and it takes 15 minutes to install. There's only one downside to the Ignitor, the Autolite and Motorcraft distributors it is designed for. These distributors employ two bushings

Carburetor Sizing Quick Reference		
Engine Displacement	Recommended Street Carburetor Sizing	Recommended Racing Carburetor Sizing
221-260ci	400-500 cfm	500-600 cfm
289-302ci	480-600 cfm	600-650 cfm
351-400ci	550-650 cfm	600-750 cfm
400-500ci	600-700 cfm	650-850 cfm

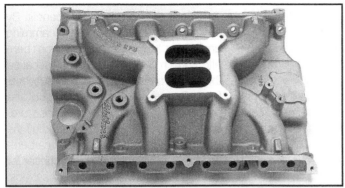
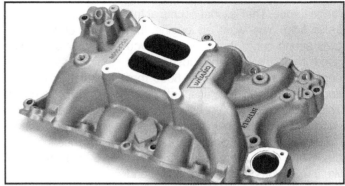

Manifolds like the Edelbrock Performer and Weiand Stealth offer outstanding low- and mid-range torque for street engines.

Don't discount used intake manifolds. Good, used dual-plane manifolds make outstanding induction systems. You can find them for as low as $50 at some swap meets. Media blast them and they look like new. Have them powdercoated in satin clear or gray for best results.

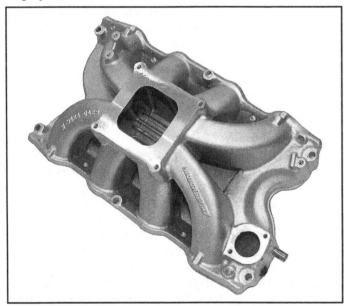

Single-plane manifolds make poor street manifolds. These manifolds do their best work at high- revs on the race track.

Size does matter. Too much carburetor can be as bad as not enough. A quick formula to remember: Small blocks up to 351 cubic inches need a maximum of 650 cfm; big blocks up to 460 cubic inches need a maximum of 750 cfm. When reliability really counts, stick with a stock carburetor. The Autolite 4100 four-barrel carburetor (not shown) is more reliable than the Holley 4160 shown. Bolt a 600 cfm Autolite 4100 atop your small block (289-351ci) or low-displacement big block (up to 390ci) and you'll love the reliability and performance.

that suffer from inadequate lubrication and therefore, they wear out quickly. The Ignitor makes huge allowances for distributor shaft side play. Points won't.

MSD, Mallory, Accel, and Jacobs Electronics all offer the enthusiast high-quality aftermarket ignition systems ranging from distributors to ignition coils and exciter packages. The result is improved performance when you mash the throttle. However, always keep in mind you're not going to see the huge performance gains these companies promise. A hotter, longer spark improves emissions, idle quality, fuel economy, and low-end torque. Anyway you slice or dice it, igni-

tion improvements enhance driveability and reliability. They're worth every penny.

Power management boils down to making the right decisions during the planning stages of your engine build. Planning for power involves consulting the right people and, ultimately, using the right parts when it's time to spin wrenches.

CHAPTER 3

CYLINDER BLOCK

The foundation for an engine build is the cylinder block. Whether it's a small or big block, selecting the proper block for your build is the single greatest decision you will make aside from choosing the right machine shop. Depending on the block you need, selecting the right one can often be a great challenge. For example, a four-bolt main Boss 302 block will be a lot tougher to find than a garden-variety 302 block. Likewise, a 427 cross bolt will be more of a challenge to locate than a 390 block. In this section, we're going to show you how to choose a block. We're also going to

show you how to tear down, inspect, and build one.

When you're shopping for a block, close inspection is vital. The cylinder bores should be sized before you go any further. Small-block Fords should never be bored beyond .040-in. oversize. Some builders have gone to .060-in. oversize, but this is not recommended. If a block is already at .030-in. oversize, you may have .010 in. more to play with. If bore taper is greater than an .011-in. variance, find another block because the only overbore choice then is .060-in. oversize. Three excep-

tions to the small-block overbore limit are the 351C, 351M, and 400M. These blocks can be bored to .060-in. oversize if they have already been bored .030-in. or .040-in. Big blocks, with the exception being the FE-series 427, can be bored to .060" oversize. The 427's limit is .030" oversize, and this is marginal.

While you're shopping for blocks, we suggest having the block sonic tested for cracking and other irregularities. Sonic testing finds irregularities in the casting the human eye cannot see. Some Ford blocks, such as the 351C, 351M, and 400M, are notorious for

Your initial block inspection should reveal obvious defects like cracks, damaged threads, damage to the cast iron or aluminum, scratched or gouged lifter and cylinder bores, flawed decks, welds in the casting, chipped or broken cylinder skirts, etc. Close inspection is important before working your plan.

cracking. Cracking is hard to see even with an antiseptic casting. Sonic testing can be expensive, but it beats the costly mistake of cleaning and machining a block only to discover it is cracked later.

Some block cracking can be repaired via welding or JB Weld. JB Weld is a two-part catalyzed product that works well with cracked cast iron. Properly mixed and cured, it will last the life of any engine block. For JB Weld to work effectively, you need a clean surface and a crack that has been carefully stop drilled at each end. Just a small 1/16-inch stop drill hole at each end slows and stops cracking. Then weld or JB Weld the crack. We suggest against the use of JB Weld on the cylinder walls and decks where stresses can be extreme. Your machine shop will know best on what call to make on repair. Some blocks are cracked beyond repair.

When you're putting together a good formula for a block, sometimes you have to opt for different main caps for a stronger build. For example, you can take the main bearing caps from a 289 High Performance block that is beyond salvage and use them on a standard 289/302 block. You can also use main bearing caps from a Mexican block 289/302 for the same purpose because they're wider and heavier. Along this same thought is the 351C block. You can convert a 351C two-bolt main block to four-bolt mains so long as you have four-bolt main caps from a trashed four-bolt main block. We do this by drilling and tapping the two-bolt main block for four-bolt mains. In the raw, the two-bolt

and four-bolt main 351C blocks are basically the same casting.

Main bearing saddle trueness is another important issue facing the budget engine builder. The alignment of the main bearing saddles is rarely a cause for concern during an engine rebuild. Align boring and honing the main bearing saddles can be expensive. But it's sound judgment. It would be wise for you to have a machine shop check the line bore for proper alignment before going any further. If the block needs to be align bored and honed, it is well worth the cost in terms of increased engine life because it gives the crankshaft a true foundation. Distorted main bearing saddle alignment puts undue stress on the crankshaft, which directly affects wear and tear. The stressed crankshaft alters connecting rod side clearances and puts stress on the main bearings. This can result in shortened engine life due to abnormal wear patterns.

With bore size and line bore out of the way, it is a good idea to check the block for cracks, obstructed water jackets and oil galleries, and other problems. Like we said earlier, cracking is something you don't want to find after the machine work is finished or the engine is assembled. Finding it early in the game is crucial. Magnafluxing and sonic testing are two means of checking for cracks. Magnafluxing is a simple test easily accomplished by a machine shop. We set up a magnetic field around the suspected area using an electromagnet, then we sprinkle iron powder over the area. Iron particles will collect at the crack, making it easy to see.

Spot checking is yet another means of crack detection. With spot checking, we use a dye and a powder developer to "spot check" cracks. The nice thing about spot checking is the ability to use it on aluminum castings as well as iron. Magnafluxing cannot be used on aluminum castings.

The most common cracking areas are block decks and main bearing webs because these areas are subject to high stress. Check these areas closely and take your time. Block decks become stressed from cylinder head bolt torque plus the high heat and pressure that take place in this area. Main bearing webs are also placed under great stress from bolt/stud torque, plus the horrific loads this area experiences. Use every means available to ensure you've found a solid block.

Obstructed coolant passages have created more than their share of headaches for engine builders. Mass engine rebuilders are sometimes guilty of knocking old freeze plugs into the water jackets to speed disassembly. Unfortunately, whoever gets this engine after the fact must deal with overheating issues because those freeze plugs knocked into the jacket obstruct coolant flow and heat dissipation. During disassembly, take a bright light and inspect cooling passages (water jackets) for any obstructions and corrosion. Passages between the heads and block sometimes become clogged with rust and iron particles. Make sure these passages are clear.

Oil galleries can become clogged with sludge, metal particles, and nylon, which starves important moving parts of oil. We mention "nylon" because failed timing sets shed nylon and aluminum particles into the oil pan clogging the pick-up and oil galleries. What's more, these particles find their way to the main, rod, and cam bearings causing excessive journal wear and engine failure. This is why close inspection of oil galleries is vital to any engine build. You're going to need a long wire brush, solvent, and water under pressure to ensure all passages are sanitary. If this seems excessive, consider the cost of engine failure and having to do this all over again.

Another area we rarely see addressed is lifter bores, but lifter bore side clearances are vital to oil control and proper lifter function. Lifter bores should be inspected for scratches and nicks, then honed as necessary. Engines that have been sitting for a long

The fate of an engine project begins here, with the bare block. First, measure the bore diameter to determine size. A standard bore with less than .011 in. of taper from top to bottom can be honed and fitted with a standard size piston. More than .011 in. of taper calls for a .020-in. or .030-in. oversize. Small blocks should never be bored any greater than .040-in. oversize. Big blocks can go to .060-in. oversize, except the 427 FE.

time often experience ceased lifters that become welded to the bores. We suggest extreme caution removing the lifters because you can permanently damage the bores. Then inspect the lifter bore for scoring, nicks, and other damage. Ceased lifters can be worked loose with WD-40 (a good soaking) and a pair of vice grips. Lifter bore side clearances should be checked using a new lifter as a reference. Side clearances should be 0.0005 to 0.0020". You may also use a small dial-bore gauge or micrometer to check lifter bore size. Check the bore diameter, then lifter diameter to determine clearance. Remember, all lifter bores should be checked because all wear differently.

BLOCK & CASTING IDENTIFICATION

Ford makes it easy for enthusiasts to identify corporate castings. Please understand that Ford casting numbers aren't always the same as part or engineering numbers. Identifying a casting is a matter of knowing what Ford part and casting numbers mean. Here's what you can expect to see.

It's easy to identify Ford castings once you understand the system because there's not only a casting number, but a casting date code that tells you exactly when the piece was cast. Not only that, a date code is stamped in the piece which tells the date of manufacture. With these two date codes, we know when the piece was cast and when it was ultimately manufactured.

Ford part numbers can be found in the Ford Master Parts Catalog on microfilm at your Ford dealer or in one of those 900-pound parts catalogs from the good old days. Because

Ford has discontinued a great many parts for vintage Fords, these part numbers don't always exist in present day dealer micro films. This is called "NR" or "not replaced" which means it isn't available from Ford any longer. However, casting numbers on parts tell us a lot about the piece.

DATE CODES

Date codes can be found two ways in Ford castings. When the four-character date code is cast into the piece, this indicates when the piece was cast at the foundry. When it is stamped into the piece, this indicates the date of manufacture.

Another area of interest to Ford buffs is where the piece was cast or forged. With Ford engines, we've seen three foundry identification marks. A "C" circled around an "F" indicates the Cleveland Iron Foundry. "DIF" indicates Dearborn Iron Foundry. "WF" or "WIF" indicates Windsor Iron Foundry. Single and double-digit numbers typically indicate cavity numbers in the mold.

CHOOSING A BLOCK

Now that you understand what to look for in a block, which block should you choose? Based on long-time experience with Ford engine castings, this

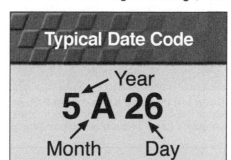

Typical Date Code

Year

5 A 26

Month   Day

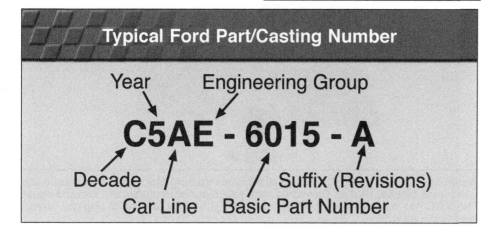

Typical Ford Part/Casting Number

Year   Engineering Group

C5AE - 6015 - A

Decade   Suffix (Revisions)
       Car Line   Basic Part Number

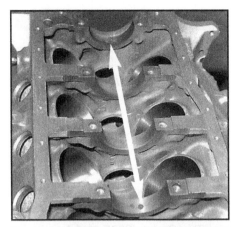

The line bore represents the main bearing saddles in the block. Any reputable machine shop can check a block for proper alignment of the line bore. Most of the time the line bore will be fine. Improper line bore calls for boring or honing. Whenever main bearing caps are replaced, the line bore must be checked and corrected with boring, honing, or both.

Block identification is important. All Ford castings will have a casting number (not always the same as the part number) and a date code (which indicates the date the piece was cast). This Ford casting number indicates a 1969-70 351W block. The date code of "0H14" tells us it was cast August 14, 1970.

Choosing the correct block goes beyond part and casting numbers. Watch for important details like accessory mounting bosses, bellhousing bolt patterns, and provisions for hydraulic lifters or roller tappets. A mechanical lifter block, for example, will not accommodate hydraulic lifters. Another example is found in an early small block which will not accommodate the serpentine belt drive with smog pump.

Most FE blocks have a "352" cast as shown. This does not always mean that you have found a 352 block. Even 427 blocks had a "352" cast in the left front and in the lifter valley.

author has observations worthy of note.

When you're searching for a 221 or 260 block, selection is quite limited because these engines were produced from 1962-64. There aren't that many survivors, nor did Ford produce many variations. The same is true for the 289 produced from 1963-67. The 302, with castings first appearing in mid-1967,

Ford small blocks cast in Mexico are desirable because they have a higher nickel content and wider main bearing caps. These blocks are identifiable at a glance because they have bosses protruding from the casting on each side at the front. They also have a Mexican Ford casting number like C6AM or C8AM, along with the casting date code.

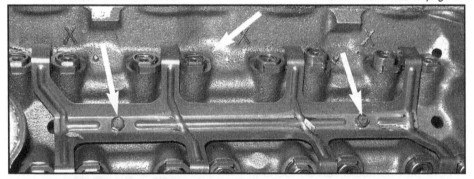

If you are building a late-model 5.0L or 5.8L engine, you should seek a roller block, identifiable by its factory spider bosses and shorter lifter bores. Stick with your vehicle's generation block whenever possible.

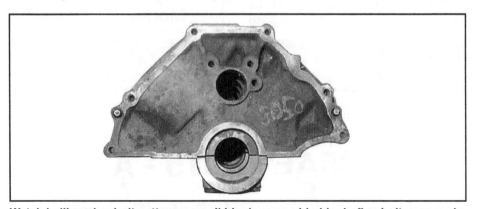

Watch bellhousing bolt patterns: small block versus big block; five-bolt versus six-bolt (small blocks). Not all Cleveland family (335-series) engines are created equal. The 351C has a small-block bolt pattern while the 351M and 400M engines have a big-block pattern.

has been in steady production for more than 30 years. The best castings were produced between 1967 and the early 1970s. Block casting quality became quite poor from 1975-84. Only a personal observation, but 1975-84 302 blocks are the ones to avoid due to cracking issues and sloppy workmanship. This period is infamous for ugly castings you'd like to hide with accessories and layers of paint.

Beginning in late 1984 with the roller blocks, 302 block casting quality improved in every respect. The downside to this is, of course, lighter, thinner castings if you're paranoid about that sort of thing. The up side is better casting techniques that have resulted in a stronger block. The 5.0L engine has an excellent reputation for durability which includes block casting quality. This block has been in regular production since late 1984 which means plenty of buildable cores.

The quality story remains the same for 351W blocks produced between 1975 and 1984. Iron casting integrity just wasn't up to par during those years. Again, these are the

Continued on page 33

Small-Block Engine Block Information

(Bold Indicates High Performance)

Displacement/ Years Available	Ford Casting Number (6015)	Ford Part Number (6015)	Bore Size	Deck Height	Other Information
221ci 1962-63	C2OE-G	C4OZ-B	3.50"	8.206"	Five-bolt bellhousing
221ci 1962-63	C3OE-A	C4OZ-B	3.50"	8.206"	Five-bolt bellhousing
260ci 1962-64	C3OE-B	C4OZ-B	3.80"	8.206"	Five-bolt bellhousing
260ci 1962-64	C3OE-C	C4OZ-B	3.80"	8.206"	Five-bolt bellhousing
260ci 1962-64	C4OE-B	C4OZ-B	3.80"	8.206"	Five-bolt bellhousing
260ci 1962-64	C4OE-D	C4OZ-B	3.80"	8.206"	Five-bolt bellhousing
260ci 1962-64	C4OE-E	C4OZ-B	3.80"	8.206"	Five-bolt bellhousing
289ci 1963-64	C3AE-N	C4AZ-B	4.00"	8.206"	Five-bolt bellhousing
289ci 1963-64	C4OE-C	C4AZ-B	4.00"	8.206"	Five-bolt bellhousing
289ci 1963-64	C4OE-F	C4AZ-B	4.00"	8.206"	Five-bolt bellhousing
289ci 1963-64	C4AE	C4AZ-B	4.00"	8.206"	Five-bolt bellhousing
289ci 1963-64	C4DE	C4AZ-B	4.00"	8.206"	Five-bolt bellhousing
289ci 1963-64 **High Performance**	**C3OE-B**	**C4OZ-E**	4.00"	8.206"	Five-bolt bellhousing
289ci 1963-64 **High Performance**	**C4OE-B**	**C4OZ-E**	4.00"	8.206"	Five-bolt bellhousing
289ci 1965-67	C5AE-E C5OZ-D C7OZ-C	C5AZ-E	4.00"	8.206"	Six-bolt bellhousing
289ci 1965-67	C5OE-C C5OZ-D C7OZ-C	C5AZ-E	4.00"	8.206"	Six-bolt bellhousing
289ci 1965-67	C6AE-C C5OZ-D C7OZ-C	C5AZ-E	4.00"	8.206"	Six-bolt bellhousing
289ci 1965-67 **High Performance**	**C5AE-E**	**C5OZ-D**	4.00"	8.206"	Six-bolt bellhousing
302ci 1968-69	C8OE-A D2OZ-C D1ZZ-C	D1TZ-E	4.00"	8.206"	Extended cylinder skirts "302" in valley
302ci 1968	C8TE-B	D1TZ-E	4.00"	8.206"	Truck block
302ci 1969	C9TE-C	D1TZ-E	4.00"	8.206"	Truck block
302ci 1970-74	D1OE-AA D2OZ-C D1ZZ-C	D1TZ-E	4.00"	8.206"	8.229" deck height in 1973-76
302ci 1971-74	D1TE-AA D2OZ-C D1ZZ-C	D1TZ-E	4.00"	8.206"	Truck block
302ci 1974	D4DE-AA		4.00"	8.206"	8.229" deck height in 1973-76
302ci 1975-81	D5ZY-AA		4.00"	8.206"	8.229" deck height in 1973-76
302ci 1975-77	D5ZY-AA		4.00"	8.206"	8.229" deck height in 1973-76
351W 1969-70	C9OE-B D1AZ-E	C9OZ-B	4.00"	9.480"	
351W 1971-74	D2AE-BA D1AZ-E	C9OZ-B	4.00"	9.480"	9.503" deck height in 1974
351W 1971-74	D4AE-AA D1AZ-E	C9OZ-B	4.00"	9.480"	9.503" deck height in 1974
351W 1975-8	D4AE-DA D1AZ-E	C9OZ-B	4.00"	9.503"	
302ci 1969-70 **Boss 302**	**C8FE**	**D1ZZ-B** **D1ZZ-C**	4.00"	8.209"	302 Tunnel-Port block
302ci 1969-70 **Boss 302**	**C9ZE**	**D1ZZ-B** **D1ZZ-C**	4.00"	8.209"	
302ci 1969-70 **Boss 302**	**D0ZE-B**	**D1ZZ-B** **D1ZZ-C**	4.00"	8.209"	
351C 1970-71	D0AE-A	D0AZ-D	4.00"	9.206"	2-bolt main block
351C 1970-71	D0AE-C	D0AZ-D	4.00"	9.206"	2-bolt main block
351C 1970-71	D0AE-E	D0AZ-D	4.00"	9.206"	2-bolt main block
351C 1970-71	D0AE-G	D0AZ-D	4.00"	9.206"	2-bolt main block

Small-Block Engine Block Information Continued

351C 1970-71	D0AE-J	D0AZ-D	4.00"	9.206"	2-bolt main block
351C 1970-71	D0AE-L	D0AZ-D	4.00"	9.206"	2-bolt main block
351C 1972-74	D2AE-DA	D0AZ-D	4.00"	9.206"	2-bolt main block
351C Australian		**D6HM-L**	4.00"	9.206"	
351C 1971	**D0AE-B**		4.00"	9.206"	4-bolt main block
	D0AE-D				
	D0AE-F				
	D0AE-H				
351C 1971 **Boss 351**	**D1ZE-A** **D1ZE-B**	D1ZZ-D	4.00"	9.206"	4-bolt main block
351C 1971-74 **Cobra Jet**	**D2AE-CA**	**D1ZZ-A** **D3ZZ-A**	4.00"	9.206"	
351C 1972 **High Output**	**D2AE-EA**	D1ZZ-D	4.00"	9.206"	4-bolt main block

FE Big-Block Engine Block Information

(Bold Indicates High Performance)

Displacement/ Years Available	Ford Casting Number (6015)	Ford Part Number (6015)	Bore Size	Deck Height	Other Information
332ci 1958		EDC	4.00"		Solid Lifter Block
332ci 1958		575063	4.00"		Hydraulic Lifter Block
332ci 1958-59		5751091	4.00"		Hydraulic Lifter Block
332ci 1959		B9AE-B	4.00"		Hydraulic Lifter Block
352ci 1958		EDC	4.00"	.046 - .066"	Solid Lifter Block
352ci 1958		575063	4.00"	.046 - .066"	Hydraulic Lifter Block
352ci 1958-59		5751091	4.00"	.046 - .066"	Hydraulic Lifter Block
352ci 1959-60		B9AE-B	4.00"	.046 - .066"	Hydraulic Lifter Block
352ci 1960 **High Performance**		EDC-B	4.00"	.036 - .056"	Solid Lifter Block
352ci 1960 **High Performance**		EDC-C	4.00"	.036 - .056"	Solid Lifter Block
352ci 1961-62		C1AE-G	4.00"	.046 - .066"	Hydraulic Lifter Block
352ci 1963		C3AE-A	4.00"	.046 - .066"	Hydraulic Lifter Block
352ci 1963		C3AE-F	4.00"	.046 - .066"	Hydraulic Lifter Block
352ci 1964		C3AE-G	4.00"	.046 - .066"	Hydraulic Lifter Block
352ci 1964		C4AE-A	4.00"	.046 - .066"	Hydraulic Lifter Block
352ci 1965		C5AE-C	4.00"	.046 - .066"	Hydraulic Lifter Block
352ci 1966		C6TE-C	4.00"	.046 - .066"	Hydraulic Lifter Truck Block
352ci 1966		C6TE-L	4.00"	.046 - .066"	Hydraulic Lifter Truck Block
352ci 1966-67		C6ME-A	4.00"	.046 - .066"	Hydraulic Lifter Block
352ci 1967		C7AE	4.00"	.046 - .066"	Hydraulic Lifter Block
360ci 1968-76		C6ME	4.05"	.046 - .066"	Hydraulic Lifter Block Truck Block
360ci 1968-76		C6ME-A	4.05"	.046 - .066"	Hydraulic Lifter Block Truck Block
360ci 1968-76		C8AE-A	4.05"	.046 - .066"	Hydraulic Lifter Block Truck Block
360ci 1968-76		C8AE-C	4.05"	.046 - .066"	Hydraulic Lifter Block Truck Block
360ci 1968-76		C8AE-E	4.05"	.046 - .066"	Hydraulic Lifter Block Truck Block
360ci 1968-76		D3TE	4.05"	.046 - .066"	Hydraulic Lifter Block Truck Block/Heavy Duty
360ci 1973-76		D3TE-1	4.05"	.046 - .066"	Hydraulic Lifter Block Truck Block
360ci 1973-76		D3TE-AC	4.05"	.046 - .066"	Hydraulic Lifter Block Truck Block/Heavy Duty
360ci 1973-76		D3TE-HA	4.05"	.046 - .066"	Hydraulic Lifter Block Truck Block/Heavy Duty
360ci 1974-76		D4TE-AC	4.05"	.046 - .066"	Hydraulic Lifter Block Truck Block/Heavy Duty

(Bold Indicates High Performance)

Displacement/ Years Available	Ford Casting Number (6015)	Ford Part Number (6015)	Bore Size	Deck Height	Other Information
360ci 1968-76		D7TE-BA	4.05"	.046 - .066"	Service Block
361ci 1958-59 Edsel Only		EDC	4.05"	.046 - .066"	Solid Lifter Block
390ci 1961-62		C1AE-C	4.05"	.010 - .030"	Hydraulic Lifter Block
390ci 1961-62		C1AE-G	4.05"	.010 - .030"	Hydraulic Lifter Block
390ci 1961 **High Performance**		C1AE-V	4.05"	.010 - .030"	Solid Lifter Block
390ci 1962 **High Performance**		C2AE-BC	4.05"	.010 - .030"	Solid Lifter Block
390ci 1962 **High Performance**		C2AE-BE	4.05"	.010 - .030"	Solid Lifter Block
390ci 1962 **High Performance**		C2AE-BR	4.05"	.010 - .030"	Solid Lifter Block
390ci 1962 **High Performance**		C2AE-BS	4.05"	.010 - .030"	Solid Lifter Block
390ci 1962		C2SE	4.05"	.010 - .030"	Hydraulic Lifter Block
390ci 1962		C3SE-A	4.05"	.010 - .030"	Hydraulic Lifter Block
390ci 1963 **Police Interceptor**		C3ME-B	4.05"	.010 - .030"	Solid Lifter Block
390ci 1963 **Police Interceptor**		C3AE-KY	4.05"	.010 - .030"	Solid Lifter Block
390ci 1963		C3AE-AY	4.05"	.010 - .030"	Hydraulic Lifter Block
390ci 1964		C4AE-D		.010 - .030"	Hydraulic Lifter Block
390ci 1964 **Police Interceptor**		C4AE-F	4.05"		Solid Lifter Block
390ci 1964		C4AE-D		.010 - .030"	
390ci 1965		C5AE-A	4.05"	.010 - .030"	Hydraulic Lifter Block
390ci 1965 **Police Interceptor**		C5AE-B	4.05"	.010 - .030"	Solid Lifter Block
390ci 1966		C6ME-A	4.05"	.010 - .030"	Hydraulic Lifter Block
390ci 1968		C8AE-A	4.05"	.010 - .030"	Hydraulic Lifter Block
390ci 1968		C8AE-C	4.05"	.010 - .030"	Hydraulic Lifter Block
390ci 1968		C8AE-E	4.05"	.010 - .030"	Hydraulic Lifter Block
390ci 1973		D3TE	4.05"	.010 - .030"	Hydraulic Lifter Truck Block
390ci 1973		D3TE-AC	4.05"	.010 - .030"	Hydraulic Lifter Truck Block
390ci 1973		D3TE-HA	4.05"	.010 - .030"	Hydraulic Lifter Truck Block
390ci 1974		D4TE-AC	4.05"	.010 - .030"	Hydraulic Lifter Truck Block
390ci 1976		D7TE-BA	4.05"	.010 - .030"	Service Block
406ci 1962 **High Performance**		C2AE-J	4.13"	.045 - .065"	Solid Lifter Block
406ci 1962 **High Performance**		C2AE-K	4.13"	.045 - .065"	Solid Lifter Block
406ci 1962 **High Performance**		C2AE-V	4.13"	.045 - .065"	Solid Lifter Block
406ci 1962-63 **High Performance**		C2AE-BD	4.13"	.045 - .065"	Solid Lifter Block Cross-Bolted Main Caps
406ci 1963 **High Performance**		C3AE-D	4.13"	.045 - .065"	Solid Lifter Block Can Be Converted To Cross-Bolted Mains
406ci 1963 **High Performance**		C3AE-V	4.13"	.045 - .065"	Solid Lifter Block Can Be Converted To Cross-Bolted Mains
410ci 1966-67		C6ME	4.05"	.015"	
410ci 1966-67		C6ME-A	4.05"	.015"	
427ci 1963 **High Performance**		C3AE-M	4.23"	.035"	
427ci 1963 **High Performance**		C3AE-AB	4.23"	.035"	
427ci 1963 **High Performance**		C3AE-Z	4.23"	.035"	
427ci 1964 **High Performance**		C4AE	4.23"	.035"	
427ci 1964 **High Performance**		C4AE-A	4.23"	.035"	

FE Big-Block Engine Block Information Continued

(Bold Indicates High Performance)

Displacement/ Years Available	Ford Casting Number (6015)	Ford Part Number (6015)	Bore Size	Deck Height	Other Information
427ci 1965 **High Performance**		C5AE-A	4.23"	.035"	
427ci 1965 **High Performance**		C5AE-E	4.23"	.035"	
427ci 1965 **High Performance**		C5AE-D	4.23"	.035"	
427ci 1965-66 **High Performance**		C5AE-H	4.23"	.035"	Side Oiler
427ci 1965-66 **High Performance**		C6AE-B	4.23"	.035"	Side Oiler
427ci 1966 **High Performance**		C6AE-C	4.23"	.035"	Side Oiler
427ci 1966-67 **High Performance**		C6AE-D	4.23"	.035"	Side Oiler
427ci 1967 **High Performance**		C7AE-A	4.23"	.035"	Side Oiler
427ci 1965-66 **High Performance**		C5JE-D		.035"	Industrial
427ci 1965-66 **High Performance**		C6JE-B	4.23"	.035"	Marine Use
427ci 1965-66 **High Performance**		C7JE-E	4.23"	.035"	Industrial
427ci 1965-66 **High Performance**		C7JE-A	4.23"	.035"	Marine Use
427ci 1968 **High Performance**		C8AE-A	4.23"	.035"	Hydraulic Lifter Block Side Oiler
427ci 1968 **High Performance**		C8AE-B	4.23"	.035"	Hydraulic Lifter Block Side Oiler
427ci 1968 **High Performance**		C8AE-H	4.23"	.035"	Hydraulic Lifter Block Side Oiler
428ci 1966-67		C6AE-A	4.13"	.015"	
428ci 1966 **Police Interceptor**		C6AE-B	4.13"	.015"	Solid Lifter Block
428ci 1966 **Police Interceptor**		C6AE-F	4.13"	.015"	Solid Lifter Block
428ci 1966-68		C6ME	4.13"	.015"	
428ci 1966-68		C6ME-A	4.13"	.015"	
428ci 1967-68		C7ME	4.13"	.015"	
428ci 1967-68		C7ME-A	4.13"	.015"	
428ci 1968-70 **Cobra Jet**		C8ME	4.13"	.015"	Heavier Main Webs

385-Series Big-Block Engine Block Information

(Bold Indicates High Performance)

Displacement/ Years Available	Ford Casting Number (6015)	Ford Part Number (6015)	Bore Size	Deck Height	Other Information
429/460ci 1968-70		C8VE-F	4.36"	10.300"	
429/460ci 1968-70		C8VY-A	4.36"	10.300"	
429/460ci 1969-70		C9VY-A	4.36"	10.300"	
429/460ci 1969-70		C9VE-B	4.36"	10.300"	
429/460ci 1970-71		D0SZ-A	4.36"	10.300"	
429ci 1970-71 **Cobra Jet Super Cobra Jet Police Interceptor**		D0OE-B	4.36"	10.300"	
429/460ci 1971-up		D1VZ	4.36"	10.310"	
429/460ci 1971-up		D1VE	4.36"	10.310"	
429/460ci 1971-up		D1ZE-AZ	4.36"	10.310"	
429/460ci 1975-up		D5TE	4.36"	10.310"	Truck Block

Continued from page 28

blocks to avoid, if for no other reason than aesthetics.

Because FE-series 352/360/390/428 big blocks haven't been in regular production since 1976, we haven't had the luxury of new block castings for a long time. However, FE block casting quality was always pretty good. Like any other Ford block casting, you have to check for cracking and other flaws. Of course the ideal situation is a new-old-stock block. These can be found around the country with different sources. Sneathen Enterprises in Cape Girardeau, Missouri is one source for NOS FE-series blocks. Perogie Enterprises in New Jersey is yet another. Because 360 truck blocks were produced right up until the end of FE production in 1976, these remain reliable and plentiful finds in salvage yards across the land. No one knows how long they will be plentiful.

This leads us to the 385-series big blocks that have been in continuous production since 1968. Because the 429/460 has always been a hardy passenger car big block, block castings tend to be true to mark in terms of quality and consistency. Where there appears to be quality issues with 302 and 351W block castings during the late 1970s and early 1980s, we've never seen much of this with the 385-series big block castings. Most have remained true to mark in terms of quality throughout their entire manufacturing history.

TEARDOWN AND INSPECTION

We have already shown you how to choose a foundation for your project, but what if you have purchased an entire engine assembly? It's a good idea to know what you're getting into before you buy an engine. Always choose a salvage yard or source that provides a written guarantee addressing engine condition. No one wants to spend $400 to $800 on a used engine, only to discover that it cannot be rebuilt. Here are a few reasons why an engine cannot be rebuilt:

- It has already been rebuilt and cannot be bored oversize.
- It has cracked castings.
- The castings are severely warped (indicating a severe overheat).

- Bolt holes are damaged beyond repair.
- It is hydrolocked with excessive cylinder or head damage.
- It has a thrown rod or broken crank with internal damage not apparent externally.

Make sure you have a written escape clause with your purchase.

You can determine if an engine has been apart by checking gasket condition. Evidence of silicone sealer is one tipoff. Also, examine bolt heads for paint chips, indicating they have been removed and retorqued. This is especially important at the head and oil pan bolts.

When it's time to disassemble an engine, organization is vital. You must catalog and properly store your engine's parts for ease of reassembly. Store parts in labeled plastic bags or food containers. This keeps dirt and moisture out. Immediately upon disassembly, it's a good idea to get these parts to a trusted machine shop for inspection and proper machine work. The block must be completely disassembled, including the removal of freeze and oil gallery plugs, cylinder head pins, oil filter adapter, and water jacket plugs. In the old days, we used to submerse castings in a lye tank which removed sludge, paint, and rust. Today, machine shops are mandated by the Environmental Protection Agency (EPA) to have modern cleaning equipment that primarily uses citric acid and hot water. There is also a shot peen system of cleaning, used after the solvent treatment, that makes cast iron look like

new. This process is recommended for best results. Also be prepared to clean the block again and again during the machining process to ensure maximum effectiveness. If your machine shop isn't willing to clean and reclean the block, then visit your local car wash and use the high-pressure washer to clean all passages. Give cooling and oil gallery passages extensive attention with high-pressure hot water.

Inspect parts first, then machine. Inspecting castings first prevents waste. If a piece is cracked or otherwise seriously flawed to the point that it can't be machined successfully, you want to find this out before expensive machine work begins. Few machine shops will refund your money if the piece is found to be flawed later. Time is money to these businesses. Ask your machine shop to inspect the part first, and call you if serious flaws are found. Inspection methods include magnafluxing, die-penetrant (also known as Spotcheck) inspection, X-ray, and sonic testing. If your machine shop is not capable of performing these inspections, then find a machine shop that can.

Once your engine block is clean, inspected, and ready for machine work, there are several machining steps a seasoned professional is going to want to follow. The block decks should be checked for warpage. Most of the time, they will need a mild cleaning with a milling machine. Milling the decks is life insurance for your head gaskets. Mill the minimum amount necessary to get the deck true. If they are true, milling is not necessary.

When the decks are milled, you will

Teardown begins with pulling accessories and subassemblies. Fastline Performance in Simi Valley, California begins a 5.0L engine build by pulling the intake manifold. She will catalog this piece and properly store it during the build.

The valvetrain is next. If you are going to reuse valvetrain components, mark the rocker arms with a Magic Marker based on the cylinder installed. Because specific wear patterns develop over time and use, parts like rocker arms and pushrods should be reinstalled in their original locations. Examine all parts for extraordinary wear. Replace each part as needed. Rocker arms with worn tips or fulcrums should be replaced.

Next, remove the cylinder heads. A pry bar is sometimes necessary to break heads loose. Gently pry the head as shown. Excessive pressure can sometimes damage the casting, so be careful.

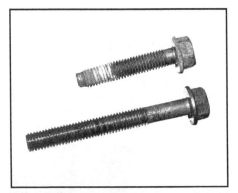

Head bolts and other hardware should be examined for damaged threads or other defects. When in doubt, replace the fastener.

Examine the block decks for evidence of water jacket leakage, a blown head gasket, or obvious cracking.

want the line bore checked next. Most of the time, the line bore will need a mild honing. In more serious situations, it will need boring and honing, just like a cylinder bore. Replace any of the main bearing caps, and the line bore must be checked and machined. If one main bearing cap needs replacement, we suggest replacement of all of them as a set. Use a complete matching set from another block.

Boring and honing the cylinder bores is the final block machining step. The machinist sets the block up in the boring machine and uses a boring bar to do the major cuts. By major cuts, we mean .025 in., which is a rough cut that trues the cylinder wall. The machinist dresses the cylinder wall with a hone to achieve a smooth finish and a crosshatch pattern, which are vital to oil

control. Each new piston has to be matched to each bore. The machinist measures the piston and cylinder bore as honing takes place. The objective is to achieve a .003-in. to .005-in. clearance between the piston and cylinder wall. We do this because pistons and cylinders must match. This clearance allows for oil flow and piston expansion as the engine warms up.

Next, remove the lifters. If you are disassembling a late-model roller tappet (1985-up) small block, remove the spider and lifter guides first. As with the rocker arms, if you are going to reuse the lifters, mark them and reinstall them in the same location.

The front dress is next. Remove the water pump pulley, water pump, drive pulley, and harmonic balancer. You will need a puller for the harmonic balancer, available from a rental store. Remove the timing cover.

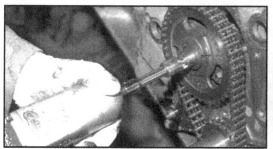 

The timing set is removed next. Always replace this assembly. It's cheap insurance when it comes to engine life.

With the machine work complete, the block must be thoroughly cleaned with high-pressure water, soap/solvent, pipe brushes, and compressed air. This step removes any contaminates, including rust and metal shavings. We suggest cleaning the block and all passages again and again until the soapy water runs clear. Then let the block dry out and clean again just for good measure. This may seem redundant, but contaminants do lodge themselves inside cooling and oil gallery passages, surfacing when the engine is fired and running. Repeated cleanings get this process under control long before fire up. Take the extra time now and sleep better later.

OTHER DETAILS

When all of the block machine work is finished, it's a good idea to chase bolt-hole threads with a thread chaser and some WD-40. While you're at it, examine those threads for damage. A thread chaser may be rented from your local auto parts store or a rental store. If you cannot afford to buy or rent a thread chaser, clean the bolts with a wire wheel and use the bolt with WD-40 to chase the threads. The objective here is clean threads regardless of how you do it.

Gasket contact surfaces can always use your attention as well. All too often engine builders don't remove all of the old gasket material, which is easily overlooked during cleaning and machining. It can leak later. A light dressing with fine sandpaper perfects gasket surfaces and prevents leaks. Start with 220 grit sandpaper and work your way up to a finer 320 or 400 grit paper. Use a block sander to ensure smooth surfaces.

Earlier we mentioned lifter bores, which virtually never get the nod during a rebuild. However, scored lifter bores will damage new lifters and sacrifice oil pressure just like a scored crankshaft journal and bearing.

Rear main seal grooves need a closer look during the cleaning process. Contaminants in the seal groove will cause a leak from that new engine. Taking the time to clean these surfaces will save you trouble later.

Check main bearing saddles for evidence of spun bearings and scoring. Check the thrust faces on the thrust bearing saddle. All of this nit-picky checking can save you time and money later on.

Remove the cam retainer plate, then gently remove the camshaft. If you are satisfied with the level of performance witnessed with the existing camshaft, have your machine shop inspect and measure the lobes for excessive wear. If wear is within limits, you don't have to replace the camshaft.

 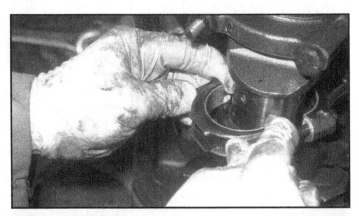

Remove the rod caps carefully as shown.

Gently drive the piston and rod assembly out through the top of the block. Mark each piston and rod for the bore it came from.

Fastline Performance measures the cylinder bores for taper. This is called "miking" the bores with an inside micrometer. This step shows if an engine has ever been bored before, plus what oversize is needed. If the block is at maximum oversize (.040-in. over for small block, .060-in. over for big block), it should be sleeved or discarded. If you are going to run the engine hard, an alternative block is your best choice.

 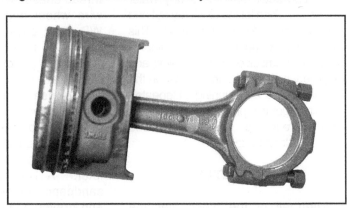

Inspect each piston/rod assembly for unusual wear patterns. This particular 5.0L engine shows evidence of abuse. These rod bearings have been hammered hard and the pistons show excessive blow-by, indicating the use of nitrous oxide during the engine's short life.

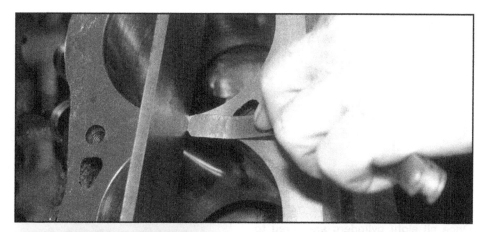

Remove the main caps and inspect them for abnormal wear and distortion. Remove the crankshaft as shown.

The block deck is checked for warpage with a machinists straight edge and feeler gauge, then milled if necessary

With all oil galley plugs and freeze plugs removed, have the block professionally cleaned. This is the first of many times the block will need to be cleaned. The block should be cleaned after each machining step. You may have to pay more for this process, but it will save you money in potential engine damage from missed metal debris.

Each cylinder is bored .025-in. oversize for trueness.

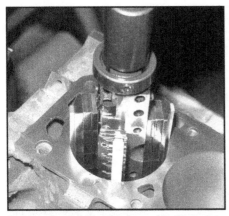

Once all eight cylinders are bored to .025-in. oversize, a hone takes each of them to .030-in. oversize. The hone provides nice crosshatch finish work.

Next the line bore is checked and bored/honed as necessary.

Where oil gallery press-in plugs have been used, have these openings tapped and fitted with screw-in plugs for oiling system security. Never use press-in plugs.

Always use brass freeze plugs — never steel. Steel freeze plugs are subject to corrosion and rot-through. Use a thin bead of silicone sealer around the perimeter, then drive the plug until the lip is flush with the block. Allow the silicone to cure.

Some oiling systems need close attention. The 351C, 351M, and 400M need a restrictor plug in the passage between the No. 1 cam bearing and No. 1 main bearing to keep oil volume and pressure where it's needed most — at the main bearings. This restrictor limits oil flow to the top end (lifters and rocker arms) where it's needed less.

Check cooling passage for obstructions.

Keep in mind that some blocks do not have provisions for hydraulic lifters, like early FE blocks and 427 FE blocks. Beginning in 1968, the 427 block accepted hydraulic lifters. Note the absence of oil gallery plugs in this mechanical lifter 427 block.

CHAPTER 4

ROTATING ASSEMBLY

What we build into an engine's bottom end directly determines durability and lifespan. Believe it or not, you can build integrity into a budget engine if you understand what counts and where to prioritize. Your focus needs to be on areas that do count. This means using the best parts available in your budget range; in short, spending money where it makes the most sense in a budget engine build.

When we're planning a budget engine, it is wise to plan for the best our budget can buy, then cost down as necessary, prioritizing as we go. For example, you might want a set of Crower Sportsman rods topped with forged pistons. When cost enters the picture, you may have to throttle back to hypereutectic pistons and modified stock rods to get the job done. Compromising down under is something you do carefully, answering yourself honestly what this engine is going to be.

Before you get started, it is important to remember there are no guarantees

when we build an engine. Anytime we build an engine, we always run the risk of engine failure due to flawed materials or faulty assembly procedures employed during the build. Additionally, there is the risk of engine failure due to abuse once in service — such as over-revving, poor tuning, or the neglect of proper maintenance like regular oil changes. The best we can do is to put quality into an engine build in the first place, then do our best to treat the mill respectfully once the chambers are warm.

Treating the mill respectfully means using common sense. Never push a cold engine, for example. Cold oil doesn't flow and coat moving parts as liberally as warm oil. Cold parts need warm-up time to expand to proper tolerances. Operating an engine in a poor state of tune is another factor. Too much timing or a lean fuel mixture is hard on an engine. Too much of either will destroy an otherwise healthy engine in seconds.

FIRST, A WORD ON BALANCING

Before we get into how to build a solid bottom end, we must first talk about balancing issues and how they pertain to Ford V-8 engines. Proper dynamic balancing is rooted in having the right combination of rotating and reciprocating parts. All Ford small-block engines, including the 351C, 351M, and 400M, are "externally" balanced. This means we counterweight the engine "externally" on the flywheel/flexplate and harmonic balancer to achieve dynamic balance.

Why go outside and externally balance? Because the crankshaft counterweights inside don't always give us sufficient weight to counter reciprocating bobweight (rods and pistons). We add counterweight to the flywheel and harmonic balancer to make up for the difference in reciprocating weight inside the block. Look at a small-block Ford flywheel, flexplate, and harmonic balancer and you can see the counterweighting. On flexplates, the counterweight is welded on. With flywheels, it's an integral part of the casting. Holes are drilled in the flywheel, often opposite the counterweight, to achieve ideal dynamic balancing. The same can be said for the harmonic balancer, which is also drilled to achieve ideal dynamic balance. We drill flywheels and harmonic balancers to remove weight where it isn't needed.

One Ford small block, the 1963-67 289 High Performance V-8, uses additional counterweighting (a slide-on counterweight) at the front of the crankshaft to allow for heavier reciprocating weight inside. If you're building a replica Hi-Po, you don't have to have this counterweight. Your machine shop can fill the crankshaft counterweights with Mallory metal or add weight to the flywheel/flexplate.

Why is all this balancing hoopla important? Whenever we're dynamic balancing an externally balanced engine, we must have the flywheel (manual transmission), flexplate (automatic transmission), and harmonic balancer present at the time of balancing. Horrible vibrations abound when we ignore this fact.

What makes the small-block "external" balance issue more complicated is 28-ounce offset balance versus 50-ounce offset. Earlier Ford small blocks like the 221, 260, 289, and 302 V-8s through 1981 were 28-ounce offset balanced. When Ford began producing the 5.0L (302) High Output V-8 in 1982, a 50-ounce offset balance was used to allow for heavier reciprocating masses inside. Small-block crankshaft flanges are drilled to allow flexplate or flywheel installation one way only. This prevents us from incorrectly installing the flywheel or flexplate, adversely affecting balance.

Ford FE big-blocks were both internally and externally balanced depending on engine type. All FE engines, except the 410 and 428, were internally balanced. Internally balanced means the crank, rods, and pistons are balanced together without concern for the flywheel, flexplate, or harmonic balancer. Internal balancing means there's enough counterweighting in the crankshaft counterweights to do the job without help from the flywheel, flexplate, or harmonic balancer.

The 410 and 428 were externally balanced because they had greater reciprocating weight than other FE counterparts. Both had heavier rods and pistons, which made it necessary to add counterweighting outside the engine at the flywheel, flexplate, and harmonic balancer. The 428 Cobra Jet has an additional slip-on counterweight at the front of the crankshaft behind the harmonic balancer to allow for heavier moving parts inside.

We'll take the FE story a step further with the FT (Ford Truck) big-block cousin. If you're using a cast or steel-forged FT truck crankshaft (affordable brute strength) in your FE engine, always remember FT engines are externally balanced which means the flywheel, flexplate, and harmonic balancer must be included in the balancing process.

All 385-series 429 and 460ci engines are "internally" balanced, which means they don't need any help outside at the flywheel, flexplate, or harmonic balancer. This is a big plus for the 385 because it makes dynamic balancing easy. When it's time to replace a clutch and flywheel, you can expect a good balancing experience because the crankshaft, rods, and pistons are independent from the flywheel, flexplate, and harmonic balancer.

STROKER KITS

Pumping up the displacement in your Ford V-8 doesn't have to be expensive. In fact, when you opt for a cast crankshaft and cast pistons, stroking your budget engine doesn't have to cost any more than a simple rebuild. Stroker kits are available from Performance Automotive Warehouse (PAW) for not much more than a budget engine kit. Ditto for Summit Racing Equipment and Ford Racing Technology.

An engine is stroked by increasing the distance the piston travels in the cylinder bore. When we increase the distance the piston travels in the bore, the bore takes on more air and fuel resulting in more power. Stroker kits vary in scope and cost. Often you can stroke an engine without buying a kit using off-the-shelf parts. For example, you can stroke a 390 to 410+ci by installing a 428 crankshaft, or turn a 429 into a 460 with a 460 crankshaft. Just offset grind a 302 or 351 crank and use the right rod and piston for increased displacement from your small block.

Stroker kits are the easiest means to displacement when off-the-shelf Ford parts won't get you there. Ford Racing, for example, offers a 347ci stroker kit (M-6013-B347) for 289/302 blocks. This kit sports a nodular-iron 3.40" stroke crankshaft, KB flattop pistons, Federal Mogul high-performance connecting rods, and Grant piston rings. You must provide all machine work and dynamic balancing. Remember, this is an externally-balanced engine. Flywheel, flexplate, and harmonic balancer must be present for balancing.

Ford Racing also offers a 514ci stroker kit (M-6013-A514) for 429/460 big blocks. This kit includes a nodular-iron crankshaft with 4.30" stroke, M-6200-A514 connecting rods, choice of TRW forged pistons, Speed Pro piston rings, and Federal Mogul bearings. Like the small-block stroker kit mentioned earlier, this kit requires externally balancing with flywheel, flexplate, and harmonic balancer present.

Stroker engines are also available from Ford Racing. You can install 600 horsepower in a weekend with the M-6007-B514 crate 514ci big-block package. This engine has been dyno tested at 600 horsepower at 6,250 rpm, which is 590 ft./lbs. of torque at 4,750 rpm.

Coast High Performance has a variety of stroker kits for Ford V-8s. The most popular is the 347ci Street Fighter small block. Several versions with either I-beam or H-beam rods are available for your application depending on budget. Coast also offers 377, 408, and 426ci stroker kits for 351W and 351C engines. If you're building a 385-series big block, Coast can help with 501, 514, and 557ci stroker kits for your monster big block.

Keep in mind that when you're ordering a stroker kit for your Ford V-8, the more expensive kits sport H-beam rods, forged pistons, and steel cranks. Rules of budgetary concern must apply here. Street engines don't need race-ready pieces. Keep your expectations realistic and an eye on the check book.

CRANKSHAFTS

It is a popular misconception that high-performance engines need steel-forged crankshafts, but nothing could be

Suggested Stroker Kits For Small- & Big-Block Fords

Manufacturer	Engine Served	CID After Stroke	Rod Type	Rod Length	Crank Type
Ford Motorsport SVO	302	347	4340 Steel	5.315"	Nodular Iron
Lunati Cams	302	347	Lunati	5.400"	Nodular Iron
Coast High Performance	302	317	Eagle	5.400"	Nodular Iron
Coast High Performance	302	331	Ford 1600	5.200"	Nodular Iron
Coast High Performance	302	347	Blue Thunder	5.315"	Steel Forged
Coast High Performance	302	347	Eagle	5.400"	Steel Forged
Ford Performance Solutions	302	326	Eagle	5.400"	Australian 302 Nodular Iron
Speed-O-Motive	302	357	Eagle	5.400"	351C Nodular Iron
Nowak Racing Engines	302	327	Eagle	5.400"	Forged Steel
Powered By Ford	302	347	Crower	5.400"	Forged Steel
Coast High Performance	351W	377	Chrysler	6.125"	Nodular Iron
Coast High Performance	351W	408	Eagle	6.200"	400M Nodular Iron
Coast High Performance	351W	426	Eagle	6.200"	400M Nodular Iron
Ford Performance Solutions	351W	408	Pro H-Beam	6.125"	400M Nodular Iron
Ford Performance Solutions	351W	426	Pro H-Beam	6.125"	400M Nodular Iron
Speed-O-Motive	351W	426	Eagle	6.125"	400M Nodular Iron
Nowak Racing Engines	351W	408	Crower	6.250"	SCAT Billet
Ford Motorsport SVO	460	600	Aluminum	6.77"	Forged Steel
Coast High Performance	460	501	Eagle	6.200"	Nodular Iron
Coast High Performance	460	557	Eagle	6.800"	Forged Steel

further from the truth. Steel crankshafts are necessary for high-stress, high-RPM racing applications that would take a toll on a nodular-iron crankshaft. Single digit quarter-mile drag racers and all-out road racers need steel crankshafts due to the extremes their engines experience. If you're building a weekend racer or a boulevard terror, you will be pleasantly surprised at what can be done with a cast-iron crank to ensure reliability. There is no place in the engine where quality is more important than in the bottom end. Building quality into your engine's bottom end is going to cost you money, but it doesn't have to cost a fortune. Wise investing in the beginning of your build will help you give your engine a bottom end that will last.

Street engines do fine with nodular iron crankshafts, and nodular iron crankshafts live well with affordable machining techniques Crankshaft journals should never be machined more than .020-in. undersize. Additionally, crankshaft trueness must be addressed. Your machine shop can check and make corrections as necessary before machining begins. Crankshafts are straightened with a hydraulic press

designed specifically for this mission. Then they're checked for trueness. The concept is simple where the crankshaft is positioned in a jig, then pressure is applied hydraulically with a hand-operated pump. With each pass, the crank is checked for trueness. At the same time, a crankshaft should be checked for cracking via Magnafluxing, Spotchecking, x-ray, or sonic testing. Magnafluxing and Spotchecking (dye penetrant) are the most affordable means.

Most crankshafts will need to be turned. Turning the crank means grinding and polishing the main and rod journals to the next undersize, which means you're going to need oversize bearings. If we grind or "turn" the crank .010" undersize, this means we're going to need .010" oversize bearings. Before turning a crankshaft, we need to check the journals for wear. Drag your fingernail over each journal surface and observe. If your fingernail snags at any scoring (lines and grooves), the crankshaft should be checked with a micrometer, then turned to the next undersize. Your machine shop will be happy to do

this. If you have a clean crankshaft with smooth journals, check the journals with a micrometer and determine course of action. If the journals "mike" clean at the current size, then have your machine shop polish the journals and stick with the current size bearings. Always check every journal.

Another way we breathe life into a crankshaft is radiusing a larger fillet at the corners of each journal. This area is where most crankshafts fail. Journals fail because a high concentration of stress occurs at the tight radii of each journal. By enlarging the radius, we distribute the load over a broader area which means less journal stress and less chance of failure.

Crankshaft repair is also an option when journals are damaged beyond normal machining technique. Machine shops use a process of pouring iron onto the superheated journal surface (this is actually a welding process), then machining the journal to specs. If your machine shop doesn't offer this service, it can probably ship the crankshaft to one that does. Before you consider repairing a

Cast or Forged?

Cast-iron (also known as nodular-iron) crankshafts don't get a fair shake in the world of high-performance engines. However, a nodular-iron crankshaft that has been properly machined, radiused, shot peened, and checked for cracking can do everything a steel crank can do and more. Believe it or not, you can spin a cast crank up to 7500 rpm, although we suggest keeping it around 6500 rpm maximum.

What makes a cast crank more forgiving than a steel crank is flexibility. A cast- or nodular-iron crankshaft flexes in extreme conditions where a steel crank will not. Steel cranks tend to snap under great stress. Another plus for the cast crank is a harder surface that is more user friendly and less subject to scoring. Where the steel crank wins against the cast crank is greater strength for extreme duty racing conditions. For the street, cast cranks are the common sense, affordable alternative. For horsepower ratings up to 400 to 450, the cast crank is the clear winner. Crank choice boils down to how your engine will be used.

Steel crankshafts are available from a number of different sources: Scat, Cola, Crower, Lunati, Ford Racing, and Coast High Performance. Most of these steel cranks are stroker pieces designed to maximize displacement and power. The nice thing about a stroker crank is that you get steel and displacement all in one stop. It just doesn't come cheaply. You can expect to spend in excess of $1800 for a steel crankshaft depending on the source. Also keep in mind there are different grades of steel cranks (material and treatment) out there. The grade you choose depends largely on your engine's mission. Talk with each of these suppliers and determine which is best for your application.

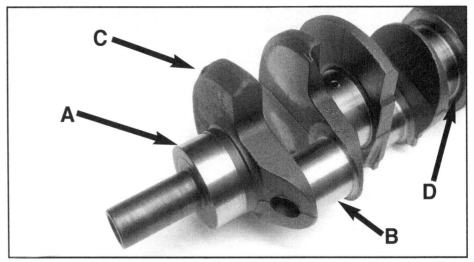

Anatomy of a crankshaft: Main journals (A), rod journals (B), counterweight (C), and thrust main journal (D). Each of the journals should be machined to the next available undersize or polished when undersizing isn't necessary. Oversized bearings are used with undersized journals. Machine the journals .010-in. undersize and you will need .010-in. oversized bearings to make up the difference.

Crankshaft evaluation begins with journal inspection. If your fingernail snags anywhere on a journal, it is sufficiently scored to need machining. The journal is then measured with a micrometer to determine wear and diameter. Begin by checking what the recommended factory dimensions are, then check with a mike as shown. Remember, the maximum you want to go is .020-in. undersize.

common crankshaft widely available, consider another crankshaft, which is often cheaper than fixing a damaged piece. Always have the machine shop contact you first before wasting time and money on a bad crank.

Chamfering the oil holes in the crankshaft journals improves oil distribution at the bearing. This is a low-cost means to longer engine life. As we said earlier, cutting a broader radius in each side of the journals distributes bearing stress more evenly. These are low-cost means to longer engine life.

One method of crankshaft improvement we haven't discussed is oven/shot peening, which cleans the surfaces and builds strength into the iron. Shot peening the iron hammers the surface with microscopic shot that compresses the molecules and makes the crankshaft stronger. When you couple oven/shot peening with the crack checking Magnafluxing offers, you're virtually writing your engine a life insurance policy.

Two other methods of improving crankshaft durability are Nitriding and cold casting. Nitriding lays down a tougher surface on nodular-iron crankshafts, but this process doesn't come cheap at typically around $100. Cold casting is a similar process to Nitriding and costs approximately the same. Ask your machine shop about these processes and determine what's best for your application.

Finally, know when to cash it in on a bad crankshaft. Crankshafts that are severely scored or already turned to .020"+ undersize need to be sidelined for a better crank. Know when to abandon a heavily-scored crank that will need expensive repair work. Commonplace crankshafts are easy to replace and usually less expensive than repair work. Unless you're building something exotic like a Boss 302 or 427 Sideoiler, crankshaft repair is virtually unnecessary.

On first sight, this journal appears to need machining. Upon checking it with a micrometer, we learned it needed only polishing.

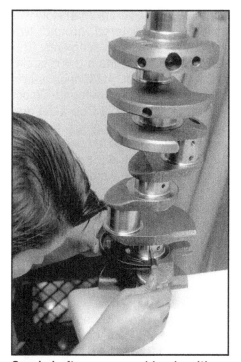

Crankshafts are machined with a crankshaft grinder. When the dimension desired is neared, the journal is measured again and polished to a smooth finish.

Ford crankshafts are identifiable through markings in the casting or forging. This is a "3M" crank for the 351W (see identification table).

Sometimes you will find identification marks like these (stamped in a crank) which indicate undersizing. The R.010/M.010 indicates .010-in. undersize on rod and main journals. We call this a "10/10" crank.

When all crankshaft machine and polish work is finished, the crank must be cleaned as shown. Run solvent through all oil passages and clean the passages with a pipe brush. Do this again and again until passages are clean. If you think this is redundant and unnecessary, consider that it only takes one stray piece of metal to score a bearing and render an engine useless.

221, 260, 289, 302, and 351W

Ford's legendary small block offers a few crankshaft choices. Because there are three small-block stroke lengths, selection is simple. The 221, 260, and 289 have a 2.87-in. stroke, while the 302 has a 3.00-in. stroke. The 351W has a 3.50-in. stroke. The only factory steel-forged crankshaft was used in the 1969-70 Boss 302 with a 3.00" stroke. The rest had nodular iron crankshafts.

Aside from the 351W, all small-block Fords had the same size main bearing journal, which makes crankshaft interchangeability across the displacements possible. You can actually fit a 302 crank into a 221/260 block (although why would you?) for a modest increase in displacement from those 3.50" and 3.80" bore blocks.

Crankshaft identification is simple with small-block Fords. The 221, 260, and 289 engines with the 2.87" stroke had "1M" nodular-iron crankshafts. Look for

221, 260, 289, 302, and 351W Crankshaft Identification

Displacement /Year	Casting/Forging Number	Stroke	Information
221/260ci 1962-64	C2OZ, C3OZ	2.87"	Marked 1M Cast-Iron Crankshaft
289ci 1963-67	C3OZ	2.87"	Marked 1M Cast-Iron Crankshaft
289ci High Performance	C3OZ	2.87"	Brinell Test Mark Also marked 1M Cast-Iron Crankshaft
302ci 1968-81	C8AZ-A	3.00"	Marked 2M Cast-Iron Crankshaft
302ci 1980-up	E0SE-AD	3.00"	Lincoln Versailles crank designed for EEC-I system
Boss 302 1969-70	D0ZE-A	3.00"	Also marked 7FE-8 Steel-Forged Crankshaft
351W 1969-72	No Casting Number	3.50"	Marked 3M or 3C
351W 1973-up	No Casting Number	3.50"	Marked 3MA

"1M" cast into the crankshaft counter-weight. The most common type of small-block Ford crankshaft is the 3.00" stroke 302 crank marked with a "2M" in the casting. Later model 5.0L nodular-iron crankshafts sport the same "2M" marking with revision codes (an example would be "2ME", which we see a lot). The 351W crankshaft with a 3.50" stroke is marked "3M". Later 351W cranks also have part number revisions like the 301/5.0L crank already mentioned.

335-SERIES: 351C, 351M, and 400M

Like the small-block V-8 mentioned earlier, the Cleveland and M-series engines were never fitted with a forged steel crankshaft either. The 351C and 351M 3.50" stroke crankshafts were marked "4M". The longer 4.00" stroke 400M crank was marked "5M" This keeps selection simple.

The 351C and 351M engines can be stroked using the 4.00" stroke "5M" nodular-iron crankshaft, machining down the counterweights, and using the right rod/piston combination. The same can be said for the 351W, which uses the "5M" crankshaft in a variety of stroker configurations.

FE-SERIES: 332, 352, 360, 361, 390, 406, 427, and 428

The FE-series big-block Fords have a more involved crankshaft history than their small-block cousins. During the FE engine's production life spanning 1958-76, dozens of crankshaft types were employed. Despite what you may believe about 427 crankshafts, not all of them were steel. Most were cast iron. Four strokes were available in the FE family: 3.30-in., 3.50-in., 3.78-in., and 3.98-in.

The shortest stroke, 3.30", was confined to the early years with the short-lived 332ci FE. The more common 3.50" stroke was used with the 352 passenger car, 361 Edsel, and 360 truck engines. The longer 3.78" stroke was common to

the 390, 406, and 427 FE big blocks. Because these engines all had the same main bearing journal size, crankshaft swapability is broad based. You can fit your 352 block with the 3.78" stroke crank for greater displacement, for example. The greatest FE stroke is 3.98" used in the 410 Merc' and 428ci big blocks. Ford achieved the 410 by dropping a 428 crankshaft into a 390 block. You can stroke your FE big block without a specialized, high-dollar stroker kit. Just go to the Ford parts bin for affordable answers.

385-SERIES: 429 and 460 BIG BLOCK

The 385-series crankshaft story is a simple one centered around two strokes and two displacements. The 429ci big block sports a 3.59" stroke thanks to a "4U" or "4UA" nodular-iron crankshaft that can be found almost anywhere. Those 429 Cobra Jet and Super Cobra Jet engines had the same "4U" or "4UA" nodular-iron crankshaft as your dad's old Mercury Marquis with the exception being Brinnel hardness testing and the appropriate markings. CJ and SCJ crankshafts were simply hand-picked and tested for strength using the Brinnel test method. This is something you can do with a bread and butter 429 crankshaft. Your machine shop should know how.

When you begin to understand the availability of 460 "2Y" and "3Y" crankshafts with a 3.85" stroke and the higher displacement, one has to wonder why you would bother with the 429 crank just mentioned. All 429 engines can be stroked to 460+ci with the 460 crankshaft. Because the 460 was produced for many years after the 429 was phased out, you have plenty of cores to choose from.

Ford's Boss 429 "Shotgun" engine was the only 385-series engine ever produced with a steel crankshaft also sporting a 3.59" stroke like the wedge 429. Because Boss 429 crankshafts are extremely rare and pricey, we're convinced your search likely won't include these pieces.

Because the 429/460 385-series big blocks are hardy engines offering fierce reliability, their nodular-iron crankshafts are trustworthy pieces you can count

351C, 351M, and 400M Crankshaft Identification

Displacement /Year	Casting/Forging Number	Stroke	Information
351C 1970-74	No Casting Number	3.50"	Marked 4M Cast-Iron Crankshaft
351C Boss & High Output 1971-72	No Casting Number	3.50"	Brinell Test Mark Also marked 4M Cast-Iron Crankshaft
351M 1975-80	No Casting Number	3.50"	Marked 1K
400M 1972-80	No Casting Number	4.00"	Marked 5M, 5MA, 5MAB

332, 352, 360, 361, and 390ci Crankshaft Identification

Displacement /Year	Casting/Forging Number	Stroke	Information
332ci 1958	EDC	3.30"	Cast-Iron Crank
332ci 1959	5752421	3.30"	Cast-Iron Crank
332ci 1958-59	C0AE-C	3.30"	Service Replacement Cast-Iron Crank
352ci 1958	EDD	3.50"	Cast-Iron Crank
352ci 1959	5752420	3.50"	Cast-Iron Crank
352ci High Performance 1960	C0AE-A	3.50"	Heavier Counterweights without grooved journals Cast-Iron Crank
352ci High Performance 1960	C0AE-D	3.50"	Heavier Counterweights without grooved journals Cast-Iron Crank
352ci 1960-62	C0AE-B	3.50"	Cast-Iron Crank
352ci 1963	C3AE-A	3.50"	Cast-Iron Crank
352ci 1964	C4AE-A	3.50"	Cast-Iron Crank
352ci 1964	C4AE-E	3.50"	(Also 330MD "FT") Cast-Iron Crank
352ci 1965	C5AE-A	3.50"	Cast-Iron Crank
352ci 1965	C5AE-B	3.50"	Cast-Iron Crank
352ci 1966-67	C6AE-B	3.50"	(Also 330MD "FT") Cast-Iron Crank
352ci 1966-67	C6AE-D	3.50"	(Also 330MD "FT") Cast-Iron Crank
361ci 1958 Edsel	EDD	3.50"	Same as 352ci engine Cast-Iron Crank
361ci 1959	5752420	3.50"	Same as 352ci engine Cast-Iron Crank
360ci 1968-76	2T	3.50"	(Also 330MD "FT") Cast-Iron Crank
360ci 1968-76	2TA	3.50"	(Also 330MD "FT") Cast-Iron Crank
390ci 1961-62	C1AE-A	3.78"	Cast-Iron Crank
390ci High Performance 1961	C1AE-D	3.78"	Heavier Counterweights with grooved journals Cast-Iron Crank
390ci High Performance 1961	C1AE-H	3.78"	Heavier Counterweights with grooved journals Cast-Iron Crank
390ci High Performance 1961	C2AE-B	3.78"	Heavier Counterweights with grooved journals Cast-Iron Crank
390ci 1963	C3AE-B	3.78"	Cast-Iron Crank
390ci 1963	C3AE-C	3.78"	Cast-Iron Crank
390ci 1963	C3AE-E	3.78"	Cast-Iron Crank
390ci Police Interceptor 1964-65	C4AE-C	3.78"	Cast-Iron Crank
390ci Police Interceptor 1964-65	C4AE-D	3.78"	Cast-Iron Crank
390ci 1965	C5AE-C	3.78"	Cast-Iron Crank
390ci 1966	C6AE-A	3.78"	Cast-Iron Crank
390ci 1966	C6AE-C	3.78"	Cast-Iron Crank
390ci 1966	C6JE-J	3.78"	Marine Use Reverse Rotation Cast-Iron Crank
390ci 1966-73	2U	3.78"	Car & Truck Cast-Iron Crank
390ci 1973-76	3U	3.78"	Trucks Cast-Iron Crank
390ci 1973-76	2UA	3.78"	Trucks Cast-Iron Crank

on. With common sense machining practices and dynamic balancing, your 385's crankshaft will serve you well high into the revs.

BEARINGS

Most of us don't give bearings much thought because we think bearings are just bearings. However, there are different grades of bearings just like there are different grades of crankshafts, connecting rods, and pistons. Although our focus here is a budget engine build, cutting corners is never suggested down under. Cutting corners to save a few bucks down under isn't really building a budget engine at all because if you have to tear it down and build it again because you didn't use quality parts, then what did you save? Specify the best stuff and save money long term.

Michigan 77 or Federal Mogul competition level bearings may cost more (nearly double), but they're worth every penny in what they save you in engine life. This is no area to compromise on quality unless, of course, you'd like to rebuild this engine again sooner than later.

HARMONIC BALANCERS

This area of an engine's bottom end is getting a lot of attention these days because the aftermarket is ablaze with all kinds of balancers. Our thinking here is simple: Budget engines don't always need sophisticated balancers.

The harmonic balancer, also known as the vibration damper, is there to help dynamic balance and dampen combustion pulse shock. Combustion pulse shock hammers the crankshaft with great consistency. The damper or balancer is there to control the vibration or pulsing, which helps increase crankshaft life and smooth out the vibration. Ideally, you will use the heaviest stock harmonic balancer available for your application. For small-block builders, this would be the 289 High Performance or Boss 302 balancer, for example. Cleveland and big-block builders aren't blessed with this kind of selection. Needing a heavier balancer means looking to the aftermarket when stock choices are unavailable.

ATI and Vibratech are two examples of aftermarket balancers available out there for Ford V-8 engine applications. Believe it or not, using the right aftermarket balancer can net you power as well as smoother operation. One drawback to aftermarket balancers is weight. Because they tend to be heavier, they do add stress to the crankshaft, sometimes breaking off the snoot and doing a lot of damage. Street engines don't always need an aftermarket balancer where a stock one will do just fine. Your machine shop or speed shop will know what's best for your mission.

CONNECTING RODS

With the crankshaft machined to specifications, we're ready to move on to the connecting rods. Connecting rods mandate your close attention to detail. Because you are building a budget engine, you're probably going to want stock connecting rods. Stock rods are stronger than you might believe. Recondition and fit them with ARP bolts, and your engine will be ready for thousands of miles of faithful service.

If you're not in the mood to spend what's necessary for ARP bolts, consider most connecting rod failure happens when bolts shear or snap. ARP bolts are designed to take up to 190,000 psi and live 30 percent longer than stock rod bolts. What's more, using stock rod bolts over again is asking for trouble. Rod bolts are good for just so many cycles (usage), then they can fail miserably. Like bearings we mentioned earlier, spending wisely here is an integral part of your Ford engine's life insurance policy.

If you're going with stock used rods, each rod must be checked carefully and machined properly. This is called the inspection and reconditioning process. Connecting rods need to be checked in three key areas: small end, large end, and trueness from end to end and side to side. Both the small and large ends can and do become egg-shaped over time. The beam can become twisted and distorted from abuse or the absence of lubrication, leaving the ends out of true. Connecting rods can even be bent in an engine that still runs, making the piston cockeyed in the bore causing extreme wear due to side loads.

When we recondition a connecting rod, we first have to make sure important dimensions are correct to begin

406, 410, 427, and 428ci FE Crankshaft Identification

Displacement/Year	Casting /Forging Number	Stroke	Information
406ci High Performance 1962-63	C2AE-D	3.78"	Cast-Iron Crank
406ci High Performance 1963	C3AE-D	3.78"	Cast-Iron Crank
427ci High Performance 1963	C3AE-G	3.78"	Cast-Iron Crank
427ci High Performance 1963	C3AE-U	3.78"	Cast-Iron Crank
427ci High Performance 1964	C4AE-B	3.78"	Cast-Iron Crank
427ci High Performance 1964	C4AE-H	3.78"	Forged-Steel Crank
427ci High Performance 1964	C4AE-AJ	3.78"	Forged-Steel Crank
427ci High Performance 1965	C5AE-C	3.78"	Forged-Steel Crank Cross Drilled
427ci High Performance 1965	C5JE-A	3.78"	Cast-Iron Crank Marine Application
427ci High Performance 1965	C5JE-B	3.78"	Cast-Iron Crank Marine/Reverse Rotation
427ci High Performance 1966	C6JE-B	3.78"	Cast-Iron Crank Marine Application
427ci High Performance 1966	C6JE-C	3.78"	Cast Iron Crank Marine Application
427ci High Performance 1966	C6JE-D	3.78"	Cast-Iron Crank Marine/Reverse Rotation
427ci High Performance 1968	C8AE-B	3.78"	Cast-Iron Crank
427ci High Performance 1969	C9AE-A	3.78"	Forged-Steel/NASCAR
410/428ci 1966-67	C6ME	3.98"	Cast-Iron Crank
428ci Police Interceptor Cobra Jet 1968-69	1U	3.98"	Cast-Iron Crank
428ci Police Interceptor Cobra Jet 1969-70	1UA or 1UB	3.98"	Cast-Iron Crank
428ci Super Cobra Jet 1969-70	1UA	3.98"	Cast-Iron Crank
428ci Super Cobra Jet 1969-70	B	3.98"	Cast-Iron Crank

429 and 460ci Crankshaft Identification

Displacement /Year	Casting /Forging Number	Stroke	Information
429ci 1968-78	4U, 4UA	3.59"	Cast-Iron Crank Marked 4U or 4UA
429ci Cobra Jet Super Cobra Jet 1970-71	4U, 4UA	3.59"	Brinell Test Mark Cast-Iron Crank Marked 4U or 4UA
429ci Boss Crank 1969-70	C9AE-A or C9AE-B	3.59"	Forged-Steel
429ci Boss Crank 1969-70	C9AE-C	3.59"	Forged-Steel
460ci 1968-78	2Y, 2YA, 2YAB, 2YABC	3.85"	Cast-Iron Crank Marked 2Y, 2YA, 2YAB, 2YABC
460ci 1979-up	3Y	3.85"	Cast-Iron Crank Marked 3Y

Small Block Connecting Rod Identification

Engine/Model Year	Part Number	Center To Center	Information
1962-63 221/260ci	C2OZ-6200-A	5.1535 to 5.1565"	5/16" Rod Bolts
1964 260ci	C3AZ-6200-D	5.1535 to 5.1565"	5/16" Rod Bolts C3AE Forging Number
1963-67 289ci	C3AZ-6200-D	5.1535 to 5.1565"	5/16" Rod Bolts C3AE Forging Number
1963-67 289ci High Performance	C3OZ-6200-C	5.1535 to 5.1565"	3/8" Rod Bolts C3AE Forging Number
1968-69 302ci	C9OZ-6200-B	5.0885 to 5.0915"	5/16" Rod Bolts C8OE Forging Number
1970-up 302ci	D1OZ-6200-A	5.0885 to 5.0915"	5/16" Rod Bolts C8OE Forging Number
1969-70 Boss 302	C9ZZ-6200-B	5.1535 to 5.1565"	3/8" Rod Bolts C3AE Forging Number Replaces 289 Hi-Po Rod
1969-up 351W	C9OZ-6200-A	5.9545 to 5.9575"	3/8" Rod Bolts C9OE Forging Number

with. We want the small and large ends to be in alignment with one another on two planes. This means the centers must be in perfect alignment from end to end. If they aren't, the rod should be disposed of. That said, we need to check the big end, the bearing bore, for proper sizing. We also have to check the big end for bearing movement. Shiny surfaces on the back of the bearing and the face of the rod are reason enough to believe we have movement. A sheared bearing tab is conclusive proof we've had bearing movement.

If we have a bearing bore that is too large, the bearing is going to spin in the big end causing engine damage and failure. This is called a "spun" bearing. To prevent a spun bearing, we have to resize the big end of the rod by machining the rod and cap mating surfaces first, then honing the bearing bore for proper resize. When reconditioned properly, the big end of the rod then accommodates the bearing comfortably. It gives the bearing just the right amount of "crush" (0.001" when the rod is torqued) to conform and do its job effectively. Reconditioning the big end of the rod should include truing and honing the bearing bore. The resulting crosshatch pattern will give the bearing something to adhere and reduce the likelihood of a spun bearing.

Whenever you're reconditioning connecting rods, you should always use the largest ARP bolts possible without violating rod strength. The small-block Ford, for example, has 5/16" bolts from the factory. Some machine shops opt for a 3/8" bolt upsize, but this has been

known to cause rod failure in some applications. A compromise bolt size, 11/32", available for GM applications, will work in your small-block Ford. Being creative in your work is a necessity as a budget engine builder. You may have to look in all of the automaker's parts bins for solutions like this one. We suggest the use of ARP bolts because they happen to be the best fasteners in the aftermarket industry. ARP has its roots in the aerospace industry, which is what accounts for the outstanding integrity we find with those fasteners.

The small end of the rod typically doesn't need much attention aside from a new bushing where floating pins are used. For press-fit applications, you need to check the inside diameter of the pin bore.

Whether to go with a stock or aftermarket rod depends on how your engine will be used. Contrary to popular opinion, most street engines don't need H-beam rods. Most of the time, they don't even need high-performance aftermarket rods like the Crower Sportsman or Blue Thunder. Just a beefed-up stock rod will do. Aftermarket I-beam rods like the Sportsman become necessary when horsepower climbs above 400 to 450, and you're planning on a lot of weekend racing.

When you recondition a stock connecting rod, it is always advisable to determine what the best stock rod is before reconditioning the ones you have. As a rule, connecting rods get better with evolution. They grow heavier big ends with broad

shoulders, and that is what you want in a connecting rod.

One other thing we can do with a connecting rod is a weight loss program. Most stock small-block rods, for example, weigh around 600-650 grams. Your weight goal should be around 500 grams. Big-block rods, being larger, will weigh more. It is important to remember our weight loss program cannot and should not compromise rod strength. We load shed with connecting rods to reduce reciprocating stress and gain power. When we remove weight from the small end of the rod, we actually gain strength (and power) because there's less weight stress here. Remove weight from the big end and less crankshaft counterweighting (still more weight loss) is needed. Connecting rod weight loss should begin with one primary rod, then modeling the rest after this rod. Weight across the board should mirror the weight of the primary rod. This happens during the dynamic balancing process. Because this is a time-intensive process, there is considerable cost involved. Your machine shop can offer insight.

Choosing the right connecting rod boils down to visible condition, too. Always bear in mind sharp edges and rough spots in the rod forging mean potential trouble because this is where fatigue cracking and failure occur. Remove rough spots with a dye grinder (carefully!) and finish out with 400 grit paper or find another connecting rod. Rods that are rusted or pitted should not be used. Pitted spots are potential failure points because they are weaknesses. Always choose rods with similar weights to begin with. This makes the dynamic balancing job for your machine shop easier.

Beef up rod strength by shot peening, just like we do with the crankshaft. Shot peening hammers the forged surface with microscopic shot which compresses the iron molecules and builds in strength.

When we look at small-block Ford connecting rods, the best rod to use is the most current 5.0L (302ci) and 5.8L (351W) rods because they're thicker on the big end than their older counterparts. FE-series big blocks benefit from the use of the 390, 406, 410, 427, and 428 High Performance and Police Interceptor short rods. These were the best FE rods. Because the 427 LeMans

351C, 351M, and 400M Connecting Rod Identification

Engine/Model Year	Part Number	Center To Center	Information
1970-74 351C	D0AZ-6200-A	5.778"	3/8" Rod Bolts 4M Code D0AZ Forging Number
1971 Boss 351C 1972 351C H.O.	D1ZZ-6200-A	5.778"	3/8" Rod Bolts High Strength Magnafluxed 4M Code D1ZX Forging Number
1975-up 351M 1972-up 400M	D1AZ-6200-A	6.58"	3/8" Rod Bolts 5M Code

FE Big-Block Connecting Rod Identification

Engine/Model Year	Part Number	Center To Center	Information
1958-66 332/352ci 1958-59 361ci	C1AZ-6200-C	6.540"	3/8" Rod Bolts Long Rod EDC Forging Code
1961-62 390ci	C1AE-6200-C	6.488"	3/8" Rod Bolts C1AE Forging Number
1963-65 390/406/427ci	C3AZ-6200-B	6.488"	3/8" Rod Bolts C2AE or C3AE
1963-65 390/406/427ci	C3AZ-6200-F	6.488"	3/8" Rod Bolts C3AE Forging Number
1966-68 428ci	C6AZ-6200-C	6.488"	13/32" Rod Bolts C6AE Forging Number
1967-68 427ci	C7OE-6200-A	6.488"	7/16" Rod Bolts C7OE Forging Number
1968-70 428ci CJ	C9ZZ-6200-A	6.488"	7/16" Rod Bolts C7AE Forging Number

385-Series Big-Block Connecting Rod Identification

Engine/Model Year	Part Number	Center To Center	Information
1968-up 429/460ci	C8SZ-6200-A	6.6050"	3/8" Rod Bolts C8VE Forging Number
1970-71 429 CJ/SCJ	D0OZ-6200-A	6.6050"	3/8" Rod Bolts High Strength Magnafluxed D0OE Forging Number
1976-up 460ci		6.6050"	3/8" Rod Bolts D6VE-AA Truck Rod Replaces D0OZ-A CJ & SCJ Rod
1969-70 Boss 429	C9AZ-6200-A	6.5480"	1/2" Rod Bolts 820-S Engines Only C9AE-A
1969-70 Boss 429	C9AZ-6200-B	6.6050"	3/8" Rod Bolts 820-T Engines Onl C9AE-B

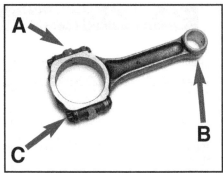

This is a typical connecting rod (small-block rod shown). When we recondition a rod, we clean up the large end (A) by cutting the cap and rod mating surfaces, then resizing the journal opening. Stock rods are mostly press fit pin types, where the piston pin is pressed into the small end (B). Free-floating types are found mostly in aftermarket rods. When you recondition a stock rod, it's a good idea to step up to larger ARP bolts (C). If you're shy about boring the bolt hole, at least use an ARP bolt of the same size.

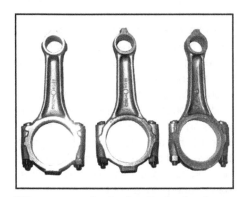

When we speak of using the best rod possible, the evolution of the 302 rod is a case in point. From left to right you can see this evolution. These are all C8OE forgings, but look at how they are machined. Note from left to right how there is more bearing and journal surface contact area as the rods evolve. On the far right is a 5.0L high output rod. Big-block connecting rods tend to follow the same refinement evolution.

rod is not a budget rod, we're not going to go there in this book. The 385-series big blocks used three basic rod forgings. The best of the three is the broad-shouldered D6VE-AA truck rod which replaced the D0OE-A Cobra Jet/Super Cobra Jet rod with broached bolt heads.

PISTONS

Selecting a piston for your budget build is probably the easiest choice you will make in the whole process. Three basic piston types are available: cast, hypereutectic, and forged. Translated into dollars, that's cheap, not so cheap, and darned expensive. Which piston is best for your application? For a budget engine build where power output is going to be no higher than one horsepower per cubic-inch, cast or hypereutectic pistons are your best choices because they're just right for street applications. They even work for some weekend racing applications. Cast and hypereutectic pistons run quieter than forged pistons They don't suffer the expansion properties of a forged piston, which run loose and noisy when cold, and they also cost considerably less than a forged piston.

Over time and use, the large end of a connecting rod becomes egg-shaped. We recondition the rod to make the large end perfectly round, yet square again. Reconditioning stock connecting rods involves cutting the cap and big end of the rod to perfect the mating surfaces, then boring a new journal. We finish up with a new pair of rod bolts and nuts. Never reuse the old bolts.

This is the Blue Thunder small-block connecting rod from Coast High Performance. As you can see, this is a heavy-duty connecting rod with broached bolts, big shoulders, and a thicker small end. A set of rods like this can cost upwards of $800 to $1,000. However, these rods are life insurance if you plan on spinning your engine above 6000 rpm

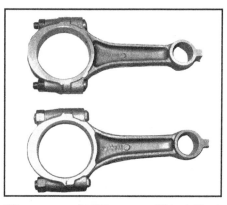

When you are building a small-block Ford, keep in mind that not all rods are alike. A C3AE forging number indicates a 221/260/289 rod (bottom). If you see a C8AE number, it's a 302 rod (top). The Boss 302 uses a 289-style "C3AE" rod forging.

H-beam rods with cap screw bolts are costly, but effective, if you have the budget. These rods will take an eight-grand spin without complaint. For a budget street or weekend racing engine, they're overkill and unnecessary.

Cast pistons are just that: low-buck cast-aluminum slugs we find in original equipment, low-performance applications. Before you dismiss cast pistons as a "no go" for your budget engine build, consider this: Most factory high-performance engines had cast pistons in the 1960s. Those 428 Cobra Jet big blocks that beat the socks off their competition in 1968-69 NHRA competition had cast pistons. The 289 High Performance V-8 had cast pistons. Both those engines could take a six grand rev without piston failure. The message here is that cast pistons are better than you think. They're perfect for the warmed-up street performance engine.

If you're still uncomfortable with cast pistons, the hypereutectic piston is the next best thing, and for just a little more money. While a hypereutectic piston is still a cast piston, it has silicon in the alu-

minum mix, which makes for a stronger piston without the high cost of forging. Cast and hypereutectic pistons afford us more flexibility when it comes to cylinder wall clearances. They are more forgiving (in their expansion properties) than forged units.

Both cast and hypereutectic pistons can withstand a 6200-rpm rev without failure. However, these pistons will get into trouble when pushed past their performance envelope. You'll want to keep the revs below 6200 rpm. Plus, no nitrous oxide or supercharging need apply with cast and hypereutectic pistons because failure is certain and swift. Nitrous and supercharged applications need forged pistons.

Another important point is piston weight. The lighter the piston, the more power your engine will produce. As a rule, you want less piston skirt, which

means less drag. Yet you want piston structural integrity. We need a balance of strength and light weight in the piston department. At the same time, we want the closest piston-to-cylinder wall clearance possible without trouble. This is where mission comes in. Engines fed with nitrous or force-fed with supercharging need greater piston-to-cylinder wall clearances due to higher combustion temperatures. Ideally, piston-to-cylinder wall clearances should be around .004-.008". Some piston alloys are more forgiving, allowing even tighter clearances, but be careful. Check with your manufacturer for details.

Despite a forged piston's ability to withstand nitrous, it will not withstand excessive nitrous use. Hammer a forged piston really hard with nitrous or supercharger boost and it will fail. Like cast and hypereutectic pistons, the forged piston

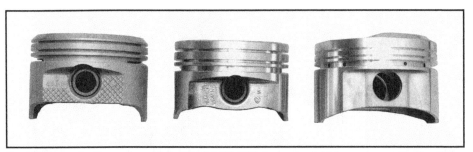

Cast, hypereutectic, or forged (left to right)? Which one is right for your application? For a budget street engine, cast and hypereutectic pistons are fine when the revs stay below 6200 rpm. Forged pistons become mandatory whenever you are planning nitrous oxide, supercharging, or frequent hard acceleration.

This is a forged piston, immediately apparent by the lines that run 360 degrees around the ring lands and dome. Forging crams those molecules closer together for a tougher chunk of aluminum. This is why forged pistons have different expansion properties.

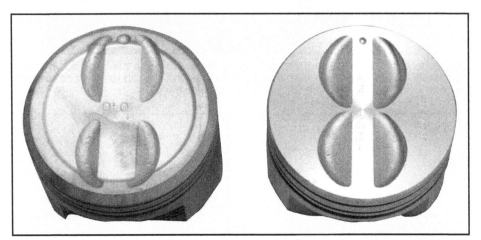

Closer inspection shows the difference between cast (left) and hypereutectic (right).

Protective coatings are also available to protect pistons from extremes, like nitrous oxide or big boosts from superchargers. This process is expensive.

Custom pistons are expensive, but sometimes necessary for an odd-duck application like special heads or specific compression ratios. This custom piston for a 351C is dished for reduced compression. Note the valve reliefs to clear huge valves.

Here's why proper piston selection is important. This cast piston got hammered hard and failed under the stress. This skirt cracking probably occurred during an over-rev under hard acceleration.

the ring end gap. This means we need a larger compression ring end gap. Nitrous applications need a greater piston ring end gap than supercharged applications because combustion temperatures are greater. Read your piston ring installation instructions for specifications.

Piston sources are plentiful for Ford V-8s. We've had excellent luck with Federal Mogul TRW pistons. Other excellent choices are JE, Aries, Ross, Wisco, and Probe Industries/Coast High Performance.

BALANCING ACT

Now that you are armed with the right information for a comfortable bottom-end marriage, it's time to think about engine assembly. Before you can assemble an engine, those spinning and reciprocating internals must be dynamic-balanced, just like you would balance a car tire and wheel to foil off vibration. The less vibration we have in an engine, the smoother it will operate and the longer it will last. Vibration is a destructive dynamic, which makes a balancing job worth every penny.

will begin to break down around the same temperature. We get great power increases from nitrous because it helps the fuel burn extremely hot. Nitrous makes your fuel mixture a rabid dog because it makes the most of the mix. Extreme heat is where we get the power. It's called thermal expansion. With nitrous, we get thermal expansion quickly, but there's a price involved called heat. Too much heat and we destroy pistons.

Another important issue to consider during piston selection is cylinder head

type. Cylinder head type is important because of the piston dome-to-chamber relationship. You must know what type of cylinder head you're going to use before selecting a piston. Once a head is selected, piston selection comes easy. Also keep compression height in mind while you're shopping pistons.

Also remember that with nitrous and supercharging comes piston ring end gaps. With the great heat loads we witness with nitrous and supercharging, piston rings expand at a greater rate closing

Dynamic balancing should be an integral part of any engine build. Balancing gets rotating and reciprocating weight in synch for smooth operation. Pistons, rings, rods, and bearings are weighed on a gram scale first to determine which weighs the least of the group. Then the rest of the rods and pistons are put on a weight-loss program. All of the pistons are carefully drilled to get their weight down to the weight of the lightest piston. The same is true for the rods, which are ground to remove weight. When we have a matching set, then we balance the crankshaft.

Bobweights that weigh the same as the piston/rod combos are fastened to the crankshaft rod journals to simulate piston/rod weight. We subtract weight by drilling metal out of the affected counterweight. We add weight by using Mallory metal in the counterweight. When piston/rod assemblies and crankshaft counterweights weigh the same, we have a perfect dynamic balance as the two whirl around inside the block.

Although we have addressed balancing issues earlier in this chapter, we cannot impress enough the importance of having matched components that will balance properly together. To achieve the right balance, we have to match the right components. Small-block Fords, for example, employ two types of balancing, depending on vintage. Prior to 1982, small-block Fords (221/260/289/302) had a 28-ounce offset balance, which means they use a different flywheel/flexplate and harmonic balancer than 1982-up 5.0L high-output engines. From 1982 and up, the 302 (5.0L) has a 50-ounce offset bal-

ance. Do not get the two confused or you will have serious vibration issues.

FE- and FT-series Ford big blocks are both internally and externally balanced as we said earlier. All FE engines except the 410 and 428 are internally balanced. FT medium- and heavy-duty truck engines are externally balanced like their 410/428 FE counterparts. The same can be said for FE- and FT-series Ford big blocks. Some are internally balanced, and some are externally balanced. Special balancing practices are required if ever you mix parts between the two types. Internally balanced

engines don't require the flywheel and balancer be present for balancing. Externally balanced engines must have the flywheel and balancer present. In short, make sure your machine shop is aware of these differences before balancing begins. When you're mixing FE and FT parts, all parts must be present for effective dynamic balancing.

BALANCERS AND FLYWHEELS

When you are packaging an engine's bottom end, both ends of the crankshaft make up an integral part of the balancing program. You will want a compatible flywheel or flexplate for the engine you are building. When you are shopping for a flywheel or flexplate, you must ascertain balancing issues as mentioned earlier, flywheel/flexplate size (number of teeth and diameter), and the appropriate bellhousing (if applicable). We stress this because Ford produced dozens of different flywheel/flexplate/bellhousing types for each engine family.

Harmonic balancers follow the same path as flywheels and flexplates. Balance issues are first and foremost, followed by fitment issues. Timing covers and harmonic balancers must be compatible (timing pointer and timing mark locations). Ford V-8 engines produced prior to 1970 have a three-bolt drive-pulley pattern. Those produced from 1970 and up have a four-bolt pattern.

Which balancer is right for your application? Balancer choice boils

All Ford V-8s prior to 1970 have three-bolt harmonic balancers.

High-performance small blocks, like the 289 Hi-Po and Boss 302, were fitted with wider harmonic balancers, which dampened vibration and added counterweight.

This is a typical small-block balancer prior to 1968.

From 1970-up, all Ford V-8s have four-bolt harmonic balancers.

Another consideration few think about is accessory drive balance. It pays to have large, heavy-drive pulleys balanced during the engine build. Out-of-balance pulleys will cause vibration, even when the rest of the engine is in balance.

Extra Weight

Some high-performance Ford V-8s, like the 428 Super Cobra Jet and 289 High Performance, had a slide-on counterweight for the front of the crank. These extra counterweights made up for the additional weight imposed by heavier connecting rods. Your machine shop can make up for this counterweight (if missing) by adding weight to the counterweights if necessary during the balancing process. See your machine shop for more details.

down to how much connecting rod you are going to run. The heavier the rod, the greater the need for counterweight. Ford did this by using a wider balancer with more counterweighting. You can do it by having your machine shop add weight to the crankshaft counterweights as necessary during the balancing process. Each machine shop uses its own preferred technique.

LUBRICATION

Working shoulder-to-shoulder with an engine's moving parts is the lubrication system. Improving lubrication is a cost-efficient process in a budget engine build-up. Blueprinting an oil pump costs virtually nothing. Chamfering oil holes in a crankshaft costs very little. Where it can get costly is the installation of a deep-sump or road-race oil pan with a modified pickup. The budget street engine doesn't need a deep-sump or road-race pan because there won't be the demands

on the engine we see in drag or road-racing conditions.

If you're going to aggressively spin your engine, we suggest a windage tray from MPG and a baffled Canton street pan, which keeps the oil where it belongs during high revs. These accessories don't come cheap, but they can prevent oil starvation. If you're building a mild cruiser, the stock pan will get the job done.

When we speak of blueprinting an oil pump, it's a simple process you can do in your shop at home. Your local machine shop can do it in less than 30 minutes, and it's time and money well spent. Oil pumps — like camshafts, pistons, rods, cranks, and other critical components — don't always arrive from the supply source in perfect condition. Camshafts don't always match the specs on the cam card; pistons aren't always the size printed on the package; and oil pumps aren't always clearanced as they should be. They need help from the builder.

Blueprinting an oil pump is just like blueprinting the rest of the engine. It is measuring and perfecting clearances just like we do with cylinder bores, heads, and other important parts. Oil pump clearances consist of rotor-side clearances mostly. Check the clearance between the rotor and the pump housing, and the rotor and the cover plate. Then machine the cover plate and/or rotor as necessary to get clearances perfected. We also need to check the pressure relief valve for freedom of movement and proper spring pressure. Nothing's more useless than a pressure relief valve that comes on too soon, or one that doesn't relieve pressure at all.

Your blueprinting should also include working the edges inside with a die grinder. Bevel the passages to ensure smooth flow. Remove ragged casting trash with the die grinder. This is what blueprinting an oil pump is all about. Do not touch the machined contact surfaces inside the pump with a die grinder or you risk rotor damage when the pump is assembled. Because some oil pump applications run close to the crankshaft counterweight, we suggest grinding the oil pump casting carefully to achieve better clearance with the counterweight. Do a mock-up and check your clearances. You'll be glad you did later.

Oiling system improvements consist of chamfering oil holes at each of the crank journals. This can be accomplished by your machine shop during crankshaft machining. Chamfering improves oil flow to the bearings and journals.

Using a high-performance oil pump drive shaft is insurance against shaft failure. Some engines — like the 351C, 351M, and 400M — suffer from oil starvation at No. 4 and No. 5 main bearings. There are two solutions for these engines. One solution is to run an external oil pressure line from the front oil pressure sending unit port to the sending unit port at the back of the block, which feeds additional oil to No. 4 and No. 5 main bearings. Another solution is to restrict oil flow to the cam bearings and top end, which improves oil flow to the No. 4 and No. 5 main bearings. A restrictor is screwed into the oil galley passage between the No.

Blueprinting an oil pump ensures smooth operation and sufficient oil pressure. Rotor-side clearances at the pump housing and cover must be perfected.

Even with new oil pumps, the relief valve should be checked for smooth operation.

1 main bearing and No. 1 cam bearing, which restricts oil flow to the cam bearings, lifters, pushrods, and rocker arms and keeps it where it's needed most, at the main bearings.

Oil galleys should be cleaned thoroughly again and again until all debris is removed. You will be amazed at the trash hidden inside. Rust and iron particles can lodge in oil galley passages, doing damage later to an engine's bearings and other moving parts. Wash the block repeatedly for best results.

Another important area is oil return flow to ensure we keep plenty of oil in the pan. Chamfering oil return passages, and primering the lifter valley

and cylinder head drain back areas, improve oil return flow to the pan. Improved oil return flow also keeps a more liberal oil supply to the timing set in front which relies on drain back flow for its lubrication.

GASKETS & FASTENERS

Gaskets are an area not enough of us think about when we're building an engine. What we want from a gasket is reliability. Gaskets fail not always due to the fault of the gasket, but the condition of casting surfaces. A warped block, cylinder head, manifold, timing cover, or water pump will contribute to gasket failure. Deck surfaces must be checked for trueness before assembly begins. Always specify the right gasket or seal for the job. Fel-Pro offers gaskets for specific duties. For example, a standard head gasket works fine for naturally-aspirated engines. Fel-Pro's Loc Wire head gasket is the ticket for supercharged and turbocharged applications. We suggest Fel-Pro gaskets because of the company's extraordinary attention to quality and abundant applications for Ford V-8s. When you're shopping head gaskets, keep cylinder bore size and water passage compatibility in mind.

Valve cover and oil pan gaskets have improved so much that oil leakage just isn't a given anymore. Opt for steel-reinforced rubber composition gaskets for your Ford. They will cost more, however, so does oil leakage. Intake manifold gasket installation warrants a reminder. Manifold end gaskets, especially with 221/260/289/302/351W engines, tend to pop out from crankcase pressure. Throw the end gaskets away and opt for a large bead of silicone gasket sealer on the block at each end of the manifold, then seat the manifold. When the silicone cures, it will expand and provide a tight seal. This will keep oil inside and out of the timing chain cover pockets on top.

Gasket makers offer a greater variety of self-sealing gaskets that don't require sealer, such as Fel-Pro's Printoseal, which not only self-seals, but doesn't stick when it's time for disassembly. When you're using silicone sealer, be sparing in your use. Many of us use too much, which can lead to sealer in places where it isn't wanted, like oil galleries and pick-up screens. A thin film of silicone sealer around water passages is all it takes with standard gaskets. Give the sealer time to cure before using the engine.

Main seals, fore and aft, mandate extra care. The front main seal should get a thin film of silicone sealer around its outside perimeter before installation. This ensures a good seal between the seal and the timing chain cover. Rear main seals need good lubrication before crankshaft installation. Non-synthetic, 30w engine oil is the best answer there.

Fel-Pro Gasket Basic Identification Chart/Small-Block

Type/Number	Application	Dimensions/Other Information
Full Set 2804	260/289/302 1962 - 11/30/82	From 12/1/82 302 and 1969-89 351W, specify individual gaskets.
Head 1011-1	260/289/302 1962-82	Pre-flattened steel wire with a steel core laminate.
Head 1011-2	302/5.0L 1983-93	Pre-flattened copper wire with a steel core laminate.
Head 1006	302/5.0L 1983-93	Loc Wire copper wire combustion seal with steel core laminate.
Intake 1250	260/289/302 1962-98	Standard, with Printoseal (no sealer required) For stock and small race-port heads.
Intake 1262	260/289/302 1962-98	Standard, with Printoseal (no sealer required) For large race-port heads.
Exhaust 1415	260/289/302 1962-93	Perforated steel core with anti-stick coating. Port Size: 1.25" x 1.48"
Exhaust 1486	J302 and K302 with dual bolt pattern.	Perforated steel core with anti-stick coating. Port Size: 1.40" x 1.40"
Exhaust 1487	Dart & TFS, E351 with dual bolt pattern, inline spread bolt Dart and TFS heads.	Perforated steel core with anti-stick coating. Port Size: 1.42" x 1.62"
Valve Cover 1613	260/289/302 1962-87	Blue Stripe/cork and rubber, 3/16" thick.
Valve Cover 1614	260/289/302 1962-87	Fel-CoPrene rubber, 5/32" thick.
Valve Cover 1645	260/289/302 1962-87	Cork-Lam cork-rubber with steel core, 5/16" thick.
Oil Pan 1809	302/5.0L 1989-98	One-piece gasket assembly.
Oil Pan 1810	260/289/302 1962-92	Rubber-coated fiber (cork)
Rear Main Seal 2901	260/289/302 1962 - 11/30/82	Premium material, 2-piece.
Rear Main Seal 2922	302/5.0L 11/30/82 - 93	Premium material, 1-piece
R.A.C.E. Set 2707-1	260/289/302 1962 - 11/30/82	Does not contain full-circle rear main seal.
R.A.C.E. Set 2718	302/5.0L 12/1/82 - 93	Does not contain full-circle rear main seal.
Head 1021	Boss 302 1969-70	Pre-flattened steel wire with steel core laminate.
Intake 1248	Boss 302 1969-70	Standard, with Printoseal (no sealer required) Port Size: 1.88" x 2.65"
Exhaust 1416	Boss 302 1969-70	Perforated steel core with anti-stick coating. 1.89" x 2.19"
Valve Cover 1636	Boss 302 1969-70	Cork-Lam cork-rubber with steel core, 1/4" thick.
Oil Pan 1809	Boss 302 1969-70	Rubber-coated fiber, 3/32" thick.
Rear Main Seal 2901	Boss 302 1969-70	Premium material, 2-piece.
R.A.C.E. Set 2707-1	Boss 302 1969-70	
Head 1021	302 SVO, 351W SVO	Pre-flattened steel wire with steel core laminate.
Head 1022/1023	302 SVO, 351W SVO with large overbore. Use 1022 left and 1023 right.	Pre-flattened steel wire with steel core laminate.
Head 1013	351C	Pre-flattened steel wire with steel core laminate.
Intake 1229	For SVO cylinder head # M-6049-A	Standard, with coating. Port Size: 1.35" x 2.20" to 1.83" x 2.20"
Intake 1265	For SVO cylinder heads #M-6049-B351, M-6049-C302, M-6049-D302.	Standard. Port Size: 1.35" x 2.20"
Intake 1253-1	For SVO "Yates" cylinder head, #M-6049-C3.	Standard w/o coating. Port Size: 1.35" x 1.95" Thickness: .030"
Intake 1253-2	For SVO "Yates" cylinder head, #M-6049-C3.	Standard w/o coating. Port Size: 1.35" x 1.95" Thickness: .045"
Intake 1253-3	For SVO "Yates" cylinder head, #M-6049-C3.	Standard w/o coating. Port Size: 1.35" x 1.95" Thickness: .060"

Fel-Pro Gasket Basic Identification Chart/Small-Block

Intake 1253-4	For SVO "Yates" cylinder head, #M-6049-C3.	Standard w/o coating. Port Size: 1.35" x 1.95" Thickness: .090"
Intake 1253-5	For SVO "Yates" cylinder head, #M-6049-C3.	Standard w/o coating. Port Size: 1.35" x 1.95" Thickness: .120"
Exhaust 1417	For SVO cylinder head #M-6049-A3	Perforated steel core with anti-stick coating. Port Size: 1.94"
Exhaust 1431	For SVO cylinder heads #M-6049-B351, M-6049-C302, M-6049-D302.	Perforated steel core with anti-stick coating. Port Size: 1.81"
Exhaust 1433	For SVO "Yates" head #M-6049-C3.	Perforated steel core with anti-stick coating. Port Size: 1.86" x 1.68"
Valve Cover 1615	For SVO aluminum cylinder heads except SVO stabilizer cover.	Blue-Stripe cork-rubber, 3/16" thick.
Valve Cover 1616	For SVO aluminum cylinder heads except SVO stabilizer cover.	Fel-CoPrene rubber, 1/8" thick
Valve Cover 1636	For SVO aluminum cylinder heads except SVO stabilizer cover.	Cork-Lam cork-rubber with steel core, 1/4" thick.
Valve Cover 1620	SVO Stabilizer Cover	Rubber coated fiber, 3/64" thick.
Oil Pan 1809	302 SVO Engine	Rubber coated fiber, 3/32" thick.
Oil Pan 1810	351W SVO Engine	Rubber coated fiber, 3/32" thick.
Oil Pan 1811	351C SVO Engine	Rubber coated fiber, 3/32" thick.
Oil Pan 1827	351W SVO Engine	Steel core gasket, 3/32" thick.
Rear Main Seal 2922	302 SVO Engine 11/30/82 - 98	Premium material, full-circle type.
Rear Main Seal 2901	302 SVO Engine	Premium material, 2-piece.
Rear Main Seal 2902	351C SVO, 351W SVO Engines	Premium material, 2-piece.
Rear Main Seal 2921	351 SVO Engine 7/10/83 - 93	Premium material, full-circle type.
R.A.C.E. Set 2707-1	302 SVO Engine	
R.A.C.E. Set 2710	351C SVO Engine	
R.A.C.E. Set 2709-1	351W SVO Engine	
R.A.C.E. Set 2331	302 SVO, 351W SVO Engines, Timing Cover Gasket	Premium material.
Head 1013	351C-4V Only	Pre-flattened steel wire with steel core laminate.
Intake 1240	351C-2V, 351M, 400M - 1970-79.	Standard, with Printoseal. Port Size: 1.50" x 2.12"
Intake 1228	351C-4V Only	Standard, with Printoseal. Port Size: 1.88" x 2.65"
Exhaust 1430	351C-2V, 351M, 400M - 1970-79.	Perforated steel core with anti-stick coating. Port Size: 1.56" x 1.98"
Exhaust 1416	351C-4V Only	Perforated steel core with anti-stick coating. Port Size: 1.89" x 2.19"
Valve Cover 1615	351C, 351M, 400M	Blue-Stripe cork-rubber, 3/16" thick.
Valve Cover 1616	351C, 351M, 400M	Fel-Co-Prene rubber, 1/8" thick.
Valve Cover 1636	351C, 351M, 400M	Cork-Lam cork-rubber with steel core, 1/4" thick.
Oil Pan 1811	351C, 351M, 400M	Rubber coated fiber, 3/32" thick.
Rear Main Seal 2902	351C, 351M, 400M	Premium material, 2-piece.
R.A.C.E. 2710	351C, 351M, 400M	

FASTENERS

Being on a budget, you're probably wondering what is the best hardware to use. ARP makes bolt kits and stud kits for main bearing caps. The use of bolts or studs is a personal thing. Of the two, studs provide greater strength and keep main bearing caps where they belong. Studs provide greater strength because they're more rigid than bolts. They keep cap movement to a minimum.

If you're going to ARP the crankcase, you should ARP everywhere else in your engine for maximum effectiveness. ARP has oil pan and pump bolt kits not to mention accessory bolt sets for the front dress. Because these hardware kits are of aerospace quality, you can feel confident about your work right away.

If cost is a huge issue and ARP bolts are out of your reach, consider the cost of a failed engine because you didn't go the extra mile. Using the best hardware to assemble your engine is like buying life insurance. It doesn't look as good as a high-rise intake or a nice set of valve covers. But it's great comfort when your foot is on the floor and the engine is spinning at 6000 rpm.

Engine fasteners remain an area of great debate and confusion for enthusiasts. Truth is, we don't treat fasteners with the respect they need, nor do we always know enough about them. During the research and development of this book, we spoke with the people at American Racing Products (ARP), which makes the best engine fasteners in the world. ARP uses high quality aircraft grade alloys in its engine fastening hardware. Any failure is unacceptable. This means you can expect aircraft grade 8740 steel alloy. It is expensive, but worth the cost difference when you consider the price of catastrophic engine failure. You may contact ARP at 800-826-3045. Check out the listings of fasteners from ARP for Ford powerplants located in this chapter.

Head studding a block isn't necessary for street applications unless you're running a supercharger or turbocharger. For racing applications, studding the block helps rigidity and tightness between the cylinder head and block. The downside is cylinder head removal and installation in a small engine compartment, which becomes impossible for a Mustang, Falcon, Fairlane, Comet, or Cougar. Engine removal becomes mandatory.

ARP Engine & Accessory kits are a great one-stop hardware source for your engine build. Everything is here

Fel-Pro Gasket Basic Identification Chart/Big-Block

Type/Number	Application	Dimensions/Other Information
Head 1020	390/406/410/427/428ci	Pre-flattened steel wire with steel core laminate.
Intake 1246	427/428ci Cobra Jet	Standard with Printoseal.
Intake 1247	390ci High Performance	Standard with Printoseal.
Exhaust 1442	All "FE" except GT head.	Perforated steel core with anti-stick coating.
Exhaust 1485	390ci GT head.	Perforated steel core with anti-stick coating.
Valve Cover 1632	All "FE"	Blue-Stripe cork-rubber, 3/16" thick.
Oil Pan 1817	All "FE"	Rubber coated fiber.
Rear Main Seal	See Master Catalog 900.	
R.A.C.E. Set 2720	All "FE"	
Head 1018	All 385-series 429/460 Gasket Bore Dia. 4.500"	Pre-flattened steel wire with steel core laminate.
Head 1028	All 385-series 429/460 Gasket Bore Dia. 4.670"	Pre-flattened steel wire with steel core laminate.
Intake 1230	All 385-series 429/460 except 429CJ and SCJ.	Standard with Printoseal, .060" thick. Port Size: 1.98" x 2.26"
Intake 1231	429CJ and SCJ only.	Standard with Printoseal, .060" thick. Port Size: 2.24" x 2.60"
Exhaust 1419	All 385-series 429/460 except 429CJ and SCJ.	Perforated steel core with anti-stick coating. Port Size: 1.50" x 2.10"
Exhaust 1420	429CJ and SCJ only.	Perforated steel core with anti-stick coating. Port Size: 1.55" x 2.35"
Valve Cover 1619	All 385-series 429/460.	Blue-Stripe cork-rubber, 3/16" thick.
Valve Cover 1617	All 385-series 429/460.	Fel-CoPrene rubber, 5/32" thick.
Valve Cover 1643	All 385-series 429/460.	Cork-Lam cork-rubber with steel core.
Oil Pan 1812	All 385-series 429/460.	Rubber coated fiber, 3/32" thick.
Rear Main Seal	See Master Catalog 900.	
R.A.C.E. Set 2712	All 385-series 429/460.	

ARP "Head Bolt Kits" Identification/Availability Chart

Application	"High Performance"			"Stainless"	
	Hex	12-Point	Pro-Series/12-Point	Hex	12-Point
260/289/302ci	154-3601	154-3701	N/A	454-3601	454-3701
260/289/302ci w/ 351W heads	N/A	N/A	254-3708	N/A	N/A
Boss 302	154-3602	154-3702	254-3702	454-3602	454-3702
351W	154-3603	N/A	N/A	N/A	N/A
351C	154-3604	N/A	254-3704	N/A	N/A
351C SVO	N/A	N/A	254-3701	N/A	N/A
332/352/360/390 406/410/427/428ci	155-3601	N/A	N/A	N/A	N/A
427 SOHC	155-3602	N/A	N/A	N/A	N/A

ARP "Cam Bolt Kits" Identification/Availability Chart

Application	Diameter	Socket Size	High Performance	Pro-Series
'68-up 302/351W/429/460ci	3/8-16	5/8"	155-1001	255-1001
332/352/360/390/406/410 427/427ci	7/16-14	5/8"	155-1002	255-1002

ARP "Main Stud Kits" Ident./Avail. Chart

Application	2-Bolt Main	4-Bolt Main
260/289/302ci	154-5401	N/A
260/289/302ci w/ windage tray	254-5501	N/A
302/5.0L Dual-Sump pan	154-5407	N/A
Boss 302	N/A	154-5602
351W	154-5403	154-5606
351W w/ windage tray	154-5503	N/A
351W SVO	N/A	154-5603
351C	154-5404	154-5604
302ci SVO	N/A	154-5605
332/352/360/390 /406/410/427/428ci	155-5401	N/A
429/460ci	155-5402	155-5501
429/460ci w/ windage tray	255-5502	255-5702

ARP "Main Bolt Kits" Ident./Avail. Chart

Application	High Performance Series	Pro Series
260/289/302ci (2-Bolt Main)	154-5001	N/A
Boss 302 (4-Bolt Main)	154-5201	N/A
351W (2-Bolt Main)	154-5003	N/A
351W (4-Bolt Main)	154-5203	N/A
351C (2-Bolt Main)	154-5004	N/A
351C (4-Bolt Main)	154-5204	N/A
351ci SVO (4-Bolt Main) w/ 3/8" outer bolts.	N/A	254-5202
351ci SVO (4-Bolt Main) w/ 7/16" outer bolts.	N/A	254-5203
332/352/360/ 390/406/410 /427/428ci	155-5201	N/A
429/460ci	155-5202	N/A

ARP "Head Stud" Identification/Availability Chart

Application	Hex Nuts	Hex Nuts/ U/Cut Studs	12-Point Nuts	12-Point Nuts/ U/Cut Studs
260/289/302ci 7/16"	154-4001	254-4401	154-4201	254-4701
260/289/302ci w/ 351W, SVO J302, SVO High Port, SVO GT-40, Edelbrock.	154-4005	254-4405	154-4205	254-4705
351W, SVO J302, SVO High Port, SVO GT-40, Edelbrock, Dart and World Products heads.	154-4003	254-4503	154-4303	254-4703
Boss 302	154-4002	N/A	154-4202	N/A
351C	154-4004	N/A	154-4204	N/A
332/352/360/390 406/410/427/428ci	155-4001	N/A	155-4201	N/A
427ci SOHC	155-4002	N/A	155-4202	N/A
429/460ci w/ SVO A429 aluminum heads	155-4003	N/A	155-4203	N/A
460ci SVO aluminum A460 and B460	N/A	255-4304	N/A	
460ci w/ Blue Thunder heads	N/A	255-4101	N/A	255-4301

ARP "Connecting Rod Bolt" Ident./Avail. Chart

Application	High Performance	High Performance (2-piece pack)	HighPerformance Wave Loc
221/260/289/302ci	154-6002	154-6022	N/A
Boss 302 & 351W	150-6004	150-6024	150-6404
351C	154-6003	154-6023	154-6403
351M/400M	154-6001	154-6021	N/A
302/5.0L Sportsman SVO	150-6005	150-6025	N/A
332/352/360/390/406/410			
427/428ci	155-6002	155-6022	N/A
428 Cobra Jet	155-6001	155-6021	N/A
429/460ci	155-6003	155-6023	N/A
Boss 429	150-6004	150-6024	N/A

ARP "Engine & Accessory Kits" Ident./Avail. Chart

(Available in Chrome Moly or Black Oxide)

Application	Hex-Head	12-Point	Stainless 300 Hex-Head	Stainless 300 12-Point
221/260/289/302ci	554-9801	554-9701	554-9601	554-9501
Boss 302	554-9802	554-9702	554-9602	554-9502
351W	554-9803	554-9703	554-9603	554-9503
351C	554-9804	554-9704	554-9604	554-9504
332/352/360/390/406/410				
427/428ci	555-9802	555-9702	555-9602	555-9502
429/460ci	555-9801	555-9701	555-9601	555-9502

to help you assemble and dress up your engine: valve covers, oil pan, intake manifold, headers, fuel pump, water pump, timing chain cover, thermostat housing, alternator bracket, coil and distributor hold-downs, and engine mounts.

ORIGINAL EQUIPMENT FASTENERS

If you're building a high-performance engine for either a concours restored or a restomod, ARP fasteners may not be for you. ARP is the undisputed leader in high-performance fasteners. However, ARP fasteners don't offer an original equipment look. AMK Products offers virtually every kind of original equipment fastener known for Ford engines. This means you can screw it together with a factory original appearance using new hardware. AMK Products isn't just about engine hardware. The company brings the restorer a wealth of different parts and subassemblies that not only outfit the engine, but the engine compartment.

For around $100, you can outfit your Ford mill with AMK's Engine Fastener Kit, which is available for all of the engines covered in this book. There's obscure hardware you can spend hours combing the salvage yards for, but why? AMK Products brings us exactly what the factory did 30 years ago, with the proper finish and markings. It's almost too good to be true.

Engine hardware is more than just exhaust manifold bolts and accessory fasteners, it's radiator and heater hose clamps, air cleaner wing nuts, fuel line brackets, decals and stickers, alternator parts, ignition wires, voltage regulators, battery cables, starter solenoids, vacuum advance units, radiator caps, even Autolite battery caps!

AMK Products will also educate you on engine hardware with its Guide To Ford Fasteners, which details hardware like no other book ever published on the subject. What's more, it's a Ford exclusive. This book details more than 10,000 different Ford fasteners, the history of each type of fastener, proper finishes, measurements, grades and accurate refinishing. No engine building project is complete without the AMK Products Guide To Ford Fasteners. For more information contact AMK.

Although not all engines have fastener kits available, complete kits will be available in time. All hardware is available separately for every engine type covered in this book. Contact AMK Products or your favorite Ford parts vendor.

ARP "Oil Pump Bolts & Studs" Ident./Avail. Chart

Application	Black Oxide Hex-Head	Black Oxide 12-Point	Stainless Hex	Stainless 12-Point
Standard Bolt Kit, 5/16"	150-6902	150-6901	450-6902	450-6901
SVO, extended oil pump, stud kit, 5/16" x 7.0"	154-7006	N/A	N/A	N/A
Oil pump to pick-up, stud kit	154-7005	N/A	N/A	N/A

ARP "Harmonic Damper Bolt Kits" Ident./Avail. Chart

Application	Diameter	Socket Size	Part Number
All V-8s except 351C	5/8"-18	5/8"	150-2501
351C	5/8"-18	5/8"	154-2501

ARP "Intake Manifold Bolt Kits" Ident./Avail. Chart

Application	Hex-Head	12-Point	Stainless 300 Hex-Head	Stainless 300 12-Point
221/260/289/302/351W	154-2001	154-2101	454-2001	454-2101
351C	154-2004	154-2104	454-2004	454-2104
332/352/360/390/406/410				
427/428ci	155-2002	155-2102	455-2002	455-2102
429/460ci	N/A	N/A	N/A	455-2101

Chamfering oil holes in the crankshaft journals enriches oil flow to the bearings and journals. Your machine shop can do this.

Some Ford V-8 engines — like the 351C, 351M, and 400M — need a restrictor installed between the No. 1 main bearing saddle and the No. 1 cam bearing, which limits oil flow to the cam bearings, lifters, pushrods, and rocker arms. This keeps oil flow where it's needed most at the main bearings.

AMK Products "Engine Fastener Kit" Chart

Kit Number/Model Year	Group Number	Other Information
C2OE-322 1965	6007	289/302 w/o A/C
C3OE-323 1965	6007	289 High Performance w/ generator
C2OE-336 1965	6007	260/289 w/ generator and A/C
C5OE-559 1965	6007	289 w/ aluminum water pump and alternator
C5OE-560 1965	6007	289 w/ aluminum water pump w/ alternator and A/C
C5OE-561 1965	6007	289 High Performance w/ aluminum water pump and alternator
B8AE-327 1965	6007	352/390 w/ exhaust lock tabs
C6AE-328 1965	6007	352/390 w/ Ramploks
C6OE-324 1966	6007	289 w/ cast iron water pump
C6OE-325 1966	6007	289 High Performance w/ cast iron water pump
C6OE-337 1966	6007	289 w/ cast iron water pump and A/C
B8AE-327 1966	6007	352/390/428 w/ exhaust lock tabs
C6AE-328 1966	6007	352/390/428 w/ Ramploks
C6OE-329 1966	6007	352/390/428 aw/ Ramploks
C6OE-324 1967	6007	289 w/ cast iron water pump
C6OE-325 1967	6007	289 High Performance w/ cast iron water pump
C7OE-562 1967	6007	289 w/ cast iron water pump and A/C
C7OE-330 1967	6007	390 High Performance w/ Ramploks
S7ME-331 1967	6007	428 Shelby GT500
C8OE-326 1968-70	6007	289/302 All
C8OE-338 1968-70	6007	289/302 w/ A/C
C8OE-332 1968-70	6007	390 High Performance
C8OE-333 1968	6007	428 Cobra Jet
S8ME-382 1968	6007	428 Cobra Jet, Shelby GT500KR
S8ME-677 1968	6007	428 Shelby GT500
C9OE-334 1969-70	6007	428 Cobra Jet

CHAPTER 5

CYLINDER HEADS

You can achieve significant gains in engine power with the proper selection and modification of cylinder heads. Cylinder head port size and shape, coupled with combustion chamber size and shape, determine an engine's power personality. The "bigger is better" theory most of us have accepted over the years doesn't always work to an engine's advantage. A street engine can have too much cylinder head, which adversely affects driveability. The same can be said for racing engines, depending upon the application. Ports that are too large hurt the low-end torque we need for effective street performance. Your challenge is to achieve the right combination of port size and camshaft profile to enhance driving pleasure. You're going to want a cylinder head/piston/induction/camshaft combination that will serve you well in regular driving as well as traffic light-to-traffic light performance.

How you intend to use the engine directly determines the type of cylinder head you should select. Budget street engines benefit more from the smaller ports we see with stock heads. They don't always need porting and polishing, either. Sometimes porting and polishing take street power away from where you need it most. Stock intake ports that are rough cast keep fuel droplets in suspension on carburetor equipped engines. This improves low-end torque. Ground and polished intake ports can actually hurt low-end torque on carbureted engines because fuel atomization and suspension are affected.

SMALL BLOCK

One of the biggest myths you will face in your Ford engine build is that the 289 High Performance head is the best head to use. This is not necessarily so. The only difference between the 289 High Performance head and the 2V/4V head is valve spring pockets and screw-in rocker-arm studs. Otherwise, port size is virtually the same. So save your

money and spruce up a set of 2V/4V heads or opt for 351W types. How? By doing some port work, opting for screw-in rocker-arm studs, and installing hardened valve seats and larger valves.

If you're building a 289 High Performance engine, opt for larger 1.94/1.60" Chevrolet valves (no one's going to know they're there but you) and a port/bowl job to achieve the most from those factory Hi-Po heads. Externally, they will look stock. Internally, they will help your 289 High Performance engine breathe like it never has before. You can also opt for 351W heads here too without anyone knowing the difference externally.

Vintage small-block Ford head choices aren't as simple as they may appear. There has been significant change in the 221/260/289/302 head over the past four decades. Some of these heads are best avoided. Others are diamonds in the rough.

The best small-block head to use is the 1969-73 351W, thanks to its larger valves and ports. It's a bolt-on swap. When a 351W head cannot be sourced, the 1965-73 289/302 head is your best bet, due to its smaller wedge chambers. We stress head use prior to 1974 because combustion chamber size remains smaller in those years, keeping compression healthy.

When you are building a set of heads, good machining technique is important. First, castings should be checked for cracks and serious warpage. Then head deck surfaces should be checked and milled as necessary. Valves and guides should be reworked or replaced. Hardened exhaust valve seats should be installed. Pushrod guide plates and screw-in rocker-arm studs should be fitted. When budget is limited, you should opt for 1965 through early 1966 heads with pushrod guides already cast. If you are running a hot camshaft, screw-in rocker-arm studs become mandatory. When screw-in studs are beyond your budget, pinning the press-in studs becomes an inexpensive alternative.

Bush Performance in Fort Smith, Arkansas offers a low-cost way to get into hot street performance with the Street Boss system (nicknamed the "Clevor", for Cleveland and Windsor). The Street Boss system puts the 351C head atop the 289/302/351W block. The

way you intend to use your engine determines which 351C head you will use. For the weekend racer, the 351C-4V head with its large ports and closed-wedge chambers makes a good high-rev head. The 351C-4V head breathes very well at high RPM like we see in drag and road-course racing. The 351C-2V head is a better street head due to its smaller ports and open-chamber design. Smaller ports give you better low-end torque. Open chambers reduce the risk of detonation with low-octane fuels.

New aftermarket heads aren't within the realm of a budget build. However, as they age and see use, they often wind up at the swap meets for considerably less than they were new. Glass beading and valve work makes them as good as new for less money. Good street heads include the Ford Motorsport SVO GT-40 iron and aluminum heads, World Products Windsor Jr. heads, and Edelbrock Performers. These are the most common, most reliable heads out there for the builder on a budget.

For those of you building late-model 5.0L and 5.8L engines, cylinder head choices tend to be different, especially if you're interested in meeting emission standards. From 1982-84, Ford used a D9AE-6049-AA cylinder head casting atop the 5.0L High Output V-8. This is not

a high-performance cylinder head although it was used on the 1982-84 5.0L High Output engines. It is, however, a workable cylinder head that will come alive with port work and larger 1.94/1.60" Chevrolet valves.

Small-block Ford heads lost yardage in the performance arena after 1978 with Ford's increasing attention to emissions and driveability. Ports became smaller for improved low-end torque and cleaner emissions. Although this works well in traffic, it doesn't do much for our engine in higher RPM ranges. Despite the D9AE casting shortcomings, you can still port these heads and make power. However, this is not maximizing what you can do with a stock cylinder head.

The biggest shortcoming with the D9AE casting is the exhaust port with Ford's infamous Thermactor injection "hump" in the port. It becomes very restrictive. However, this hump can be ground out and all restriction taken away with some Saturday afternoon labor on a work bench. For 1985 only, Ford went to the E5AE head, which was little more than a modified D9AE casting designed for easy roller tappet removal with the head installed. It is identifiable by the reliefs notched in the head at the lifter valley. Otherwise, it is virtually identical to the D9AE casting.

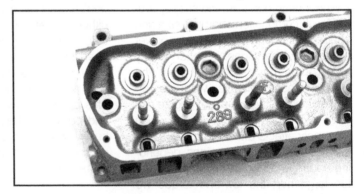

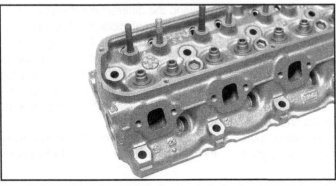

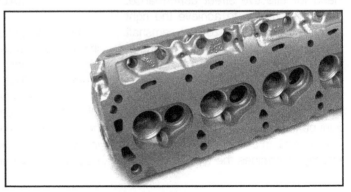

The 1965-66 289-2V/4V head is the best choice for 289/302ci engines due to its 57cc chambers and cast-in-head pushrod guides. Port size is limited, however. For the engine builder on a strict budget, this head needs minimal rework.

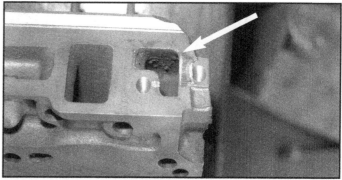

The 1969-73 351W head is a budget performance bolt-on for 289/302ci engines due to its larger valves and ports. The only important difference to watch for is the dog-leg coolant passage between the intake manifold and cylinder head on early 351W heads. This can pose leak problems if you use the wrong intake gasket. Use the 351W intake manifold gasket.

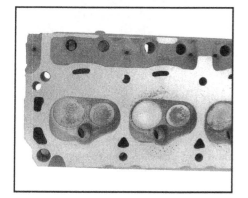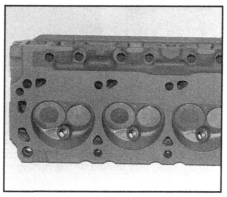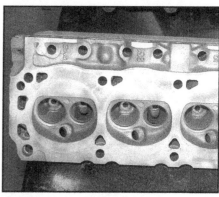

Chamber size is critical to performance. Small-block Ford engine evolution includes larger combustion chambers after 1973, which lowers compression. For best results, stick with 57-64cc chambers in your engine build. The quickest way to identify the smaller chamber is the shrouded 18mm spark plug hole shown here.

Ford heads after 1973 grew larger chambers like these for reduced compression. Look for the 14mm spark plug holes common from 1975-up.

The 351W head has larger chambers than the 289/302 head. This is a 1969-73 head with 18mm spark plugs.

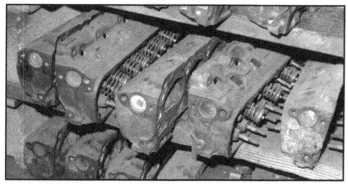

Head castings can be found at any swap meet or seasoned machine shop. Some machine shops, like Fastline Performance in Simi Valley, California, keep large inventories of used cylinder heads.

Ford began making improvements to the 5.0L/5.8L head in 1986 with the "high-swirl/fast burn" E6AE and E6TE castings. This head saw widespread use from 1986-88 depending on vehicle application. A shrouded intake valve was trademark to the "high-swirl/fast burn" concept. Thing is, the E6AE/E6TE head didn't do much for power.

The E5TE and E7TE heads introduced for 1987 are undoubtedly the best late-model castings because the "high-swirl/fast burn" chamber is eliminated. This is more a return to the 1985 High Output/Truck head with improved water jacket passages. For you the engine builder, this head is good for an easy bonus 25-30 horsepower.

The 1993-95 Cobra GT-40 head is little more than a marine head with larger valves and ports. This fact all by itself makes the GT-40 a good,

economical head for 5.0L/5.8L performance. Economical because it is a common head. Just look for 1.84/1.54" valves, "GT" markings, and F3ZE/F4ZE casting numbers. Ford part numbers are F3ZZ-A and F4ZZ-A. These heads are also available from Ford Racing as M-6049-L302. Properly outfitted, these heads use the F3ZZ-6564-A roller rocker arm with a 1.7:1 ratio.

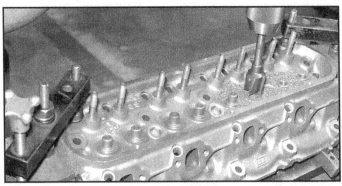
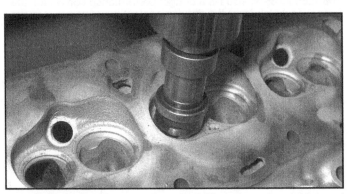

Head work involves more than just grinding and seating valves. Performance and reliability come from installing new valve guides and cutting in hardened exhaust valve seats. Heads are checked and leveled on the milling machine prior to machine work.

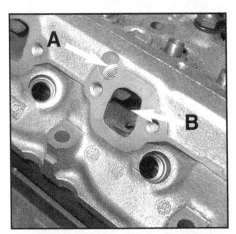

One head to avoid is the 1966-68 289/302 Thermactor head for California emissions engines. These heads have Thermactor injection ports that disturb exhaust flow. These ports can be plugged (A) and their humps (B) ground smooth for better flow.

Head deck surfaces should be milled for trueness.

Unless your budget is very limited, we suggest the installation of hardened exhaust valve seats. This involves cutting out the iron seats and pressing in hardened seats. Hardened exhaust valve seats help engines live longer with unleaded fuel use.

Putting 351C heads on a 289/302/351W block is nothing new. Ford did it first with the 1969-70 Boss 302 engine, which has modified 351C heads on a four-bolt main bearing 302 block. The "Street Boss" from Bush Performance Engines is a budget trip to awesome power from your 289/302/351W.

This is the 1963-67 289 High Performance head with valve spring pockets and screw-in rocker-arm studs. What makes this head a high-performance piece isn't huge port size, but reliability mods like the spring pockets and screw-in studs. Port and valve size is exactly the same as the 289-2V/4V head. The value of a "Hi-Po" head is rooted in rarity, not performance. If you're seeking performance, don't waste your money.

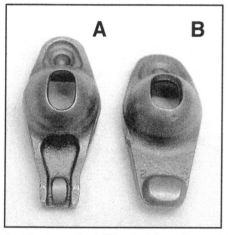

Another important difference in early small-block heads is rail (A) versus conventional (B) style rocker arms. Beginning May 8, 1966 in production, Ford began using the rail-style rocker arm on 289 small blocks, with a new head casting that eliminated the pushrod guide hole in the cylinder head. These rocker arm types cannot be interchanged. Heads with rail-style rocker arms can be equipped with screw-in rocker-arm studs and pushrod guide plates for use with conventional rocker arms.

An effective, affordable modification is screw-in rocker-arm studs with pushrod guide plates. Your favorite machine shop can handle this one. This process involves removing the press-in studs, machining down the bosses, and cutting threads for the screw-in studs.

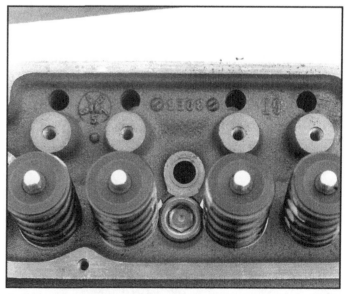

Late model 5.0L GT heads can be adapted to any 221/260/289/302 block. Remember, these heads have larger 64-68cc chambers, which reduces compression. Have a plan in tow to increase compression when you're using GT and GT-40 heads. From a performance standpoint, not much power will be gained from using these heads unless you keep compression in the 9.5:1 to 10.5:1 range.

To install pushrod guide plates and screw-in rocker-arm studs, the press-in studs must be removed. After the stud bosses are milled the width of the guide plate, threads are cut in the cylinder head for screw-in studs.

With screw-in rocker-arm studs and guideplates, you dramatically improve the integrity of the valvetrain.

Valve spring pressure must match the aggressiveness of the camshaft profile. Spring pressures must be set accordingly. If there is not enough spring pressure, you will experience valve float at high revs. Too much spring pressure can wipe a camshaft.

The more aggressive the camshaft, the more heavy-duty your rocker arms must be. Roller-tip forged rockers like these are designed to withstand aggressive camshaft profiles.

You can farm out head porting to a machine shop, or you can do it yourself using a grinder and some home porting techniques. Because head porting involves extensive labor, it's expensive. For a street engine, limit your porting to port and bowl work. Polishing is unnecessary for street heads because the heads will carbon up with use, rendering the polish job useless.

The 351C-4V head employs closed-wedge chambers with huge intake and exhaust ports for healthy high-RPM breathing. We emphasize "high-RPM breathing" because this is a poor street head. Large ports do their best work at high revs when velocity increases. At low RPM, they don't make the torque you need for traffic-light-to-traffic-light performance. Those small-wedge chambers tend to aggravate detonation with today's low-octane fuels.

The 351C-2V head makes the best street head thanks to its open-chamber design and smaller ports. Smaller ports do their best work at lower revs typically experienced with street use. For coming out of the hole, this is a great head. The large open chamber reduces the chance of detonation.

This is the 351C/351M/400M and Boss 302 valve cover first used in 1969. A cast aluminum valve cover is also available.

AFTERMARKET SMALL-BLOCK STREET HEADS

Life has never been better for the small-block Ford builder. Thirty years ago, we had to settle for 351W heads atop the 260/289/302 small block to improve air flow, and this isn't a bad thing. The 351W head has been responsible for significant increases in power for 260/289/302 small blocks. However, manufacturers like Edelbrock and Ford Racing have made it easier for Ford buffs to get into better performance without extensive head improvement labor.

Although the 351W head is a cheap alternative, we have to rework this head to achieve best results. When you turn to Edelbrock, the work has already been done for you with better port and valve sizing right out of the box. The nice thing about Edelbrock Performer series aluminum heads for small-block Fords is their street legal status, which means they will pass a smog check in all 50 states. Here's what you get with an Edelbrock street legal Performer head: high-performance valve springs, retainers, and keepers that will withstand up to .575" valve lift, CNC port-matched intake runners, exhaust crossover passages, 1.94/1.60" or 2.02/1.60" stainless steel valves, and screw-in rocker arm studs with guide plates. All you have to supply is roller rocker arms, lock nuts, and pushrods.

Three basic types of street heads are available from Edelbrock for the small-block Ford. The Edelbrock Performer head for the 289/302/351W V-8 with Thermactor is available with either 1.90/1.60" or 2.02/1.60" valve sizes depending upon piston-to-valve clearance. Chamber size is 60cc. The Performer RPM head is designed more for the 289/302/351W without Thermactor. This leads us to the Performer 5.0/5.8L for late-model, fuel-injected V-8 engines. This head is designed for late-model, bolt/fulcrum rocker arms, which makes these a bolt-on swap. What's more, they're street legal in all 50 states. Whenever you're shopping swap meets and classified for Edelbrock Performer series heads, keep in mind what makes these heads different and applicable to a specific engine type. No one wants to find out the hard way they purchased the wrong head for their application, especially if a failed smog check confirms this fact. Examine a potential buy closely before laying down the cash.

Edelbrock comes through for you with valvetrain components and cylinder head hardware that makes your job as a performance improvement engineer a snap. Because the Performer series cylinder heads are designed to fit both 260/289/302 and the 351W engines, head bolt bushings (#9680) are required for the 260/289/302 that take a smaller head bolt (7/16") than the 351W (1/2"). Valves, guides, and seals are also available from Edelbrock for these heads.

Think of Edelbrock as a one-stop shop for all of your valvetrain needs. Pushrod guide plates, hardened steel

Small-Block Cylinder Head Identification

(Bold Indicates High Performance or change in valve/port size)

Displacement/ Year	Casting Number	Chamber Size	Valve Size	Port Size
221ci 1962-63	C2OE-A	45 - 51cc	1.59" Intake	1.76" x 1.00" Intake
	C2OE-B		1.39" Exhaust	1.24" x 1.00 Exhaust
	C2OE-C			
	C2OE-D			
	C2OE-E			
	C3OE-A			
260ci 1962-63	C2OE-F	52 - 55cc	1.59" Intake	1.76" x 1.00" Intake
	C3OE-B		1.39" Exhaust	1.24" x 1.00" Exhaust
260ci 1964	**C4OE-B (1964)**	**52 - 55cc**	**1.67" Intake**	**1.76" x 1.00" Intake**
Exhaust			**1.45" Exhaust**	**1.24" x 1.00"**
289ci 1963-67	C3AE-F	52 - 55cc	1.78" Intake	1.94" x 1.04" Intake
	C3OE-E		1.45" Exhaust	1.24" x 1.00" Exhaust
	C3OE-F			
	C4AE-C			
	C5DE-B			
	C6DE-G			
	C6OE-C (Thermactor)			
	C6OE-E (Thermactor)			
	C6OE-M			
	C7OE-A (Thermactor)			
	C7OE-B (Thermactor)			
	C7OE-C			
	C7OZ-B (Thermactor)	63cc		
	C7ZE-A (Thermactor)			
	C8OE-D (Thermactor)			
	C8OE-L (Thermactor)			
	C8OE-M (Thermactor)			
289ci 1963-67 High Performance	**C3OE** **C4OE-B** **C5OE-A** **C5AE-E**	**52 - 55cc**	1.78" Intake 1.45" Exhaust	1.94" x 1.04" Intake 1.24" x 1.00" Exhaust
Service Head	C7ZZ-B (Part No.)	52 - 55cc	1.78" Intake	1.94" x 1.04" Intake
			1.45" Exhaust	1.24" x 1.00" Exhaust
302ci 1968-	C7OE-C	63cc	1.78" Intake	1.94" x 1.04" Intake
	C7OE-G		1.45" Exhaust	1.24" x 1.00" Exhaust
	C8OE-F (4V Head)	**53.5cc**		
	C8OE-J			
	C8OE-K (Thermactor)			
	C8OE-L (Thermactor)			
	C8OE-M			
	C8AE-J	58.2cc		
	C8DE-F			
	C9TE-C (Truck Head)			
	D0OE-B			
	D1TZ-A (Truck Head)			
	D2OE-BA			
	D5OE-GA	69cc		
	D5OE-A3A			
	D5OE-A3B			
	D7OE-DA			
	D8OE-AB			

Small-Block Cylinder Head Identification

(Bold Indicates High Performance or change in valve/port size)

Displacement/ Year	Casting Number	Chamber Size	Valve Size	Port Size
302ci 1969-70 **Boss 302**	C9ZE-A C9ZE-C	**61 - 64cc**	2.23" Intake 1.71" Exhaust	2.50" x 1.75" Intake 2.00" x 1.74" Exhaust
	D0ZE-A **D1ZE-A**	**58cc**	2.19" Intake 1.71" Exhaust	2.50" x 1.75" Intake 2.00" x 1.74" Exhaust
351W 1969-80	C9OE-B C9OE-D D0OE-C D0OE-G	60cc	1.84" Intake 1.54" Exhaust	1.94" x 1.76" Intake 1.24" x 1.00" Exhaust
	D5TE-EB (Truck Head) D8OE-AB (302 Head)	69cc	1.78" Intake 1.45" Exhaust	1.94" x 1.04" Intake 1.24" x 1.00" Exhaust
302ci 1985	**E5AE-CA**	67 - 70cc	1.78" Int. 1.46" Exh.	1.94" x 1.04" Intake 1.24" x 1.00" Exhaust
351C 1970-74	D0AE-E (2V) D0AE-J (2V)	74 - 77cc	2.04" Intake 1.67" Exhaust	2.02" x 1.65" Intake 1.84" x 1.38" Exhaust
	D0AE-G (4V) D0AE-H (4V) D0AE-M (4V) D0AE-N (4V) D0AE-R (4V)	61 - 64cc	2.19" Intake 1.71" Exhaust	2.50" x 1.75" Intake 2.00" x 1.74" Exhaust
	D1AE-AA (2V) D1AE-CB (2V)	74 - 77cc	2.04" Intake 1.67" Exhaust	2.02" x 1.65" Intake 1.84" x 1.38" Exhaust
	D1AE-GA (4V) **D1ZE-DA (CJ)** **D1ZE-B (BOSS 351)**	61 - 64cc **73 - 76cc** **64 - 67cc**	2.19" Intake 1.71" Exhaust	2.50" x 1.75" Intake 2.00" x 1.74" Exhaust
	D2ZE-A (High Output)	73 - 76cc	2.19" Intake 1.71" Exhaust	2.50" x 1.75" Intake 2.00" x 1.74" Exhaust
	D3ZE-AA (CJ)	73 - 76cc	2.19" Intake 1.71" Exhaust	2.50" x 1.75" Intake 2.00" x 1.74" Exhaust

Guide To Ford Racing Small-Block Street Heads

Head Type	Details	Chamber Size	Part Number
GT-40 Turbo-Swirl Street Legal	Bare Head Aluminum	64cc	M-6049-Y302
GT-40 Turbo-Swirl Street Legal	Complete Aluminum	64cc	M-6049-Y303
GT-40P Hi-Flow Explorer	Complete Cast Iron	65cc	M-6049-P303
GT-40X	Bare Head Aluminum	64cc	M-6049-X302
GT-40X	Complete Aluminum	64cc	M-6049-X303
GT-40X	Bare Head Aluminum	58cc	M-6049-X304
GT-40X	Complete Aluminum	58cc	M-6049-X305
GT 5.0L H.O.	Complete Cast Iron	65cc	M-6049-M50

pushrods, head bolt kits, and even Performer-series camshaft kits are available from Edelbrock for your engine project. With Edelbrock, you can plan your performance agenda as a package, which makes shopping for cylinder heads, induction, and valvetrain systems easy. All you have to do is chat with Edelbrock's knowledgeable sales staff who can get you steered in the right direction.

Ford Racing offers the enthusiast a variety of cylinder head types depending upon budget. The GT-40 "Turbo-Swirl" head mentioned earlier in this chapter is available two ways: cast iron or aluminum. We suggest the aluminum head whenever you're pushing compression higher and are concerned about detonation. Aluminum heads carry away more heat than their iron counterparts, which reduces the chance of detonation. These 64cc chamber heads have 1.94/1.54" valves. The nice thing about these heads is their stock appearance and easy bolt-on nature. They have a thicker deck, which means they can be milled for increased compression. What's more, they sport a stock exhaust port configuration, which makes them compatible with stock exhaust manifolds and headers alike.

Ford Racing claims a 40 horsepower increase with the GT-40 heads. We're skeptical. Because these heads are conservative in port and chamber sizing, we're convinced they're good for 20-25 horsepower. If you combine them with an aggressive street camshaft and induction system, you may be able to pull 40 more horsepower. However, it takes a team approach with the right combination of camshaft, heads, induction, and exhaust systems. Forty horsepower comes as a package, not just one bolt-on.

One important note is this head's compatibility with some Ford small blocks. The GT-40 head will not fit the 1986 5.0L H.O. engine due to valve-to-piston clearance with flattop pistons. You will also need a cylinder head bolt kit (M-6065-C289) to bolt this head on your 289/302 engine.

The Ford Racing GT-40P Hi-Flow cylinder head is a cast-iron Explorer piece right off the production line. This head does not have angle spark plug holes like previous 289/302/351W cylin-

Head Type	Details	Chamber Size	Part Number Complete	Part Number Bare
Performer	1.90" Intake 1.60" Exhaust	60cc	6032	6031
Performer	2.02" Intake 1.60" Exhaust	60cc	6035	6034
Performer For Fel-Pro Loc Wire Head Gasket	2.02" Intake 1.60" Exhaust	60cc	6027	N/A
Performer RPM (Non-Emissions)	1.90" Intake 1.60" Exhaust	60cc	6022	6021
Performer RPM (Non-Emissions)	2.02" Intake 1.60" Exhaust	60cc	6025	6024
Performer RPM (Non-Emissions) For Fol-Pro Loc Wire Head Gasket	2.02" Intake 1.60" Exhaust	60cc	6026	N/A
Performer 5.0/5.8L	1.90" Intake 1.60" Exhaust	60cc	6037	6036
Performer 5.0/5.8L For Fel-Pro Loc Wire Head Gasket	1.90" Intake 1.60" Exhaust	60cc	6028	N/A
Performer 5.0/5.8L	2.02" Intake 1.60" Exhaust	60cc	6039	6038
Performer 5.0/5.8L For Fel-Pro Loc Wire Head Gasket	2.02" Intake 1.60" Exhaust	60cc	6029	N/A

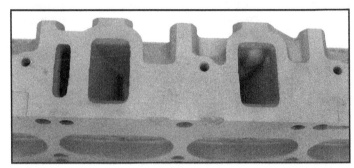

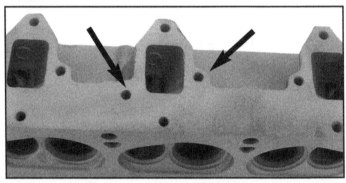

Port and chamber size determine performance. Configuration determines application. The best FE heads to use are the 390 High Performance, 427 Medium Riser, and 428 Cobra Jet. These heads sport the largest valve and port sizes. Exhaust port configuration is important, especially when your application is a Mustang, Cougar, Fairlane, or Cyclone. Heads for these applications have two exhaust manifold bolt patterns. The pattern shown (arrows) allows for bolt clearance in Ford compact and intermediate applications.

This is a typical FE-series big-block head. Shown here is a C1AE-A casting for the 1961-63 352/390. Casting numbers tell us a lot about what we have found. Port, valve, and chamber size are what performance is all about.

der heads. As a result, there isn't much in the way of exhaust headers available for this head. Custom header fabrication may be required. If you're using this head on a 1986-93 Mustang, you may order Ford Racing M-9430-P50 headers, which will work with this head. These heads do come complete with 16 valves, springs, and other hardware. Like the GT-40 Turbo-Swirl head, the GT-40P head does not clear pistons on 1986 5.0L H.O. engines. If you're mounting these heads atop a 351W block, cylinder head bolt holes in the head must be drilled to 1/2".

The GT-40X Xtra-Performance Turbo-Swirl aluminum cylinder heads are an improved GT-40 head with smaller 58cc chambers and revised intake and exhaust runners. Intake and exhaust flow is greatly improved in the GT-40X head.

One common thread we see with the Ford Racing street heads is 1.94/1.54" valve sizes, which can be improved upon to 2.02/1.60" sizes with some work. Your favorite machine shop can help. Port and bowl work will also make a difference in performance using Ford Racing street heads as a foundation.

FE CYLINDER HEADS

Although there are many types of FE cylinder head castings, there aren't as many differences as you might believe. There are exceptions like the 427 High Riser head, which is primarily a racing head with "High Riser" spe-

cific manifolds. The High Riser head has larger valves and ports. However, where this head really differs is port angle, which tends to raise the intake manifold higher, hence the name. This is a high-RPM racing head that has no business in street use. The High Riser's high price keeps it out of the budget arena, but you never know what a swap meet or garage sale might bring. To Aunt Mildred, whose drag racing husband passed away 25 years ago, those dusty C3AE-K or C4AE-F castings are chunks of iron that will be of no benefit to her in the nursing home. Sometimes you can find them for a song. Keep in mind this is not a street head; it's a head for high-revving racing engines.

FE Cylinder Head Identification

(Bold indicates high performance application or change in valve/port size)

Displacement/ Year	Casting Number	Chamber Size	Valve Size	Port Size
332/352ci 1958	EDC or EDC-E	69 - 72cc	2.02" Intake 1.55" Exhaust	2.34" x 1.34" Intake 1.84" x 1.28" Exhaust
332/352ci 1958	5752142	70 - 74cc	2.02" Intake 1.55" Exhaust	2.34" x 1.34" Intake 1.84" x 1.28" Exhaust
361ci 1958-59 Edsel	5752142	70 - 74cc	2.02" Intake 1.55" Exhaust	2.34" x 1.34" Intake 1.84" x 1.28" Exhaust
332/352ci 1959	5752143	70 - 74cc	2.02" Intake 1.55" Exhaust	2.34" x 1.34" Intake 1.84" x 1.28" Exhaust
361ci 1959 Edsel	5752143	70 - 74cc	2.02" Intake 1.55" Exhaust	2.34" x 1.34" Intake 1.84" x 1.28" Exhaust
352ci 1960	C0AE-C	73 - 76cc	2.02" Intake 1.55" Exhaust	2.34" x 1.34" Intake 1.84" x 1.28" Exhaust
352ci 1960 **High Performance**	C0AE-D	59 - 62cc	2.02" Intake 1.55" Exhaust	2.34" x 1.34" Intake 1.84" x 1.28" Exhaust
352/390ci 1961-63	C1AE-A	71 - 74cc	2.02" Intake 1.55" Exhaust	2.34" x 1.34" Intake 1.84" x 1.28" Exhaust
352/390ci 1961	C1SE-A	71 - 74cc	2.02" Intake 1.55" Exhaust	2.34" x 1.34" Intake 1.84" x 1.28" Exhaust
390ci 1962-63 **High Performance**	C2SE-A	65 - 68cc	2.02" Intake 1.55" Exhaust	2.34" x 1.34" Intake 1.84" x 1.28" Exhaust
406ci 1962-63 **High Performance**	C2SE-B	64 - 67cc	2.02" Intake 1.55" Exhaust	2.34" x 1.34" Intake 1.84" x 1.28" Exhaust
406ci 1962-63 **High Performance**	C2SE-C	64 - 67cc	2.02" Intake 1.55" Exhaust	2.34" x 1.34" Intake 1.84" x 1.28" Exhaust
406ci 1963 **High Performance**	C3AE-C	64 - 67cc	2.02" Intake 1.55" Exhaust	2.34" x 1.34" Intake 1.84" x 1.28" Exhaust
427ci Low Riser 1963 **High Performance**	C3AE-D	64 - 67cc	2.08" Intake 1.64" Exhaust	2.34" x 1.34" Intake 1.84" x 1.28" Exhaust
427ci Low Riser 1963 **High Performance**	C3AE-G	73 - 76cc	2.08" Intake 1.64" Exhaust	2.34" x 1.34" Intake 1.84" x 1.28" Exhaust
427ci Low Riser 1963 **High Performance**	C3AE-H	73 - 76cc	2.08" Intake 1.64" Exhaust	2.34" x 1.34" Intake 1.84" x 1.28" Exhaust
427ci Low Riser 1963 **High Performance**	C3AE-J	73 - 76cc	2.08" Intake 1.64" Exhaust	2.78" x 1.38" Intake 1.78" x 1.30" Exhaust
427ci High Riser 1963 **High Performance**	C3AE-K	73 - 76cc	2.18" Intake 1.72" Exhaust	2.78" x 1.38" Intake 1.78" x 1.30" Exhaust
352/390ci 1964-65	C4AE-A	71 - 74cc	2.02" Intake 1.55" Exhaust	2.34" x 1.34" Intake 1.84" x 1.34" Exhaust
352/390ci 1964-65	C4AE-G	71 - 74cc	2.02" Intake 1.55" Exhaust	2.34" x 1.34" Intake 1.84" x 1.34" Exhaust
427ci High Riser 1964-65 **High Performance**	C4AE-F	73 - 76cc	2.18" Intake 1.72" Exhaust	2.78" x 1.38" Intake 1.78" x 1.30" Exhaust
427ci Medium Riser 1965-67 **High Performance**	C5AE-F	88 - 91cc	2.18" Intake 1.72" Exhaust	2.78" x 1.38" Intake 1.78" x 1.30" Exhaust
427ci Medium Riser 1965-67 **High Performance**	C5AE-R	88 - 91cc	2.18" Intake 1.72" Exhaust	2.78" x 1.38" Intake 1.78" x 1.30" Exhaust
427ci Medium Riser 1965-67 (Canadian) **High Performance**	SK35369	88 - 91cc	2.18" Intake 1.72" Exhaust	2.78" x 1.38" Intake 1.78" x 1.30" Exhaust
427ci Medium Riser 1966-67 (Aluminum) **High Performance**	C6AE-F	88 - 91cc	2.18" Intake 1.72" Exhaust	2.78" x 1.38" Intake 1.78" x 1.30" Exhaust
427ci Medium Riser 1965-67 (Aluminum) High Performance	XE	88 - 91cc	2.18" Intake 1.72" Exhaust	2.78" x 1.38" Intake 1.78" x 1.30" Exhaust

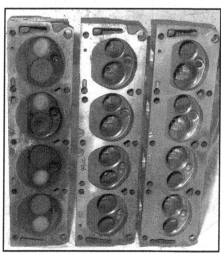

Ford produced three basic 427 head types: (from left) Low-Riser, Medium-Riser, and High-Riser. Because these heads are quite pricey, you probably won't be using them for your FE big-block project. However, the 427 Low- and Medium-Riser heads are best for street applications thanks to their port and valve sizing. They make good low- and mid-range torque, and they breath very well on the high end. The 427 High-Riser head is a race-only head, due to its large ports and valves, and high-rise induction.

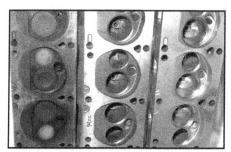

Closer inspection of 427 heads shows us key differences in chambers. The 427 Low-Riser (left) sports chambers similar to the High-Riser (right). The 427 Medium-Riser (center) has a larger quench area, making it the best street head for an FE big block. The 427 Medium-Riser head is nearly identical to the 428 Cobra Jet head.

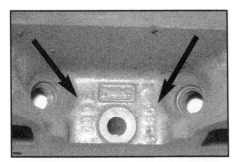

FE heads are identified by their casting numbers found here, between the two center exhaust ports.

Even more rare than the High Riser is the 427 Tunnel Port head, which is a NASCAR specific piece with its own manifolds. These are not heads you would apply to a budget big block unless they fell off a truck at the foot of your driveway. At that, we couldn't recommend them for street use. The Tunnel Port head is the best FE racing head if that's what you intend to do with your FE big block. Rarity dictates price, however. This is a head that can cost thousands of dollars depending upon condition.

If the idea of a pair of 428 Cobra Jet heads excites you, consider the facts. The 428 Cobra Jet head is little more than a 427 Low Riser head with the same modest port sizing and the same valve size. Port angle and restriction are somewhat better with the CJ and Medium Riser heads, but when these pieces are priced high, budget-minded builders have to consider alternatives that will work just as effectively.

This leads us to the rest of the FE lineup. The most common FE head is the garden variety 352/360/390 type. There are many individual types out there with different casting numbers. However, they all have similar port and valve sizes. In fact, the earliest FE heads we find on the 332, 352, Edsel 361, and the 390 all have the same port and valve sizes. It is the Low Riser 427 head that has larger valves, yet port size remains much the same as the engines mentioned earlier. Because Ford was doing a lot of development work with the 427 at the time in its dynamometer laboratory in Dearborn, Michigan, 427 heads evolved into something new almost weekly. Chamber size became smaller first. Then valve and port size increased. You want the ultimate evolution of the 427 Low Riser head: the C3AE-J casting.

FE Cylinder Head Identification (con't)

(Bold indicates high performance application or change in valve/port size)

Displacement/ Year	Casting Number	Chamber Size	Valve Size	Port Size
352/390/410/428ci 1966	C6TE-B	71 - 74cc	2.02" Intake 1.55" Exhaust	2.34" x 1.34" Intake 1.84" x 1.34" Exhaust
352/390/410/428ci 1966	C6TE-G	71 - 74cc	2.02" Intake 1.55" Exhaust	2.34" x 1.34" Intake 1.84" x 1.34" Exhaust
352/390/410/428ci 1966	C6AE-K	71 - 74cc	2.02" Intake 1.55" Exhaust	2.34" x 1.34" Intake 1.84" x 1.34" Exhaust
352/390/410/428ci 1966-67	C6AE-A C6AE-AA	71 - 74cc	2.02" Intake 1.55" Exhaust	2.34" x 1.34" Intake 1.84" x 1.34" Exhaust
352/390/410/428ci 1966-67 (w/ Thermactor)	C6AE-D	71 - 74cc	2.02" Intake 1.55" Exhaust	2.34" x 1.34" Intake 1.84" x 1.34" Exhaust
352ci 1966-67	C6AE-R	71 - 74cc	2.02" Intake 1.55" Exhaust	2.34" x 1.34" Intake 1.84" x 1.34" Exhaust
352/390ci 1966	C6AE-J	71 - 74cc	2.02" Intake 1.55" Exhaust	2.34" x 1.34" Intake 1.84" x 1.34" Exhaust
352/390ci 1966	C6AE-RVL	71 - 74cc	2.02" Intake 1.55" Exhaust	2.34" x 1.34" Intake 1.84" x 1.34" Exhaust
352/390ci 1966	C6AE-AB	71 - 74cc	2.02" Intake 1.55" Exhaust	2.34" x 1.34" Intake 1.84" x 1.34" Exhaust
390ci 1966-68	C6AE-L	67 - 70cc	2.02" Intake 1.55" Exhaust	2.34" x 1.34" Intake 1.84" x 1.34" Exhaust
390ci 1966-68	C6AE-U	67 - 70cc	2.02" Intake 1.55" Exhaust	2.34" x 1.34" Intake 1.84" x 1.34" Exhaust
390ci 1966-68	C6OE-R	67 - 70cc	2.02" Intake 1.55" Exhaust	2.34" x 1.34" Intake 1.84" x 1.34" Exhaust
390ci 1966-68 (w/ Thermactor)	C6OE-H	71 - 74cc	2.02" Intake 1.55" Exhaust	2.34" x 1.34" Intake 1.84" x 1.34" Exhaust
390ci 1966-68 (w/ Thermactor) **High Performance**	C6OE-AB	67 - 70cc	2.02" Intake 1.55" Exhaust	2.34" x 1.34" Intake 1.84" x 1.34" Exhaust
390ci 1966-68 **High Performance**	C6OE-Y	67 - 70cc	2.02" Intake 1.55" Exhaust	2.34" x 1.34" Intake 1.84" x 1.34" Exhaust
390ci 1966-68 **High Performance**	C6OE-AC	67 - 70cc	2.02" Intake 1.55" Exhaust	2.34" x 1.34" Intake 1.84" x 1.34" Exhaust
390ci 1966-68 (w/ Thermactor) **High Performance**	C6OE-AA	67 - 70cc	2.02" Intake 1.55" Exhaust	2.34" x 1.34" Intake 1.84" x 1.34" Exhaust
390ci 1966-68 (w/ Thermactor) **High Performance**	C7AE-A	67 - 70cc	2.02" Intake 1.55" Exhaust	2.34" x 1.34" Intake 1.84" x 1.34" Exhaust
352/390/410/428ci 1967	C7AE-A	71 - 74cc	2.02" Intake 1.55" Exhaust	2.34" x 1.34" Intake 1.84" x 1.34" Exhaust
427ci Tunnel Port 1967 **High Performance**	C7OE-K	88 - 91cc	2.25" Intake 1.72" Exhaust	2.17" x 2.34" Intake 1.78" x 1.30" Exhaust
427ci Tunnel Port 1967 **High Performance**	C8AX-A	88 - 91cc	2.25" Intake 1.72" Exhaust	2.17" x 2.34" Intake 1.78" x 1.30" Exhaust
360/390/428ci 1968 (w/ Thermactor)	C8AE-A	67 - 70cc	2.02" Intake 1.55" Exhaust	2.34" x 1.34" Intake 1.84" x 1.34" Exhaust
360/390/428ci 1968 (w/ Thermactor)	C8AE-B	67 - 70cc	2.02" Intake 1.55" Exhaust	2.34" x 1.34" Intake 1.84" x 1.34" Exhaust
360/390/428ci 1968 (w/ Thermactor)	C8AE-H	67 - 70cc	2.02" Intake 1.55" Exhaust	2.34" x 1.34" Intake 1.84" x 1.34" Exhaust
390ci 1968 (w/ Thermactor) **High Performance**	C8OE-A	67 - 70cc	2.02" Intake 1.55" Exhaust	2.34" x 1.34" Intake 1.84" x 1.34" Exhaust
390ci 1968 **High Performance**	C8OE-B	67 - 70cc	2.02" Intake 1.55" Exhaust	2.34" x 1.34" Intake 1.84" x 1.34" Exhaust
390ci 1969 **High Performance**	C8OE-F	68 - 71cc	2.02" Intake 1.55" Exhaust	2.34" x 1.34" Intake 1.84" x 1.34" Exhaust
390ci 1969 **High Performance**	C8OE-XX	68 - 71cc	2.02" Intake 1.55" Exhaust	2.34" x 1.34" Intake 1.84" x 1.34" Exhaust

Displacement/ Year	Casting Number	Chamber Size	Valve Size	Port Size
428ci 1968-70 (w/ Thermactor)	C8AE-F	68 - 71cc	2.02" Intake 1.55" Exhaust	2.34" x 1.34" Intake 1.84" x 1.34" Exhaust

(Bold Indicates high performance application or change in valve/port size)

Displacement/ Year	Casting Number	Chamber Size	Valve Size	Port Size
427ci Low Riser 1968 (w/ Thermactor) **High Performance**	C8AE-J	73 - 76cc	2.08" Intake 1.65" Exhaust	2.34" x 1.34" Intake 1.84" x 1.34" Exhaust
427ci Low Riser 1968 (w/ Thermactor) **High Performance**	C8AE-N	73 - 76cc	2.08" Intake 1.65" Exhaust	2.34" x 1.34" Intake 1.84" x 1.34" Exhaust
427ci Low Riser 1968 (w/ Thermactor) **High Performance**	C8WE-A	73 - 76cc	2.08" Intake 1.65" Exhaust	2.34" x 1.34" Intake 1.84" x 1.34" Exhaust
428ci Cobra Jet 1968 (w/ Thermactor)	C8OE-H	73 - 76cc	2.08" Intake 1.65" Exhaust	2.34" x 1.34" Intake 1.84" x 1.34" Exhaust
428ci Cobra Jet 1968-70 (w/ Thermactor)	C8OE-N	73 - 76cc	2.08" Intake 1.65" Exhaust	2.34" x 1.34" Intake 1.84" x 1.34" Exhaust

The C3AE-J Low Riser head was the first FE head to sport larger ports along with increased valve size. This fact, coupled with the smaller chamber, makes the head what it is. This is a casting to watch for at swap meets and garage sales. The C3AE-J head is a good casting to use for your 352/360/390 build. With port and bowl work, it can yield significant increases in power.

When we look at 332/352/361/390 heads across the board, there aren't enough differences to get excited over. Port and valve sizes are common to all of these engines. The 1961-63 390 High Performance head employs some port revisions and

429/460 Cylinder Head Identification

(Bold Indicates high performance application or change in valve/port size)

Displacement/ Year	Casting Number	Chamber Size	Valve Size	Port Size
429/460ci 1968-72	C8VE-A		2.09" Intake 1.65" Exhaust	2.18" x 1.87" Intake 1.99" x 1.30" Exhaust
429/460ci 1968-72	C9VE-A		2.09" Intake 1.65" Exhaust	2.18" x 1.87" Intake 1.99" x 1.30" Exhaust
429/460ci 1968-72	D0VE-C		2.09" Intake 1.65" Exhaust	2.18" x 1.87" Intake 1.99" x 1.30" Exhaust
429/460ci 1968-72	D3AE-A2A	88cc	2.09" Intake 1.65" Exhaust	2.18" x 1.87" Intake 1.99" x 1.30" Exhaust
429ci Cobra Jet 1970-71	D0OE-R		2.19" Intake 1.73" Exhaust	2.51" x 2.11" Intake 2.25" x 1.30" Exhaust
429/460ci 1972-74 **Police Interceptor**	D2OE-AA	88cc	2.19" Intake 1.73" Exhaust	2.20" x 1.93" Intake 2.06" x 1.31" Exhaust
429/460ci 1972-74 **Police Interceptor**	D2OE-AB	88cc	2.19" Intake 1.73" Exhaust	2.20" x 1.93" Intake 2.06" x 1.31" Exhaust
460ci Only 1973-74 **Police Interceptorx**	D3AE-FA	88cc	2.19" Intake 1.73" Exhaust	2.20" x 1.93" Intake 2.06" x 1.31" Exhaust

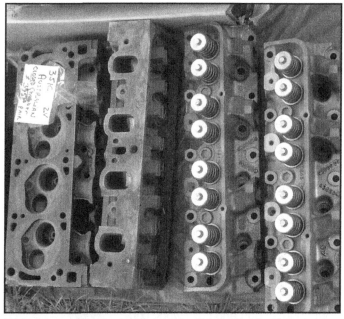

FE heads remain plentiful long after the engine family's demise. When you're cruising the swap meets, be mindful of casting numbers and take this book with you.

FE heads should always be checked for warpage at all surfaces, then milled only as necessary. Keep your milling efforts to a minimum.

Port and bowl work, regardless of head type, make a difference in performance. This head was worked by Valley Head Service in Northridge, California.

smaller combustion chambers for increased compression. What makes this head a Hi-Po head is chamber size primarily. This is what you want when you're shopping FE cylinder heads. Increased compression is what gives us power. Thing is, you have to achieve a balance here. Too much compression is bad in an era of lower octane fuels that won't perform well with 11.0:1 compression. Your FE big block needs a compression ratio around 10.0:1 to perform effectively. This means a dished piston or modified head gasket thickness to get compression down.

385-SERIES BIG BLOCK

The venerable 385-series 429/460ci big blocks yield a limited number of head types. The most popular, of course, are the 1970-71 Cobra Jet heads. Because these tend to be scarce — and expensive — we're faced with making the most of the mainstream castings available. However, mainstream isn't a bad thing when it comes to the 429/460. The mainstream 429/460 head has 2.09-in. intake and 1.65-in. exhaust valves with "right-size" ports that move air and make torque. These characteristics alone make the 429/460 a great head.

Like the FE-series big blocks just mentioned, the 429/460 head can net a wealth of torque and horsepower with some budget port and bowl work, coupled with the installation of larger valves. Because most heads could use new valves with hardened exhaust valve seats, the cost difference won't be much.

A nice alternative to the expensive 1970-71 Cobra Jet head is the 1972-74 Police Interceptor head, because valve size (2.19-in. intake and 1.73-in. exhaust) is the same. The Cobra Jet head has larger ports, however port and bowl job on the Police head can net you similar results for less money.

AFTERMARKET HEADS

The automotive performance marketplace offers you an abundance of cylinder head types to choose from. Edelbrock has embraced the FE-series big block with the Performer 390 cylinder head. The Performer 390 is on a par with the 427 Medium-Riser/428 Cobra Jet head with the advantage of lightweight aluminum. This is an outstanding head for FE performance gains. Because Edelbrock has produced a lot of them, used pieces can be found at swap meets and freshened up for a fraction of the cost of new pieces.

Why opt for an Edelbrock head for your big-block Ford? Because Edelbrock burns the midnight oil with extensive engineering time and research on the flow bench, making the most of a big-block Ford's potential. Edelbrock fine tunes heads using the right kind of valve that will work hand-in-hand with port design and camshaft profile.

The Performer 460 aluminum cylinder head is a terrific street head for 385-series big blocks thanks to 2.19/1.76" valve sizes. Two types of Performer 460 heads are available for the 429/460 big block. Early 429/460 engines produced from 1968-71 need the #6067 head with 75cc chambers. Later versions from 1972-up need the #6066 head with larger 95cc chambers. We like the Performer 460 because it is such a versatile piece. It can make 500+ horsepower at up to 6500 rpm, which makes it good for the street stormer and weekend racer. The Performer 460 is a beautiful piece any way you slice or dice it

This is a typical 429/460 head with closed-wedge chambers and oval ports. The best 385-series head to use is the 429 Police Interceptor or the 460 head. Both have larger valves and ports. Best of all, these heads don't carry the high Cobra Jet price tag. Because Ford produced so many 460 engines, these heads are plentiful and cheap.

Because most 429/460 heads were produced from 1971-up, they are already fitted with hardened exhaust valve seats. However, leave nothing to chance: Check your exhaust valve seats. If they're iron, fit them with hardened steel valve seats.

Port and bowl work will net you significant gains with 460 heads.

The Cobra Jet (M-6049-B429) aluminum head from Ford Racing Technology is an excellent street head for 385-series big blocks. Check your favorite swap meets for used pieces costing half the price of new ones.

HOW TO DO A VALVE JOB

because it accepts both factory and aftermarket valvetrain parts.

Look to Edelbrock to support all of your cylinder head and valvetrain needs. Valves, guides, seals, pushrod guide plates, hardened-steel pushrods, and even cylinder head bolt kits are available for your big-block Ford. Edelbrock advises the use of Champion RC12YC spark plugs with its heads for improved clearance around headers. Edelbrock also advises you to use an antiseize thread lubricant anytime you're installing spark plugs in aluminum heads.

Ford Racing (formerly Ford Motorsport SVO), for example, offers the aluminum Cobra Jet head for the 385-series big block, which is modeled after the 1971 429 Cobra Jet head. This seems to be the most popular aftermarket aluminum head for 385-series engines. This head is fitted with 2.000" intake and 1.760" exhaust valves, Ford Racing springs, and retainers. Although it sports smaller valve sizes than the Edelbrock Performer 460, it remains a very popular head with performance buffs.

Before a cylinder head can be improved, it must first be cleaned, then inspected for flaws. Rebuilding a cylinder head is simply improving how the head functions and performs. We improve function by checking the castings for cracks and warpage, replacing or refacing the valves, refacing or replacing the seats, and renewing the guides.

Heads are checked for cracks by Magnafluxing the castings, which will yield any flaws. Warpage is checked with a straight edge or dial indicator. While some cracks can be fixed, many will make the piece beyond repair. Warpage is corrected by milling the mating surfaces.

Cylinder sealing is perfected by improving valve-to-seat contact. We grind or replace the valves and seats to achieve a perfect seal. Valve guides are replaced or bushed to control oil flow and stabilize valve travel. You should seriously consider hardened exhaust valve seats for use with today's unleaded fuels.

Valves and seats need to be inspected for damage. We grind valves to improve their mating surfaces. Valve seats are ground for the same reason. When the cast-iron valve seats are too far gone (valve seat recession), we install hardened-steel valve seats which will outlast original equipment. As a rule, it is a good idea to replace all 16 valves and install hardened exhaust valve seats for durability. Even if regrinding the valve faces perfects those mating surfaces, we still have the valve stem to consider. Valve stems must enjoy a good marriage with the valve guides or problems will persist. Loose valve stem-to-guide tolerances cause uneven wear and loss of oil control. Oil control at the

guides and stems will be a substantial problem when the engine is cold. Some rebuilders like bronze valve guides, which tend to be a Band-Aid fix. Others opt for new steel guides, which have proven themselves in regular use. We suggest new steel guides with your valve job for best results.

Another thought with valve stems and guides is oversize valve stems. The machine shop bores out the valve guide bores and installs .025 to .030" oversize valves. This eliminates the need for new guides. From an economic perspective, you're better off with new steel guides and new standard-sized valves.

There are different trains of thought on how to machine the valve seats. We suggest a standard three-angle valve job, which any machine shop can do. A three-angle valve job gives us three different angles at the seat and valve face for better cylinder sealing. This may cost you more, but it is worth every penny.

Installing hardened exhaust valve seats begins with cutting out the old iron seat. The iron seat is integral with the casting. We're actually cutting a pocket for the hardened steel seat.

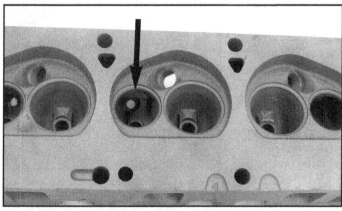

The steel seat is pressed into the iron pocket (arrow). Once installed, the hardened steel seat is precision ground for a solid marriage with the exhaust valve.

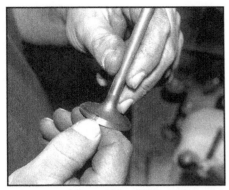

Valves are ground for smooth mating with the seats. For best results, install new valves and guides to ensure uniformity. Used valves (depending on how used) suffer from worn stems and faces. Regrinding the valve faces will improve seating. However, stem wear remains an issue. Check stem dimensions prior to any valve refacing.

Valve spring pressures must jibe with camshaft specifications. Springs that are too stiff will wipe the cam lobes. Springs not stiff enough can cause valvetrain failure at high revs. Spring stiffness must match the cam profile, which is why we suggest buying a camshaft kit that includes matching springs, retainers, and keepers. Then set your spring pressure properly.

Completed cylinder heads that have been properly machined and assembled are your best insurance for performance and reliability. This head has been milled to true the mating surfaces. A valve job using new valves, hardened seats, and steel guides makes a cylinder head like new.

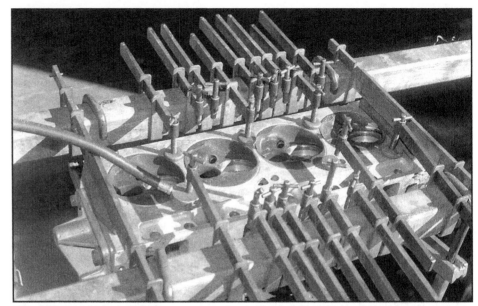

This 5.0L small-block head is pressure checked for leakage by Fastline Performance in Simi Valley, California. Any flaws are examined and the head's direction determined.

PORTING

Porting is the process of removing iron or aluminum from intake and exhaust ports to improve air flow in and out of the combustion chamber. Iron or aluminum is removed using a grinder and media to enlarge and smooth out the passages. As a rule, porting removes the irregularities of a cylinder head casting that interfere with air flow. Because automakers and cylinder head manufacturers don't have time to perfect port design, this process is left to the engine builder. Most of us have heard about porting and polishing in the pursuit of performance. We're going to explain the benefits and myths associated with porting and polishing so you may follow the best course during your engine build.

John Da Luz of John's Mustangs & Classics in San Diego, California has vast experience with Ford engine building. He has demonstrated what can be done with a stock Ford cylinder head casting — given time and sweat. There are different levels of porting you can achieve doing this yourself. You can do a simple gasket match port job, which doesn't take much time and allows for smooth flow between castings. A full-scale port and bowl job is time consuming, but good for significant air flow improvements from stock heads. John's objective with a full-scale street/race port job is to take port dimensions as far

as he can without getting into the water jacket. With stock Ford heads, there is a lot of room for improvement.

With most Ford heads, the area just inside the intake and exhaust valves is where we lose most air flow. Irregularities in the casting are what create interferences with air flow just inside the valve seats. John's objective is to make the air flow path as straight as possible without hurting the casting. He begins with a gasket match and works his way into the port. This allows the fuel/air mix to follow a smooth path. He then works the bowl to reduce restriction there too. The objective is to improve air flow without reducing velocity. We want to remove valve shrouding where possible without hurting structural integrity. When we remove valve shrouding, we remove restrictions that hurt air flow.

This exhaust manifold gasket shows us how much room there is for improvement. We can open up this exhaust port at the exit with a simple gasket match, or we can open up the entire port.

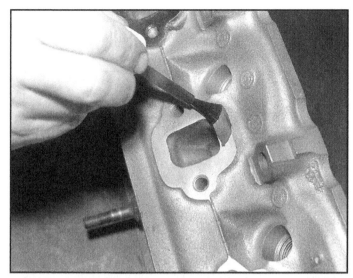

John Da Luz teaches us that cylinder head porting begins with applying Prussian Blue or a similar dye around the port as shown, then laying down a gasket as a template and marking with a scribe.

Intake ports get a healthy workout as well. Always keep those important limits in mind. Go too far and you will get into the water jacket.

Look what an afternoon's worth of exhaust port massaging can do for you! John has worked these ports and taken them to the maximum possible. The Thermactor port hump in the exhaust port is gone, which improves exhaust flow dramatically.

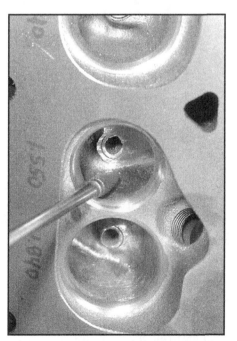
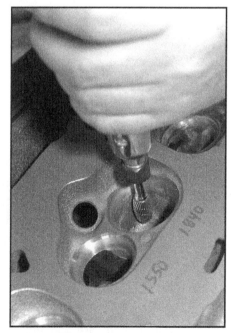

Intake manifolds should always be port-matched to the cylinder head. Follow the same procedure, using the gasket as a template to set limits.

Good bowl work beneath the valve heads makes a huge difference, too. John works these areas aggressively, and look at the result!

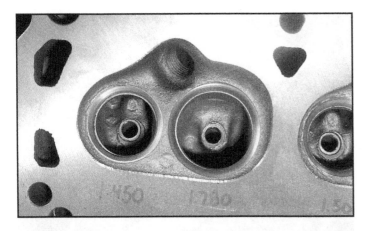

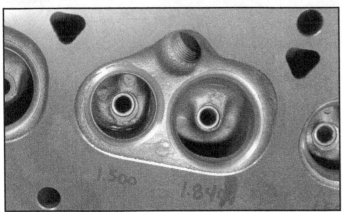

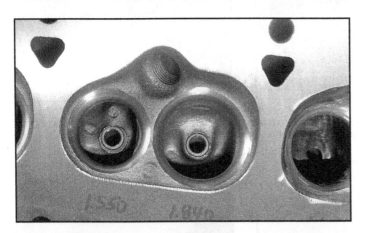

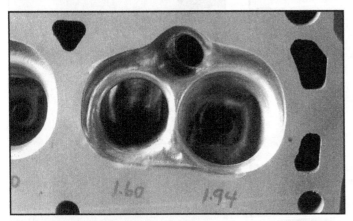

John's Mustangs & Classics shows us the actual differences in valve sizing and how large you can go with a stock head. From top to bottom are the differences: 1.45/1.780 in., 1.50/1.84 in., 1.55/1.84 in., and 1.60/1.94 in. See your machine shop for more details on valve sizing and port work.

Proting Does Make a Difference

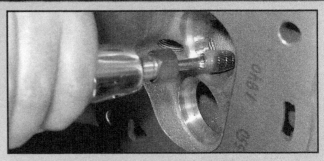

As you can see from the results below, you can improve air flow, make power, and save money with a stock Ford cylinder head. These results are from a 1967 Ford 289 cylinder head casting with four different port jobs and valve sizes tested by John's Mustangs & Classics on a flow bench. If you are impressed with these results, just imagine what you can do with a 351W cylinder head, which easily bolts onto a 260/289/302 mill. The same is true for other Ford V-8 cylinder head types.

With our test heads, we gained 57 cfm on the intake side with larger 1.94-in. Chevrolet valves with good port and bowl work. Even greater gains occurred on the exhaust side with larger 1.60-in. Chevy valves with good port and bowl work with a 60 cfm gain. A simple gasket match port job will gain you 3 cfm through both ports using stock valves. Gains vary depending upon casting types and porting proficiency. Our point is simple: You can improve air flow and power without the expense of aftermarket heads. See John's Mustangs & Classics for more details.

Head Porting/Valve Sizing Air Flow Results
(1967 289 Small-Block Iron Heads (C6AE, 49-state) at 28" Of Vacuum)

Stock Ports Stock Valve Size	1.78" Intake	1.45" Exhaust
0.2	96	64
0.3	124	88
0.4	155	98
0.5	160	100
0.6	165	112
Gasket Match Larger Valves	1.84"	1.50"
0.2	110	68
0.3	130	92
0.4	162	110
0.5	168	115
0.6	168	115
Street Port Larger Valves	1.84"	1.55"
0.2	126	82
0.3	151	112
0.4	182	125
0.5	188	132
0.6	193	145
Street/Race Port Larger Chevrolet Valves	1.94"	1.60"
0.2	121	101
0.3	173	126
0.4	205	146
0.5	215	159
0.6	222	172

CHAPTER 6

CAMSHAFT AND VALVETRAIN

The camshaft and valvetrain directly determine not only an engine's personality, but how reliably it will perform throughout its service life. Unfortunately, a lot of folks have more misconceptions about camshafts than they have facts. Hopefully, in the following pages we can set you straight on the myths and get you headed in the right direction.

To understand how to pick a camshaft and valvetrain, you must first understand how it all works. Choosing a camshaft profile must be based on how you want an engine to perform. Are you building a streetable engine where low- and mid-range torque are important? Or are you building a high-performance racing engine that makes peak torque in the high revs? Whatever the application, it is vital for you to choose the right combination of components.

A camshaft manufacturer's catalog lists dozens of camshaft types for the same type of engine. This is where it gets mighty confusing for the novice. We see words like lift, duration, lobe separation, base circle, lobe centerline angle, and valve overlap. What does all of this information mean and how will it affect your engine's performance?

CAMSHAFT SHOP TALK

What makes one camshaft different from another? Call it profile. Profile refers to the lobe's design, dimension, and positioning, as well as its functionality. Functionality refers to when the lobe opens the valve, when it closes the valve, how long it keeps the valve open, and how much it opens the valve. All of these factors influence an engine's performance.

Following are a few terms that you will hear in the shop when talk turns to camshafts. Lift is the maximum amount a lobe will open a valve. Duration refers to how long the lobe will keep the valve open. Lobe Separation or centerline is the time or duration between intake and exhaust valve action. Overlap plays into lobe separation because it is the period when the exhaust valve is closing and the intake valve is opening. The Ramp is the ascending or descending side of the cam lobe coming off the base circle when lift begins to occur. The Flank is the ascending or descending portion of the lobe past the base circle nearest maximum lift. The camshaft's Base Circle is the portion of the lobe that doesn't generate lift. The bottom-most portion of the lobe is called the Heel.

Flat-tappet camshafts work differently than roller-tappet camshafts, which means you have to think differently with each type. Flat-tappet camshafts limit what you can do with lobe profile if you want streetability. If you want an aggressive profile with flat tappets, you can only go so far with a street engine or suffer with poor driveability (rough idle, low manifold vacuum). If you want an aggressive profile in a street engine, we suggest stepping up to a roller camshaft, which can handle the aggressive profile better using roller tappets.

Quick Review: Camshaft Terminology

Lift: Maximum amount a valve-lifter-pushrod combo can be raised off the base circle. Lift is measured in thousands of an inch (.000-in.). Lobe profile determines how quickly this occurs. It can either be smooth or abrupt, depending upon lobe profile.

Duration: The amount of time the valve is open, beginning when the valve unseats. By this, we mean the number of degrees the camshaft will rotate when cam lobe lift begins. Duration typically begins at .004-in. of cam lobe lift, or when the lifter begins to ride the ramp coming off the base circle. "Duration at fifty" means duration begins at .050-in. of cam lobe lift. Duration at fifty is the industry standard for determining camshaft lobe duration. When you are reading camshaft specs, duration at fifty is the specification you will see.

Lobe Separation (also known as lobe centerline): Distance (in degrees) between the intake-lobe peak and the exhaust-lobe peak. Lobe separation generally runs between 102 and 114 degrees (camshaft degrees).

Intake Centerline: Position of the camshaft in relation to the crankshaft. For example, an intake centerline of 114 degrees means the intake valve reaches maximum lift at 114 degrees after top dead center (ATDC).

Exhaust Centerline: Essentially the same thing as intake centerline. This is when the exhaust valve reaches maximum lift before top dead center in degrees (BTDC).

Valve Overlap: Period of time when both the intake and exhaust valves are open to allow for proper cylinder scavenging. Overlap occurs when the exhaust valve is closing and the piston is reaching top dead center. The intake charge from the opening intake valve pushes the exhaust gasses out. Valve overlap is also known as lobe separation. Camshaft grinders can change lobe separation or "valve overlap" to modify the performance of a camshaft. Sometimes they do this rather than change lift or duration.

Adjustable Valve Timing: The ability to dial in a camshaft by adjusting valve timing at the timing sprocket. By adjusting the valve timing at the sprocket, you can increase or decrease torque. Advance valve timing and you increase torque. Retard valve timing and you lose torque.

STREET CAM FACTS

Based on everything we have seen in nearly 30 years of experience, the best street performance cams are ground with a lobe separation between 108 to 114 degrees. When you keep lobe separation around 112 degrees, you improve driveability because the engine idles smoother and makes better low-end torque. This is what you want from a street engine. Any time lobe separation is below 108 degrees, idle quality and streetability suffer. However, there is more to it than just lobe separation.

Compression and cam timing must be considered together because one always affects the other. Valve timing events directly affect cylinder pressure. Long intake valve duration reduces cylinder pressure. Shorter duration increases cylinder pressure. Too much cylinder pressure can cause detonation (pinging). Too little and you lose torque. You can count on cam manufacturers to figure stock compression ratios into their camshaft selection tables, which makes choosing a camshaft easier than it has ever been. Plug your application into the equation and you will be pleased with the results most of the time.

The greatest advice we can offer the layman is to be conservative with your cam specs if you want reliability and an engine that will live a long time. Stay with a conservative lift profile (under .500-in. lift). A high-lift camshaft will beat the daylights out of a valvetrain, and will put valve-to-piston clearances at risk. Watch duration and lobe separation closely, which will help you be more effective in camshaft selection. Instead of opening the valve more (lift), we want to open it longer (duration) and in better efficiency with piston timing (overlap or lobe separation).

Always bear in mind what you are going to have for induction, heads, and exhaust. The savvy engine builder understands that in order to work effectively, an engine must have matched components. Cam, valvetrain, heads, intake manifold, and exhaust system must all work as a team. If you are opting for stock heads, your cam profile doesn't need to be aggressive. Select a cam profile that will give you good low- and mid-range torque. Torque doesn't do you any good on the street when it happens at 6500 rpm. Choose a cam profile that will make good torque between 2500 and 4500 rpm. Otherwise, you are just wasting engine.

The thing to remember with camshaft selection is how the cam will work with your engine's cylinder heads. We need to take a close look at valve lift with a particular head and determine effect. Some camshafts will actually lose power with a given head because there's too much lift or duration. This is why it is important to understand a given cylinder head before choosing a camshaft. You want to seek optimum with any cylinder head/camshaft combination. This means having to really do your homework before making a decision. Part of building a successful budget engine is doing a lot of the homework yourself because you cannot afford a wasteful experience.

What type of fuel do you intend to run in your engine? This also affects camshaft selection. We can actually raise compression if we're running a mild camshaft profile or using a higher octane fuel. It all has to work together. Camshaft timing events must be directly tied to actually raise compression if we're running a mild camshaft profile or using a higher octane fuel. It all has to work together. Camshaft timing events must be directly tied to compression ratio. The longer our duration, the lower the cylinder pressure and resulting compression. The shorter the duration, the less air we're going to bring into the cylinder, which also affects compression. Our objective needs to be the highest compression without detonation, which will harm the engine. With this in mind, we want the most duration possible without compression extremes. Duration is what gives us torque as long as compression is sufficient.

Valve overlap, as we have stated earlier, is the period between exhaust stroke and intake stroke when both valves are slightly open. This occurs to improve exhaust scavenging by allowing the incoming intake charge to push remaining exhaust gasses out via the closing exhaust valve. Were the exhaust valve completely closed, we wouldn't get scavenging. The greater the overlap in a street engine, the less torque the engine will make down low where we need it most. This is why we want less valve overlap in a street engine and more in a racing engine, which will make its torque at high RPM. Increased valve overlap works best at high RPM.

Street engines need 10 to 55 degrees of valve overlap to be effective torque powerhouses. When valve overlap starts wandering above 55 degrees, torque on the low end begins to go away. A really hot street engine will need greater than 55 degrees of valve overlap, but not much greater. To give you an idea of what we're talking about, racing engines need 70 to 115 degrees of valve overlap.

For a street engine, we want valve overlap to maximize torque, which means a conservative approach in the first place. Push overlap as far as you can without compromising torque. We also have to figure in lift and duration with valve overlap to see the complete power picture.

Lobe separation angle is another area of consideration in street cam selection. This camshaft dynamic is chosen based on displacement and how the engine will be used. Rule of thumb is this. Consider lobe separation based on how much displacement and

valving you're going to be using. The smaller the valves, the tighter (fewer degrees) lobe separation should be. However, tighter lobe separation does adversely affect idle quality. This is why most camshaft manufacturers spec their cams with wider lobe separations than the custom grinders.

Duration in a street engine is likely the most important dynamic to consider in the selection process. We increase duration whenever less lift is desired. Why? Because we get air flow into the cylinder bore two ways: lift and duration. We can open the valve more and for less time to get air flow. Or, we can open the valve less and keep it open longer via duration to get air flow. Each way will have a different effect on performance. Duration is determined by how much cylinder head and displacement you have, and how the engine will be used. Excessive duration hurts low-end torque, which is what we need on the street. So we have to achieve a balance by maximizing duration without a loss in low-end torque. We do this by using the right heads with proper valve sizing. Large valves and ports don't work well at all for street use. Mix in too much duration and you have a real slug at the traffic light.

So what does this tell us about duration? Plenty. We want greater duration

whenever displacement and valve sizing go up. Increasing duration falls directly in line with torque peak and RPM range. This does not mean we necessarily gain any torque as RPM increases. It means our peak torque simply comes in at a higher RPM range. An example of this is if our engine is making 350 ft./lbs. of torque at 4500 rpm and we increase duration. We may well be making that same amount of torque at 5200 rpm. In short, increased duration does not always mean increased torque.

Compression has a direct effect on what our duration should be. When we're running greater compression, we have to watch duration closely because it can drive cylinder pressures too high. Sometimes we curb compression and run greater duration depending on how we want to make power. When we have greater duration, our engine is going to make more power on the high end and less on the low end. This is why you must carefully consider duration when ordering a camshaft. Higher compression with a shorter duration helps the engine make torque down low where we need it most in a street engine. The thing to watch for with compression is detonation and overheating. Maximum street compression should be around 10.0:1.

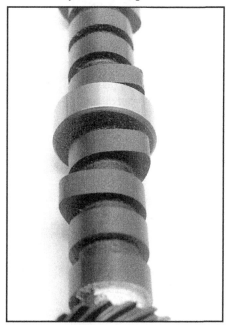

Camshaft design can be confusing. Think of the cam lobe in geographical regions as it travels against the lifter: opening ramp, opening flank, nose, closing flank, closing ramp, then the heel. The base circle is the part of the lobe that doesn't generate lift.

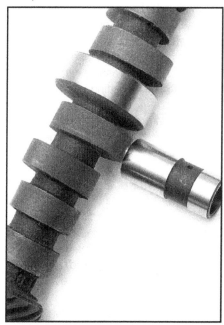

This is a flat-tappet camshaft. Notice the cam lobe profile (shape). It is more aggressive by nature even with a stock grind. Streetability suffers when lift and duration are increased, making the idle rough and eroding manifold vacuum.

Valve lift is an issue we must think about as it pertains to an engine's needs. Small blocks generally need more valve lift than big blocks. As we increase lift, generally we increase torque. This is especially important at low- and mid-RPM ranges where it counts on the street. Low-end torque is harder to achieve with a small block because these engines generally sport short strokes and large bores. Your objective needs to be more torque with less RPM if you want your engine to live longer. Revs are what drain the life out of an engine more quickly.

To make good low-end torque with a small block, we need a camshaft that will offer a combination of effective lift and duration. As a rule, we want to run a longer intake duration to make the most of valve lift. We get valve lift via the camshaft to be sure. However, rocker arm ratio is the other half of the equation. The most common rocker arm ratio is 1.6:1, which means the rocker arm will give the valve 1.6 times the lift we have at the camlobe. When we step up to a 1.7:1 ratio rocker arm, valve lift becomes 1.7 times that which we find at the lobe.

When we're spec'ing a valvetrain, it is best to achieve balance all around. If you run a high-lift camshaft with a 1.7:1 rocker arm ratio, you may be getting too much lift, which means excessive wear and tear. It is best to spec on the side of conservatism especially if you're building an engine for daily use. Whenever you opt for an aggressive camshaft with a lot of lift, you're putting more stress on the valve stem, guide, and spring. The constant hammering of daily use with excessive lift is what kills engines without warning.

We will take this excessive wear logic a step further. It is vital that you ascertain proper centering of the rocker arm tip on the valve stem tip when you're setting up the valve train. We do this by using the correct length pushrod for the application. Buy a pushrod checker at your favorite speed shop if ever you're in doubt. A pushrod checker is little more than an adjustable pushrod that you can use to determine rocker arm geometry. If the pushrod is too long, the tip will be under-centered on the valve stem, causing excessive side loads toward the outside of the cylinder head.

If the pushrod is too short, the rocker arm tip will be over-centered, causing excessive side loading toward the inside of the head. In either case, side loads on the valve stem and guide cause excessive wear and early failure. This is why we want the rocker arm tip to be properly centered on the valve stem for smooth operation.

One accessory that will reduce valve stem tip wear and side loading is the roller-tip rocker arm. Roller-tip rocker arms roll smoothly across the valve stem tip virtually eliminating wear. Stamped-steel, roller-tip rocker arms are available at budget prices without the high cost of extruded or forged pieces.

DUAL-PATTERN CAMSHAFTS

You've undoubtedly heard the term "dual-pattern" camshaft. A dual-pattern camshaft runs different profiles on the intake and exhaust side to meet the need. We tend to run dual-pattern profiles whenever we're pushing the revs up. Typically, a dual-pattern camshaft will run a shorter exhaust valve duration due to less time required to scavenge the exhaust gasses at high RPM. It is also beneficial whenever we're running nitrous or supercharging/turbocharging where exhaust scavenging is rapid and furious. Running a dual pattern camshaft on the street doesn't make much sense because we lose torque and fuel economy at low- and mid-RPM ranges. Keeping the exhaust valve open longer is what helps a street engine.

RACING CAMSHAFTS

If you are building an engine for racing, it's no longer a budget endeavor. However, you can build a competitive engine without spending a fortune. For example, camshafts for racing applications don't cost any more than street

Roller camshafts are identifiable by their lobes. Note the shine and more rounded shape. Roller camshafts are more flexible because they allow for a more aggressive amount of lift and duration without disturbing idle quality. Lift can be as much as .540 in. with only minor changes in idle quality.

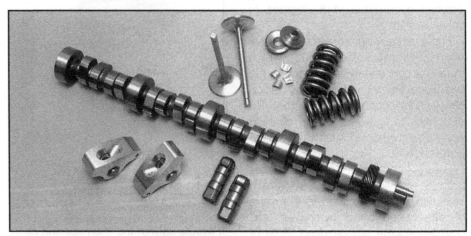

It is always best to source a camshaft in kit form, like this one from Crane Cams. A camshaft kit includes lifters and valve springs. The valve springs are of a matched pressure compatible with the camshaft profile.

cams. Camshaft profile in a racing engine depends upon the type of racing you are going to do, vehicle weight and type — even the type of transmission and rear axle ratio.

Drag racing mandates a different camshaft profile than road or circle-track racing. Vehicle weight, transmission type, and axle ratio all determine where power will be needed most. A short-track engine will need to be able to produce huge amounts of torque in short order, for example. The same is true for a drag racer. These issues teach us something about engine breathing — breathing effectiveness is determined by camshaft profile.

Lobe separation for the drag-racing camshaft should be between 104 and 118 degrees — a broad range, actually, because drag racing needs can vary quite a bit. This is where you have to customize your application with a camshaft grinder. Most camshaft grinders have computation charts that show the right cam for your application. As your needs change, so must the camshaft profile.

If you are going road racing, lobe separation becomes more specific in the 106-degree range. Some cam grinders push lobe separati on higher for the circle-track engine, depending on conditions. Generally, the higher the lobe separation, the broader the torque curve (more torque over a broader RPM range).

DEGREEING A CAMSHAFT

Degreeing a camshaft should always be an integral part of your engine building plan. Degreeing or dialing in a camshaft eliminates all doubt. It tells us valve timing events and cam lobe specs in great detail. Believe it or not, cam grinders do make mistakes. Camshafts get mis-boxed, and they don't always get ground to the specs on the card. Degreeing your camshaft is a fact-finding mission.

When you degree a camshaft, you are determining valve-timing events as they relate to crankshaft

position. The crankshaft makes two complete revolutions for every one revolution of the camshaft. One full revolution of each is 360 degrees. This means the crank turns 720 degrees and the cam 360 degrees. Think of rotation like a pie: A half turn is 180 degrees; a quarter turn is 90 degrees.

Duration is the number of degrees of rotation the camshaft will make from the time the valve begins to open until the time it closes. When we see 244 degrees of duration, that means 244 degrees of camshaft rotation from valve unseat to valve seat. Overlap, or lobe separation, is the number of degrees between maximum valve lift intake and maximum valve lift exhaust. With all this in mind, you can degree the camshaft timing events in time with piston travel.

When you advance or retard camshaft timing, you do it in the number of degrees of crankshaft rotation. Out-of-the-box camshafts typically have some degree of valve

We degree a camshaft using a degree wheel bolted to the crankshaft, as shown. Align the degree wheel with the crankshaft's top-dead-center (TDC) timing mark. Turn the crank and get No. 1 piston to TDC using a piston stop for accuracy. Turn the crank, moving the piston down in the bore. Then turn the crank and bring the piston to TDC. Examine the degree wheel. Turn the crank in the opposite direction, then bring the piston back to TDC. Examine the degree wheel again. Split the readings between the two findings to determine true TDC. With the piston against the stop, adjust the degree wheel to zero. Double-check the readings.

Use a dial indicator (these can be rented) at the pushrod or lifter as shown. Zero the dial indicator with the lifter or pushrod at the heel of the cam lobe (valve completely closed). Reading the cam card, slowly turn the crankshaft (which turns the camshaft) and watch the valve timing events. At what degree of crank rotation does the intake valve begin to open? At what degree of crank rotation is the valve at maximum lift? Do the same with the exhaust valve lobe. You can learn lobe separation during this process. Double-check the dial indicator positioning and do this again — twice! Your numbers should match the numbers on the cam card. If not, recheck twice. The savvy engine builder will do this on every cylinder bore. It may be time-consuming, but so is replacing a faulty camshaft after the engine is already in the car.

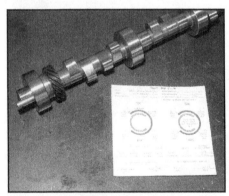

This is a cam card, which contains all of the cam specifications. These specs should jibe with degree events.

timing advance programmed in by the manufacturer. When you time a camshaft "straight up," this means you are keeping the cam in the manufacturer's suggested position on the spec card. Call this point zero, then advance or retard valve timing from there.

VALVETRAIN

The valvetrain is likely the most tortured collection of moving parts in your engine. At 6000 rpm, valves slam against their seats 3000 times a minute. Exhaust valves not only reciprocate vigorously at half the speed of the crankshaft, but they are subjected to combustion temperatures of approximately 1,800 degrees F. Lifters, pushrods, rocker arms, and valve springs take a similar amount of punishment. Of all your engine's parts, valvetrain components are the most likely to fail. Many a broken valve spring or failed keeper has silenced the mightiest of engines. This is why your attention to this area is vital.

A valvetrain's greatest ally is stability. Valvetrain systems must have matched components for stable operation. This is why camshaft manufacturers have gone to camshaft kits in recent years. They make it easy to package your valvetrain system. Packaging a valvetrain depends on how you want your engine to perform. If you are building a street engine that will be operating in the 2500 to 5500 rpm range, camshaft specifications need to be conservative on the side of torque. As a result, lifters, pushrods, rocker arms, and springs need to follow suit. Run a spring that is too soft for your camshaft and your engine will experience valve float (not enough spring pressure to close the valves) at high RPM. Likewise, run a spring that is too stiff and you can wipe the cam lobes from excessive pressure against the lobe. This is why running matched components is so important.

LIFTERS

Four basic lifter (tappet) types are used in Ford V-8s: flat tappet, hydraulic, and mechanical; and roller hydraulic and mechanical. Ford used flat-tappet lifters until 1985. It was then that roller tappets were first used and they were used increasingly in Ford factory V-8 engines after 1985. More and more engine builds are witnessing the use of roller tappets because there's less friction, smoother operation, and the ability to run a more aggressive profile

without the drawbacks of a radical flat-tappet camshaft.

Roller tappets are more costly than flat tappets due to tolerances and increased number of parts. Their cost puts them outside of the budget engine category, but they're worth every penny in what they save in wear and tear. They also give you the advantage if your desire is to run a more aggressive camshaft profile.

Although hydraulic lifters saw more widespread use beginning in the 1960s, they date back to the 1920s. Hydraulic lifters don't require periodic adjustment like a mechanical or solid lifter. As the camshaft and valvetrain wear, hydraulic lifters expand with the wear and take up clearance. This keeps operation quiet and reliability sound. Hydraulic lifters do well until camlobe and valve stem wear is so excessive the lifter can no longer take up the clearance. That is when you hear the tell-tale "click" of rocker-arm noise, especially when the engine is cold. Sometimes the click is a faulty lifter (leaking down hydraulic pressure) or an excessively worn rocker arm. Rocker arm wear that results in noise generally happens at the tip at the valve stem. This is especially common with rail-style rocker arms (small-block Fords from late-1966 through 1977) that have worn down to the rails.

Lifter and cam lobe wear and failure are rarely caused by a manufacturing defect. They fail because we don't give them a good start. Flat-tappet camshafts must be broken in properly or failure is inevitable. Moly coat must be applied to the cam lobe and lifter when you are installing a flat-tappet camshaft. The engine must be operated at 1500-3000 rpm for 20 to 30 minutes after fire-up to properly wear in the lobes. Synthetic engine oil should not be used until after the break-in period. During this period, check the pushrods for proper rotation.

Roller tappets don't require break-in because rollers and cam lobes enjoy a good marriage to begin with. The lobes are already hardened and rollers provide a smooth ride. Roller tappets can even be reused with a new camshaft if they are in good condition. If you are building a high-mileage engine, we suggest the use of new roller tappets with a new camshaft.

Flat-tappet mechanical camshafts are

terrific for high-revving engines where the inaccuracies of hydraulic camshafts (lifter collapse) are unacceptable. Mechanical camshafts give us accuracy because there's nothing left to chance. The lift moves with the camlobe with solid precision. Given proper valve lash adjustment, mechanical lifters do their job very well. However, mechanical flat and roller tappets have to be adjusted periodically, which can be annoying on a daily driven street engine. This is where you will need to do some soul searching before selecting a camshaft.

ROCKER ARMS & PUSHRODS

The pushrod and rocker arm are what transfer the camlobe's energy to the valve stem. Think of the rocker arm as the camshaft's messenger because the rocker arm multiplies lift, which makes the valve open further than the camshaft's lobe lift. Rocker arm types range from stock cast affairs all the way up to extruded and forged pieces with roller bearings and tips. Forged or extruded roller rocker arms are quite costly, which generally leaves them out of the budget engine program. However, this doesn't mean you have to settle for stock cast or stamped-steel pieces either.

Stock cast or stamped-steel rocker arms don't perform well under the heavy demands of radical camshaft profiles. An aggressive camshaft profile will break a stock rocker arm in short order. This is why it is always best to err on the side of heavy duty whenever you're building an engine. Stamped-steel, ball-stud, roller-tip rocker arms are a good first step toward valvetrain durability whenever you opt for a higher lift camshaft. The roller tip reduces the stress we experience with stock rocker arms. When we increase lift and valve spring pressures, a stamped-steel or cast roller-tip rocker arm doesn't always stand up to the test, especially when spring pressures climb to over 350 pounds. Even the best stamped-steel, roller-tip rocker arm will fail when overstressed.

When lift and spring pressures go skyward, you're going to want a roller pivot, roller-tip forged rocker arm for your budget engine build. Going that extra mile with a super durable rocker arm will ensure longer engine life, especially if you're going to drive it daily. For

Hydraulic lifters have parts inside that contain oil pressure, which takes up the clearance between rocker arm, pushrod, and lifter. This pressure is called lifter preload, and enables the lifter to take up clearance between the rocker arm and the valve stem.

Flat tappets sit on the cam lobe like this. As the cam lobe spins, it spins the lifter in the bore to evenly distribute wear.

This is a roller lifter for an FE-series big-block Ford. Roller lifters ride the cam lobe dead-center like this one. Small-block lifters are retained with a spider assembly bolted to the block, or they are joined like these where a spider is not possible.

Mechanical (solid) tappets offer precise valve action events. These are solid, with no internal parts. Valve-lash adjustment happens at the rocker arms.

the weekend racer, stepping up to a better rocker arm is like writing a life insurance policy because marginal rocker arms will not stand up to the high-revving task. Roller pivot, roller-tip rocker arms also ensure valvetrain precision and accuracy when the revs get high.

We suggest looking to Crane Cams, Comp Cams, or Crower for your Ford engine rocker arms and pushrods. These companies all have a lot of valuable experience with valvetrain components and offer wide selection. A good rule of thumb is to run the same brand of rocker arm and camshaft. See your favorite camshaft company or speed shop for more details.

When it comes to valvetrain adjustment, small-block Fords have flexibility in available, aftermarket adjustable studs where adjustable studs were not original-

ly used. The same is true for the 351C/351M/400M middle blocks and 429/460 big blocks. FE-series big-block engines with their shaft-mounted rocker arms have a couple of options. One option is adjustable rocker arms from early 332/352/361/390/406/427 engines with mechanical lifters. With these, you get the 1.7:1 rocker arm ratio, which gives you the lift advantage. For non-adjustable rocker arm shafts, you're forced to live with variable length pushrods. Opt for the use of a pushrod checker before buying a set of pushrods that don't fit. Adjustable pushrods are also available for the FE-series engine family.

Early small-block Fords (1962-67) had adjustable, stud-mounted rocker arms. From 1968-77, they had no-adjust, positive-stop rocker-arm studs. From 1978-

Lifters usually fail due to dirty oil or the absence of lubrication. The absence of lubrication can make the lifter seize in the bore, which stops the lifter from spinning on the cam lobe.

Small-block Ford rocker arms looked like this from 1962 through early 1966 (prior to May 8, 1966). This design employs pushrod guides cast into the cylinder head.

From May 8, 1966 through 1977, small-block Fords had rail-style rocker arms, which use rails cast into the rocker arm to keep the rocker arm centered on the valve. Problems arise when the rocker-arm tip wears and the rails touch the valve spring retainer. This causes clicking and potential engine failure.

Beginning in 1978, small-block Fords were equipped with stamped-steel rocker arms with a bolt/fulcrum arrangement. These are not adjustable.

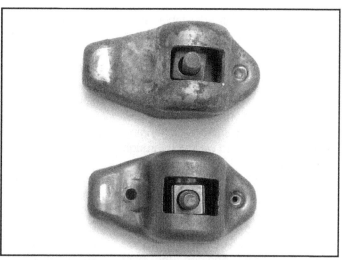

Cleveland (351) and Modified/Midland (351/400) engines have bolt/fulcrum rocker arms that are not adjustable. The exception is the 1971 Boss 351 and the 1972 351 high output, which have adjustable rocker arms (mechanical lifters).

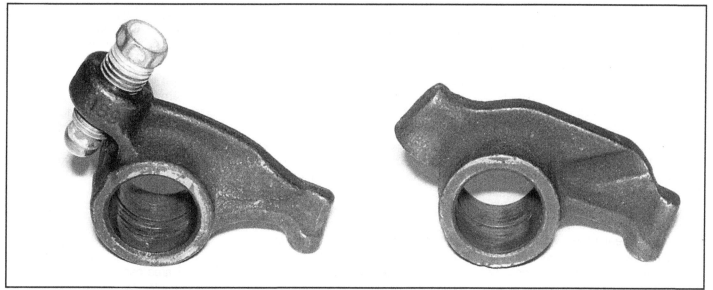

The FE engine family was equipped with two different types of ductile iron rocker-arm assemblies. Those with mechanical lifters had adjustable rocker arms unlike those with hydraulic lifters and no-adjust rocker arms. The adjustable rocker arms have a more aggressive 1.76 ratio for increased lift, and you can use them with hydraulic lifters.

present, the rocker-arm stud was replaced with a new-design stamped-steel rocker arm, fulcrum, and bolt.

Small-block Fords from May 1966 up had rail-style rocker arms, which eliminated the pushrod guide in the cylinder head. The rocker arm's side rails keep the rocker arm centered on the valve stem. The problem is, as the rocker-arm tip wears at the valve stem, the rails move closer to the valve spring retainer. As the rails push down on the retainer, the risk of keeper failure increases. When the keeper fails, the valve drops into the cylinder, causing major engine failure. Excessively worn rail-style rocker arms cause a tell-tale "clicking" during engine operation. Close examination of

the valve spring retainer will reveal wear marks from the rails if wear is excessive. Rail-style rocker arms don't perform well with high-lift camshaft profiles because the rails can contact the retainer. Sometimes these rocker arms pop off to one side or the other at high revs, pressing on the retainer and risking engine failure. During a rebuild, we suggest the use of 1962-66-style rocker arms with screw-in studs and pushrod guide plates for best results.

The 335-series small-block engine family (351C, 351M, 400M) has had two types of rocker-arm arrangements. The Boss 351 (1971) and 351 High Output (1972) had adjustable, stud-mounted rocker arms. The rest had bolt/fulcrum,

no-adjust rocker arms.

FE-series big-block Fords have always had shaft-mounted rocker arms. Those with hydraulic lifters had no-adjust rocker arms. Those with mechanical lifters had adjustable rocker arms with a 1.7:1 ratio. Hydraulic lifter clearances were adjusted using various pushrod lengths.

The 385-series 429 and 460ci engines have employed two basic rocker-arm arrangements throughout their production history. All but the 429 Super Cobra Jet have bolt/fulcrum, no-adjust rocker arms. If adjustment is necessary, it is done by using different pushrod lengths to achieve the goal. The 429

Super Cobra Jet has adjustable, stud-mounted rocker arms due to the use of mechanical lifters.

ROCKER ARM ADJUSTMENT

Ford V-8s sport an array of rocker arm combinations depending on engine family. We're going to walk you through how to do valve lash adjustment on each. Small-block Fords from 1962-67 have adjustable ball-stud rocker arms. There are different theories on how these should be adjusted. Adjustment depends on how your engine will be used. For street engines, the best approach is to turn the rocker arm stud nut clockwise until the rocker arm contacts the valve stem, then tighten the nut 1/2 to 3/4-turn.

For high-revving engines, there's yet another approach some racers use. With the engine hot idling around 1000 rpm, fit a thickness gauge (.010") between the valve stem and the rocker arm. Adjust the valve lash (turning the nut clockwise) until the lifter bottoms out. At this point, you will hear a subtle miss (putt-putting) at the tailpipe. This is caused by an unseated valve. Back off slowly until the miss vanishes. This practice requires your closest attention because overtightening the adjustment can be a bad thing. A valve that doesn't seat from overtightening will ultimately burn and fail. Valves need contact with the seat not only for the obvious — compression — but for heat transfer to the seat and water jacket. The .010" we give the rocker arm at the valve stem gives us the necessary allowance for safe operation.

Ford small-blocks from 1968 up have no-adjust rocker arms, which makes adjustment impossible. However, modifying 1968-up heads with screw-in studs and guideplates makes adjustment possible.

The 335-series engines also have a no-adjust, bolt-fulcrum rocker arm setup with the exception being the Boss 351C with mechanical lifters and adjustable ball/stud rocker arms. The 385-series big blocks have the same bolt-fulcrum rocker arm setup with the exception being the 429 Super Cobra Jet with mechanical lifters and adjustable ball/stud rocker arms.

FE-series big blocks had two types of shaft-mounted rocker arms. Early and high-performance FE engines had adjustable, 1.7:1 ratio rocker arms. The rest had 1.6:1, no-adjust rocker arms. The no-adjust rocker arms can be adjusted using various length pushrods. The goal with no-adjust rockers and hydraulic lifters should be depressing the lifter by one-half. This can be accomplished with a pushrod checker.

FE engines with adjustable rocker arms should be adjusted as follows. With the engine hot, both intake and exhaust valve lash should be .025". Engine cold, intake and exhaust valve lash should be .028". Stick with these specifications unless the cam manufacturer specifies otherwise.

When you're shopping pushrods, we suggest a lightweight 5/16" welded ball tip chrome moly piece for the best reliability. Regardless of budget, we must have components that will withstand the torture of valvetrain vibration and oscillation or it gets unpleasant quickly. A failed pushrod at high RPM can do extensive engine damage to a point where you will forget all about all that money you were trying to save.

Proper pushrod length is a very serious consideration for any engine builder. As we said earlier, it can mean the difference between long engine life and having to pull heads in a few thousand miles. A pushrod that's too long will push the rocker arm tip under-center, causing excessive side loading to the valve stem and guide. Likewise, a pushrod that's too short will do the same thing on the opposite side. A pushrod checker will help you make the right decision for not much money. You can find one of these at your favorite speed shop and get right to work in your search for the correct length pushrod.

When you're checking pushrod length, you want the rocker arm tip to be close to center on the valve stem tip. Remember, the rocker arm tip is going to walk across the valve stem tip when we come up on the high side of the camlobe. Take a black felt-tip marker and darken the valve stem tip. Then install the rocker arm and pushrod. Hand crank the engine and watch the valve pass through one full opening and closing. Get down alongside the rocker arm and valve spring and watch how the rocker arm travels. Then inspect the black marking for a wear pattern. This will show you exactly where the

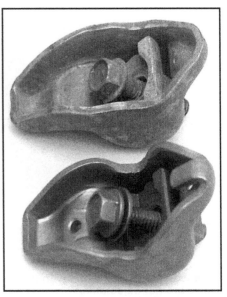

The 385-series engine family uses two basic rocker-arm types: bolt/fulcrum, no-adjust rockers on the 429/460 and 429 Cobra Jet (1970-71). The 429 Super Cobra Jet (1970-71) has an adjustable rocker-arm arrangement (not shown).

rocker arm tip has traveled across the valve stem tip. The pattern should be centered on the valve stem tip. If it runs too much toward the outside of the valve stem tip, the pushrod is too short. If it runs toward the inside of the valve stem tip, the pushrod is too long.

VALVES AND SPRINGS

Valves and springs play an important role in power and reliability. Weak spots in either area can rob you of power or lead to engine failure, so choosing the right valves and springs is important. Most cam manufacturers offer a variety of valve spring combinations designed to work well with the camshaft you have chosen. In fact, the best way to shop and buy a cam is to purchase a camshaft kit, which includes valve springs, retainers, and keepers matched to the camshaft profile chosen. We match a cam and springs because we want a compatible spring for the profile. More radical cams call for stiffer springs. Milder camshaft grinds need less valve spring pressure. Too much spring pressure can wipe the cam lobes. Too little can cause valve float (valve seating doesn't keep up with the revs) at high revs.

Choosing the right valve spring is strictly a matter of following a camshaft grinder's recommendations. Most springs are applicable to hydraulic or

Valve spring installed height looks like this. Always check your spring specs with the retainer installed.

This is a single valve spring arrangement like we see in stock applications. Some are equipped with dampeners (as shown) for spring stability.

Dual-valve springs are available for more aggressive camshaft profiles.

mechanical lifters. Some are specific only to roller camshafts. Crane Cams, for example, offers dozens of different valve spring types. The part number you select depends on camshaft profile. See your cam grinder for more details.

When you opt for a camshaft kit, knowing you have the comfort of knowing that the manufacturer has matched the springs to the camshaft profile. Most of the homework has been done for you. There won't be concern about coil binding, or too much or too little spring pressure. The best time to check for coil bind is when you are degreeing the camshaft. Do this before permanently bolting on the heads. Most cam grinders will tell you the recommended installed spring height and

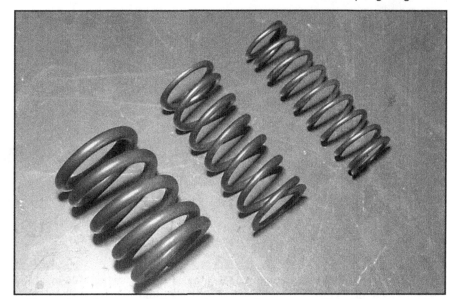

Triple valve springs from Crane Cams ensure positive valve closure with the most aggressive cam profiles. Chances are you won't be using these in your budget application.

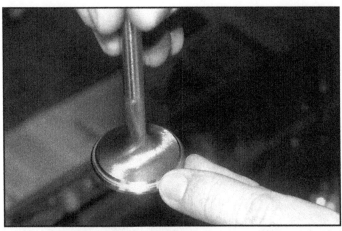

When valves are lapped, you should see a perfectly consistent line around the face of the valve like this. This means a solid seal when the valve is seated.

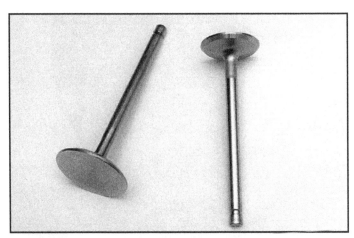

Stainless steel valves are fine for most street and mild race applications.

When spring pressure (and the appropriate number of shims) is established, the valve and spring are installed in the head. Installed height is checked here.

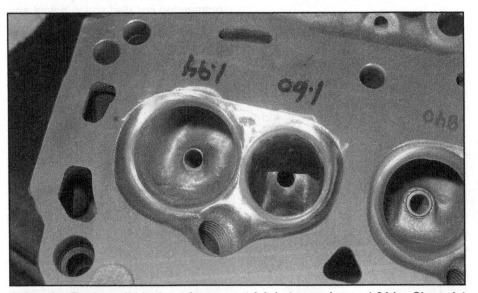

A popular Ford small-block performance trick is to use larger 1.94-in. Chevrolet valves. Upsizing the valves is one answer to power improvement without spending a lot of money. Performance Automotive Warehouse (PAW) installs the larger Chevy valves in its 289/302 small-block budget kits.

seat pressure. Correct installed height and spring pressure are achieved with the use of shims as necessary. Coil bind is checked by checking coil spacing with the valve at maximum lift. There should be no less than .040 in. between the coils at full-valve lift. Retainer-to-valve guide clearance at full lift is the same — no less than .040". This clearance is vital because coil bind or retainer contact with the head will cause valvetrain failure. The .040" we give it allows for thermal expansion of metal parts and any camshaft aggressiveness at high revs.

Another huge consideration is piston-to-valve clearance whenever you are installing a camshaft with greater lift and duration. The most common practice is to press modeling clay into the piston valve reliefs, temporarily install the head and valvetrain, then turn the crank two full revolutions. If you feel any resistance, back off and remove the head. Chances are you have piston-to-valve contact. Forcing the crank will bend the valve and damage the piston. If no resistance is felt in two turns of the crankshaft, remove the head and examine the clay. Slice the clay at the valve relief and check the thickness of the clay. This is your piston to valve clearance.

Finally, whenever you are rebuilding cylinder heads, remember the valve guides and valve-to-guide clearances. Loose valve-to-guide clearance leads to loss of oil control. Precise valve-to-guide clearance and healthy seals make every difference.

CHAPTER 7

INDUCTION SYSTEMS

One true measure of an engine's potential sits on top when it's time to button up the mill. The induction system — also called the intake manifold, carburetor, or fuel injection — influences an engine's performance as much as the camshaft and cylinder heads. Under ideal circumstances, you will have a perfect marriage between heads, camshaft, induction, and exhaust system. In the power picture, it is all about the proper packaging of parts that work well together. Not enough of us are getting that right.

CARBURETED INDUCTION

Carbureted street engines need long intake runners in order to produce good low- and mid-range torque. Longer intake runners are found in dual-plane intake manifolds like the Edelbrock Performer and Weiand Stealth. Installing an aftermarket manifold like the Performer or Stealth improves performance because it improves airflow

velocity into the combustion chambers. This is likely one of the best modifications you can make to a street engine without selling off the farm.

Dual-plane/high-rise manifolds don't always have to be new ones, either. Vintage Cobra and Edelbrock dual-plane/high-rise manifolds yield the benefits of low-end torque and high-RPM breathability, and they can be readily found at swap meets. They do well on the street in stop-and-go driving, and they yield plenty of power when it's time to rock. Single-plane intake manifolds like the Edelbrock Torker, Torker II, Tarantula, and even the Streetmaster are not the best street manifolds because they are designed to make torque at 3000 to 7000 rpm, yet we see them on a wide variety of street engines where a good dual-plane manifold would work much better.

Long intake runners and a dual-plane design are but two reasons why we can achieve good low- and mid-range torque from a carbureted engine. We

also want cool air both ahead of the carburetor and beneath it. To get cool air before the carburetor, we need to source cool air from outside. Underhood air is much hotter than the ambient air outside. If we can drop the intake air temperature by 50 to 80 degrees F, this will make a considerable difference in thermal expansion inside the combustion chamber. We can net nearly 10 percent more power this way.

We get cooler air with a hood scoop or a ram-air scoop at the leading edge of the vehicle. Ram air can be sourced through the radiator support or beneath the front bumper. Ram-air kits can be purchased from Summit Racing Equipment, Performance Automotive Warehouse (PAW), or your favorite speed shop. The choice is yours.

Getting cool induction air after the carburetor takes closing off the manifold heat passages from the exhaust side of the cylinder head. We do this during intake manifold installation by installing the manifold heat block-off plates included in most intake manifold gasket kits. Manifold heat is needed only when the outside air is really cold. A cold intake manifold allows the fuel to atomize as well as it does in a hot manifold which causes hesitation and stumbling. We curb this problem by adjusting the choke to remain on for a longer period of time. Then, when the engine is warm, we still have a cooler manifold that offers us better performance.

A popular myth is that we make more power by removing the air cleaner. The truth is, removing the air cleaner allows dirt and grit inside your engine which shortens engine life. We want a low restriction air cleaner that will effectively filter out dirt while allowing healthy breathing at the same time. K&N air filters meet the mission effectively, but they don't come cheap. Filters for carbureted applications cost around $45 each retail. They can be washed and reused, which actually saves you money long term because K&N claims these filters will last a million miles. What's more, they outperform the nearest competitor by a wide margin. A K&N air filter is money well spent in terms of performance and longevity. The new K&N filter with a separate filter in the lid improves breathing even more.

One of the biggest mistakes enthusiasts make is overcarburetion. Engines don't need as much carburetion as you might think. The formula is simple, and without a lot of complex engine math. Small blocks ranging from 221 to 302 cubic inches need no more than 500 cfm. The 351W and 351C need 500 to 600 cfm. Big blocks displacing 352 to 390 cubic inches need 600 to 650 cfm. Larger big blocks of 406 to 428 inches need 650 to 750 cfm. These numbers may sound modest, but they are all a healthy street engine needs. We have to laugh whenever we see a mildly modified street small block with a 750 cfm Holley double-pumper. That's way too much carburetor.

The exception to our carburetion formula is racing applications. When we're going racing, our engine needs more carburetor if it's going to make torque. Small blocks can tolerate 600 - 650cfm in racing applications. Middle- and big-block applications up to 390ci need 700 - 850 cfm. Beyond 390ci, we need 850 - 1050 cfm. Performance tuning is where

we learn how much carburetor we're going to need.

Overcarburetion wastes fuel and pollutes the air. Too much fuel is also hard on an engine. It washes precious lubricating oil off the cylinder walls and fouls spark plugs. Your performance objective should include being environmentally responsible. Plan and tune for cleaner air, not just power. There are three objectives in engine performance: efficiency, cleaner emissions, and power.

Through the years, we have seen and used a wide variety of carburetors on Ford V-8s. Although the Holley 1850, 4150, and 4160 are legendary performance carburetors, they don't enjoy the reliability of an Autolite 4100 — that plain-Jane four-throat carburetor Ford installed on a wide variety of V-8s from 1957-66. The 4100 is fiercely reliable and it offers the same level of performance we're used to with the Holley. Holley carburetors struggle with bowl leakage and metering block difficulties. Metering block passages tend to clog easily, causing idle and driveability problems. We don't see these problems on the Autolite 4100. Some Holley carbs perform well for years, while others tend to be high maintenance. The 1850, 4150, and 4160 can be challenging due to their small metering block passages that tend to become clogged. The 600cfm 1850 series Holley is the biggest culprit for driveability problems shortly after it comes out of the box or through a rebuild. When this carburetor won't idle right and won't adjust, remove the metering block and its plugs. You will find the idle/air bleeds plugged with dirt. Deal with this size issue with either periodic metering block cleanings or a different metering block with larger passages. This is a problematic issue common to most Holley carburetors.

Anyway you look at Holley carburetors, they are high maintenance despite what all of the Holley die-hards will tell you. Because racing and performance driving tends to be high-maintenance by nature, Holley's engineering woes tend to be lost in the shuffle. Despite these observations about the Holley, it remains the most widely used performance carburetor in the world because it is easy to service and understand. Jet, power valve, and metering block swaps are

simple with the Holley, which makes it popular with racers.

For street engines, we suggest a Holley with vacuum secondaries for a smooth transition into high power. Vacuum secondaries work better in street use because they function only when we need them at wide-open throttle. Mechanical secondaries make more sense in racing use because they come into play more quickly in a linear fashion.

Our message here for the street buff is simple: Be realistic about how you will use your engine. Most of your driving will be normal stop and go with open highway tossed in for good mix. Weekend drag racing will be the exception, not the rule. Build an engine you can live with on a daily basis, then make tuning changes for weekend fun. You need an intake manifold and carburetor that will give you good acceleration and driveability coupled with clean emissions. Companies like Edelbrock and Weiand have done extensive research to improve the performance of their products, including improved emissions. Good dual-plane street manifolds like the Performer and Stealth get the job done nicely.

The Autolite 4100 mentioned earlier is a better street performance carburetor than the Holley from a reliability standpoint. It delivers plenty of power on demand and will go for years without much in the way of service. The only exception to this rule is California with its destructive oxygenated fuels that harm older fuel systems. You can expect failing gaskets, seals, and rubber hoses with the California fuel additive MTBE. For California vehicles, we suggest hard lining your fuel system between the fuel pump and carburetor and the use of steel-reinforced hoses where necessary to prevent fuel leakage and fires.

When your performance requirements mandate something more aggressive than the Autolite 4100, opt for that weekend Holley racing experience with a simple carb swap when you want to go racing. Holley and Autolite carburetors are easily interchanged in an afternoon, which enables you to live peacefully with both.

Where carbureted induction systems become tricky is late-model 5.0L High Output V-8 engines because we must build an engine that will pass both a visual and tailpipe emissions smog check. Although you might be tempted to dig your heels in on this one, your goal should always be cleaner emissions for the daily driver.

Ford first began using cast-aluminum intake manifolds in 1979 atop the 302-2V V-8. In 1979, it was a dual-plane, two-barrel manifold. In 1980-81, it was a 255ci small block with different cylinder heads and a 255-specific intake manifold. The 255ci small block had different intake ports than we find on the 302 (smaller for improved torque from less displacement). For 1982, the 5.0L High Output V-8 had a cast-aluminum, two-barrel, dual-plane intake manifold not much different than what we had in 1979.

Ford used two basic types of carburetors in 1977-81 atop small-block V-8s. The Motorcraft Variable Venturi (VV) two-barrel carburetor is an interesting chapter in Ford V-8 history. Known as the Motorcraft 2700VV, this carburetor family is nothing like a conventional carburetor because, as its name implies, the venturis vary in size depending on load and the demand for power. Venturi size depends on throttle position. Metering rods tied to the venturis determine fuel delivery. The VV carburetor is not a popular fuel metering device, so we won't go into much detail here. Suffice it to say this carburetor was conceived for cleaner emissions, not performance. Because VV cores are outrageously priced at $500+, they don't fall inside the guidelines for a budget V-8. If you can get by without using a 2700VV carburetor, do it.

At the same time, Ford also used the Motorcraft 2150 two-barrel carburetor (depending on where the vehicle was delivered new). Like the earlier Autolite and Motorcraft 2100 carburetor, the late-model 2150 is a fiercely reliable carburetor due to its simple design. We're convinced you probably won't be using this carburetor on your high-performance budget small-block. However, emission laws being what they are in different parts of the country, you could be forced to use original equipment to pass a smog check.

For 1983-85, Ford used a dual-plane, cast-aluminum manifold that incorporated four-barrel Holley carburetion. The most important thing to remember about the Holley 4180 carburetor is this:

Guide To Late-Model Small-Block Ford Manifolds

Carbureted Only

Model Year/Type	Ford Part Number	Information
1979-85 5.0L V-8 (302ci)	E0VY-A	Two-Barrel Cast Aluminum Dual Plane. Also used with CFI from 1980-85.
1980-81 4.2L V-8 (255ci)	E0AZ-E	Two-Barrel Cast Aluminum Dual Plane.
1981-82 4.2L V-8 (255ci)	E1SZ-C	Two-Barrel Cast Aluminum Dual Plane.
1982 5.0L High Output (302ci)	E0VY-A	Two-Barrel Cast Aluminum Dual Plane.
1983-85 5.0L High Output (302ci)	E4ZZ-E	Four-Barrel Cast Aluminum Dual Plane.

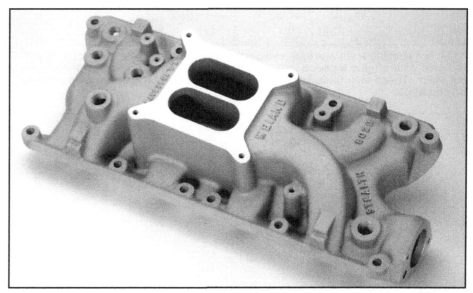

Street engines need long intake runners such as those found in the Weiand Stealth dual-plane intake manifold. This manifold fits comfortably underneath any hood using a stock or aftermarket air cleaner. A Holley 1850, Carter AFB, or Autolite 4100 carburetor will work fine with this manifold.

Edelbrock offers complete power packages like this Performer RPM manifold, carburetor, and camshaft kit for the small-block Ford. This package is also available for the 351W, FE-series 390/428 and 429/460 big blocks. It offers you plenty of low-end torque and good driveability.

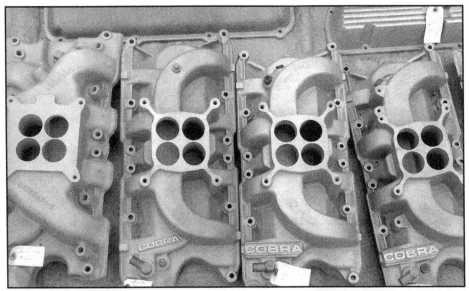

If you are seeking a vintage look and performance, swap meets give you options. Old Cobra and Edelbrock high-rise manifolds will give your engine a period look. You can have a lot of fun here with multi-carburetion setups and the like from the muscle car years. These manifolds are expensive, however. Vintage Cobra high-rise manifolds can fetch upwards of $300, depending on condition.

Ford produced its share of suitable factory performance manifolds. Here's a 1983-85 aluminum four-barrel intake for the 5.0L High-Output V-8, which is suitable for nearly any small-block Ford. Watch the coolant passages for proper sizing, however.

Although not as available as aftermarket high-rise manifolds, stock four-barrel intake manifolds work well for those trying to keep a low profile. These can be pricey, depending upon who is selling. The Autolite 4100 is the perfect carburetor for this application.

Although it looked similar to the time-proven Holley atomizers we've been playing with for more than 40 years, it is not a compatible carburetor with other Holley four-throaters. In fact, it is a Ford-designed carburetor produced by Holley for Ford exclusively. Holley produced a similar emissions/performance carburetor for Chevrolet's 305ci small blocks of the period as well, much like Ford's 4180C. The 600cfm Holley 4180C was not a feedback carburetor like a lot of carburetors of the period. This means there was no computer control aboard the 1983-85 Mustang GT, Capri RS, and LTD models fitted with the 5.0L-4V engine.

The 1983 5.0L-4V Holley 4180C is easily identified by the "LIST 50223"

number stamped in the front of the air horn like other Holley carburetors. From 1984-85, the number changes to "LIST 50265". The Holley 4180C was fitted on 5.0L High Output V-8s with five-speed transmissions. Those fitted with AOD automatic transmissions received Central Fuel Injection instead of Holley carburetion.

The Holley 4180C is not a performance carburetor despite its Holley name. It is configured for lean, clean emissions operation hence its reputation for flat spots and poor off-idle performance. You can make improvements to the metering block, power valve, and accelerator pump to net some improvement. In states with tough emission laws and regular smog checks, there is only so

much you can do. Because the Ford/Holley 4180C has a Ford-specific metering block, it is not interchangeable with other Holley metering blocks.

On the secondary side of the 4180C, there is some interchangeability with other Holley carbs. The Holley 34-6 improvement kit enables you to improve the secondary metering side. However, because the fuel transfer tube is a tad short, you will have to use two "O" rings at the secondary side. The bottom line with the 4180C is that it is not a good performance carburetor. It is a Ford/Holley venture designed with clean emissions in mind. Holley does have some performance improvement parts for this carburetor, but it remains a very limited carburetor. See Holley for more details.

Although many of these got tossed long ago in favor of aftermarket Holley carburetion, the Autolite 4100 is undoubtedly the best four-barrel carburetor for your street application. These guys come from Pony Carburetors, in sizes ranging from 480 to 600 cfm. They offer reliability and performance for small blocks (except the 351C/351M and 400M) and FE-series big blocks.

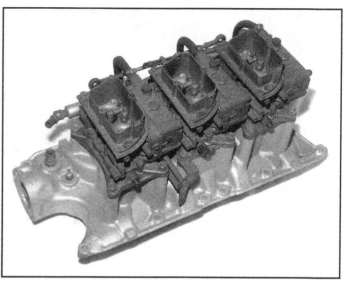

Multi-carburetor setups, like this small-block tri-power, look terrific and make a lot of power. However, they're temperamental and require ongoing tuning. Original setups like this one are attractive, but costly.

Smog laws in some areas mandate the use of original equipment. This underhood look at a 1982 Mustang GT 5.0L High Output shows us this engine was fitted with factory two-barrel carburetion. Changing this manifold is illegal in some states. Check your local emission laws before making changes.

This is the Autolite/Motorcraft 4300 four-barrel carburetor. This carburetor first saw use in 1967 atop small- and big-block Fords. It is primarily an emissions carburetor and not big on performance. Early versions are less than 500 cfm, even on big blocks. Ford stepped up the airflow to 600 cfm in 1968 for big blocks. We suggest the use of the Autolite 4100 mentioned earlier, or the Holley 1850 (500, 600 and 650 cfm).

This is an anti-stall dashpot on a Holley 4160, which controls throttle closure to prevent stalling and decrease emissions. Most Autolite 2100 and 4100 carburetors on automatic transmission-equipped Fords had these.

Holley built a special center-float pivot 715 cfm road race carburetor for Carroll Shelby. It was standard equipment on most of Shelby Mustangs and Cobras during the 1960s.

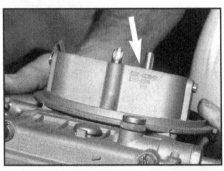

Holley carburetors are easily identified via this number found on the air horn (arrow).

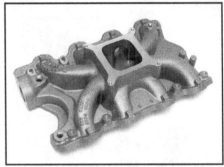

This is a single-plane 351W intake manifold from Bush Performance. Its shorter, larger intake runners help an engine do its best work at high revs. Engines need lots of air at high RPM where a manifold like this is most beneficial. Remember: Short runners for high revs (racing), long runners for low-to mid-range RPM (street use).

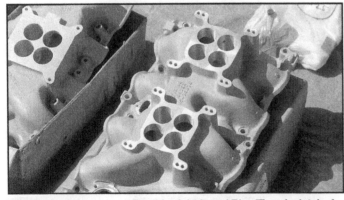

Multi-carburetion setups, like this eight-barrel Blue Thunder intake for the 429/460 big blocks, make terrific show pieces for street engines, but you will be disappointed with the performance. A single, correctly-sized four-barrel carburetor will actually give you more power.

Despite the obsolete nature of the FE big block, there is so much available for these engines both new and used. Edelbrock is your source for new Performer 390 dual-plane intake manifolds. Swap meets usually offer an array of vintage pieces, like the old Shelby Sidewinder aluminum intake manifold. This manifold is good for low- and mid-range torque, plus it makes plenty of power on the high end.

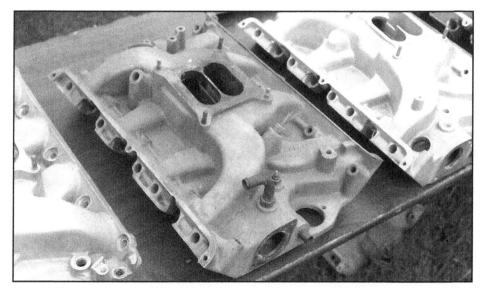

The Ford 390/428 Police Interceptor manifold is an excellent factory piece for FE builders who would like less weight on top. Painted, it looks like a cast-iron intake and no one knows it's there but you. It's an easy lightweight bolt-on.

Cast aluminum intake manifolds can be ground and polished for this result. It's easier to keep clean. Powdercoat it in clear or seal it with clear engine enamel for outstanding longevity.

Carburetor Sizing Quick Reference Chart

Engine Displacement	Suggested Carburetor Size
221, 260, 289, 302	500 cfm 4V (600 cfm if fitted with high-performance camshaft and heads)
221, 260, 289, 302	500 cfm 4V (600 cfm if fitted with high-performance camshaft and heads)
351W, 351C, 351M	500 - 600 cfm (600 - 650 cfm if fitted with high- performance camshaft and heads)
351W, 351C, 351M	500 - 600 cfm (600 - 650 cfm if fitted with high-performance camshaft and heads)
352, 360, 390, 400M	600 - 650 cfm (650 - 700 cfm if fitted with high- performance camshaft and heads)
352, 360, 390, 400M	600 - 650 cfm (650 - 700 cfm if fitted with high-performance camshaft and heads)
406, 410, 427, 428	650 cfm (700 - 750 cfm if fitted with high- performance camshaft and heads)

A WORD ON PORT SIZING/MATCHING

Ford small-block engines were cursed with small ports from the factory. Some big blocks weren't much better. Engine families like the 335-series Cleveland and Midland tended to have too much port. This is where you have to be selective — and wise — about head/manifold choice. Because we have already talked about head selection elsewhere in this book, we're not going to get into it here at any length.

If you want a small block to breathe well while yielding good driveability, it's wise to top it with 351W heads. We suggest a good porting job that includes matching the intake manifold and head ports. If you are building a 351C-4V engine and want good low-end torque, opt for the 351C-2V/351M-2V/400M-2V head and a matching intake manifold. The 351C-2V/351M/400M head employs smaller ports and open-chambered heads. Edelbrock appears to be the only aftermarket performance company which offers a four-barrel/high-rise intake manifold for 351C-2V/351M/400M heads.

CENTRAL FUEL INJECTION

Beginning in 1980, after a brief and unpleasant experience with feedback carburetion, Ford began using throttle body fuel injection in Lincolns and Thunderbirds known as "CFI" or Central Fuel Injection. At the same time, the AOD (Automatic Overdrive) debuted to work hand-in-hand with fuel injection for better efficiency. At the time, Ford had a long way to go.

CFI incorporates a two-barrel throttle body (Ford called it the "fuel charging assembly") with twin 48 lb./hr. fuel injec-

tors that pulse in time with engine speed and the demand for power. As we open the throttle, the pulse width increases (injectors stay open longer) which increases fuel delivery. Fed by dual electric fuel pumps (one in the tank and one in-line), this is a speed density system similar in function to what Ford was using (SEFI) between 1986-88 (49-state) prior to the mass-air metering system.

CFI is not a flexible system for the performance buff because any modifications, like a hot camshaft or serious head porting, only serve to confuse the computer causing erratic operation. The computer is programmed to function with stock components, including camshaft. It does not like anything outside of that Ford programmed window.

If performance isn't a priority, you can use this system atop your budget Ford small block. All you need is the ECM (electronic control module), wiring harness and all of the components required to make the system function. These items can be sourced from a parts car and incorporated into your Ford if this is what you desire. Despite the availability of CFI on loads of parts cars across the land, we can't honestly recommend CFI for your budget engine buildup, especially if it's a high-performance engine in a vehicle not originally equipped.

Perhaps you're building a budget Ford small block that was fitted with CFI from the factory. If your objective is mild-mannered factory performance, then CFI will work just fine. When the demand for performance increases, CFI will not work effectively for your applica-

Observe the differences between the 351C-2V intake manifold (top) and the 351C-4V unit (bottom). The 4V manifold sports huge ports that work well only at high RPM. The smaller 2V ports offer better velocity (and torque) at lower RPM ranges.

tion because the system is programmed for a stock camshaft, throttle body, and cylinder heads. When we go more toward a radical camshaft or better heads, the CFI system is not programmed to work hand-in-hand with these components.

SEQUENTIAL ELECTRONIC FUEL INJECTION

It is difficult to believe now, but Ford's Sequential Electronic Fuel Injection (SEFI) was quite foreign to us when it first appeared on the 1986 Mustang GT. Many viewed SEFI as the beginning of the end of a tunable Mustang. Nothing could have been further from the truth; it was only the beginning.

The late-model Mustang performance market has surpassed the vintage movement by a landslide, and with good reason. SEFI offers efficiency, cleaner emissions, and vastly improved performance. Just imagine building an 11-second quarter-mile street Ford you can drive to work daily. That's what fuel injection has brought us: performance you can tune from the driver's seat with a laptop computer. Summing it up, SEFI has been the single greatest performance improvement to a Ford V-8 since the roller tappet in 1985.

For proper operation, SEFI relies on continuous feedback from sensors positioned in and around the engine. Based on information (signals) from those sensors, it manages fuel delivery (amount) and spark curve (timing). Fuel delivery depends on throttle position, intake manifold vacuum, engine coolant and intake air temperatures, air flow, and exhaust gas mixture. Sensor operation is little more than a variable resistor (like a volume control on your sound system) or simply an on/off switch. Both serve a function of "telling" the computer or ECM (electronic control module) current conditions. Of course, sensors don't really "tell" the computer anything — they merely regulate the flow of electricity (micro voltage) to ground from the computer, which then regulates the flow of electricity to the electrically-fired fuel injectors and electronic spark control. This, of course, is an oversimplification, but suffice it to say SEFI is a system that can work very well in any vintage or late-model Ford.

With SEFI, fuel is electronically sprayed into each intake port as the intake valve opens in time with the engine's firing order. The nice thing about this system is efficiency. It does not waste fuel and it makes the most of each intake fuel charge. A single throttle body meters air into the intake manifold (also known as a plenum). A throttle position sensor "tells" the ECM where the throttle is. As the throttle is opened, the throttle position sensor gives feedback to the ECM, which adjusts spark and fuel curve accordingly. The ECM advances the spark as RPMs increase. It also increases injector pulse width (injector "open" time). Other sensors that sense manifold air pressure (vacuum) and temperature, coolant temperature, exhaust oxygen content, mass-air intake flow, and crank position give the ECM feedback. The ECM makes adjustments to spark and fuel curve to achieve optimum performance.

Between 1986-88 (49 state) and 1986-87 (California only), SEFI was a speed density system that was as inflexible as CFI. Swap the camshaft with a more radical stick and you're in trouble. Port the heads and the computer gets confused. You're limited to stock components with a speed density system. Beginning in 1988 (California only) and 1989 (49 state), mass-air metering took the place of speed density with outstanding results because it is more in touch with what's happening underhood. Mass-air understands what the engine needs via the mass-air sensor. Speed density does not. Speed density is a factory-programmed system with a limited window. It does not get along well with aftermarket modifications like mass-air does.

The speed density system has two throttle body sizes. For 1986, it's a 58mm throttle body that flows 541 cfm at wide-open throttle. For 1987-88, it's a larger 60mm throttle body that flows 580 cfm. Mass-air systems have a 65mm throttle body with a 70mm mass-air sensor for 638 cfm. Aftermarket throttle bodies are 70, 75, and 90mm for 675, 750, and 1100 cfm respectively.

We improve performance by upgrading in stages. Likely the most predictable upgrade directly from the factory is the 1993-95 GT-40 induction system which consists of the 70mm mass-air sensor, 65mm throttle body, 24 lb./hr. injectors, upper and lower intake, and the GT-40 cylinder heads.

Whenever you're shopping fuel injectors, there are six basic types for Ford applications. The 14 lb./hr. injector is gray in color and designed for 5.0L SEFI engines in nonperformance applications. Next step is the 19 lb./hr. injector, yellow in color, standard for the 5.0L High Output SEFI V-8. GT-40 5.0L applications get the 25 lb./hr. injector which is light blue in color. Red is the 30 lb./hr. injector found on the 2.3L Turbo OHC

1980 EEC ELECTRONIC FUEL INJECTION SYSTEM

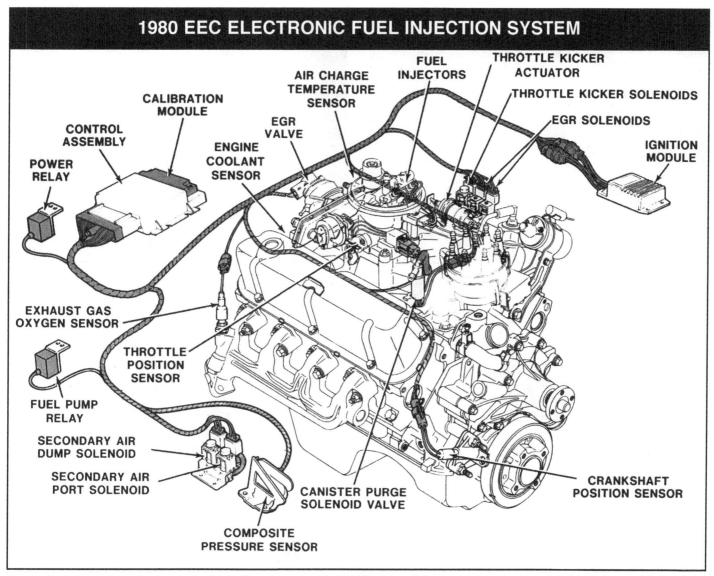

POWER RELAY

CONTROL ASSEMBLY

CALIBRATION MODULE

ENGINE COOLANT SENSOR

EGR VALVE

AIR CHARGE TEMPERATURE SENSOR

FUEL INJECTORS

THROTTLE KICKER ACTUATOR

THROTTLE KICKER SOLENOIDS

EGR SOLENOIDS

IGNITION MODULE

EXHAUST GAS OXYGEN SENSOR

THROTTLE POSITION SENSOR

FUEL PUMP RELAY

SECONDARY AIR DUMP SOLENOID

SECONDARY AIR PORT SOLENOID

CANISTER PURGE SOLENOID VALVE

CRANKSHAFT POSITION SENSOR

COMPOSITE PRESSURE SENSOR

Ford's first attempt at electronic-fuel injection began with throttle-body injection (known as central-fuel injection). Like SEFI (multi-port injection), central-fuel injection (CFI) takes feedback from multiple sensors to control fuel delivery and spark curve. Two injectors positioned over two throttle bores fire at a rate determined by the ECM, which relies on sensor feedback.

four-cylinder engines. The 1984-86 Mustang SVO 2.3L turbo four has brown 35 lb./hr. injectors. Finally, there's a dark blue 35 lb./hr. injector we've also seen. For your budget application, you're going to want to use a 24 lb./hr. injector which can even be used in a 5.0L High Output.

Performance improvements in SEFI come from time-proven hotrodding tricks, plus a few new things common to fuel-injected engines. To increase power, we increase air and fuel flow into the engine — and we play with the ECM to adjust fuel and spark curve. This is done with a laptop computer or a revised ECM. In addition, there are other ways to improve air flow: different heads, better exhaust scavenging, different valve-timing events, etc.

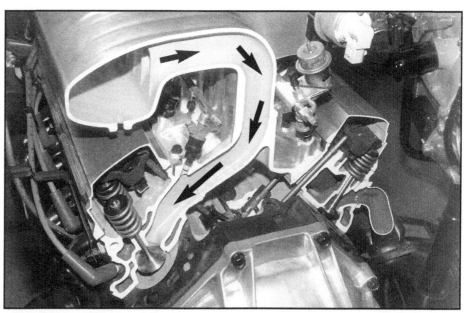

SEFI employs eight fuel injectors which are time-fired by the ECM, which gets its feedback from sensors positioned in and around the engine.

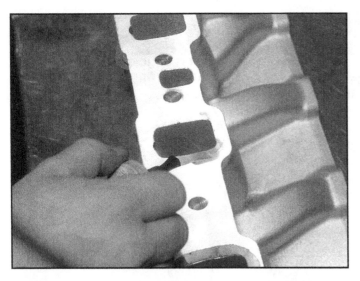
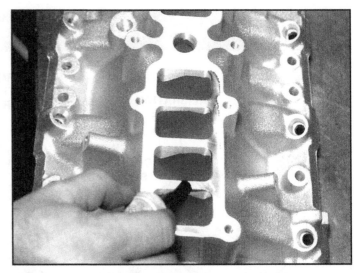
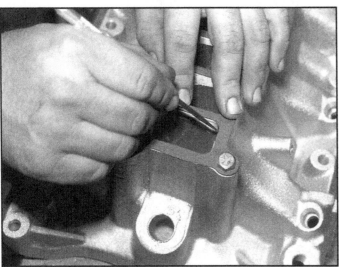

Want to make the most of your SEFI system? Fastline Performance in Simi Valley, California suggests port matching the upper and lower intakes to the cylinder heads. Cleaning up the passages can make a significant difference in power.

The Edelbrock Performer 5.0 manifold is a quick means to better performance. Compliment this package with high-flow injectors and a larger throttle body.

M-9424-D51

Ford Racing Technology's (FRT) GT-40 upper and lower intake manifolds offer a modest improvement in performance. We suggest the entire package — injectors, throttle body, mass-air sensor, ECM, cam, and heads — for best results. Remember, proper packaging is everything.

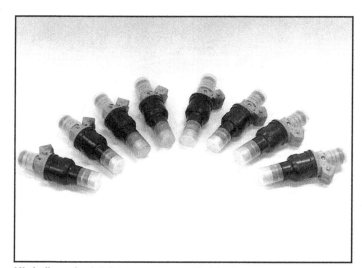

High-flow fuel injectors are available in a variety of rates. They offer increased fuel delivery to compliment a larger manifold, more radical camshaft, and larger valves/ports.

The 65mm throttle body from Ford Racing Technology is a good first step toward better performance at a modest investment.

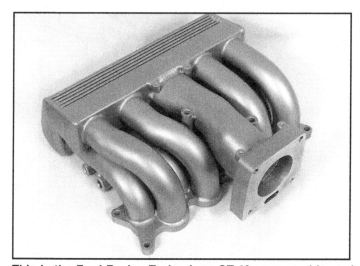

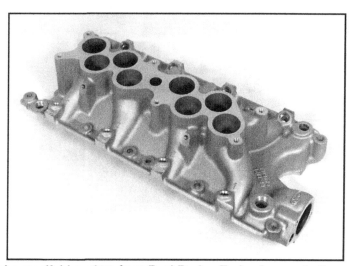

This is the Ford Racing Technology GT-40 upper and lower intake manifold system from Ford Racing Technology — bolt-on pep for your 5.0L engine. These are still available new from FRT, or used at your favorite swap meet.

NITROUS OXIDE INJECTION

Never has there been a faster path to power than nitrous oxide injection (N2O). You can add 100- plus extra horsepower to your arsenal with the punch of a button, surprising family and friends in seconds, but is nitrous for you? Chemically, nitrous oxide is two parts nitrogen attached to one part oxygen. It is a non-toxic gas that isn't harmful to the atmosphere. You have probably been exposed to nitrous oxide and didn't even know it in your dentist's office — laughing gas.

For performance automobiles, nitrous oxide is stored under high pressure in a bottle, typically located in the trunk area. It is administered to the engine electronically via the intake manifold when the engine is at wide-open throttle. Nitrous oxide can

be fed into the engine in a variety of ways. One way is through a carburetor spacer. Another is through nozzles at each intake port. Because we're talking budget performance here, carb spacer nitrous is all you're going to be able to afford.

When nitrous oxide escapes to the atmosphere under pressure, it is very cold, around -128 degrees F. At this super cold temperature, nitrous is a liquid. Because nitrous oxide is 50-percent richer in oxygen than the air we breathe, it enables an engine to generate greater amounts of power from the fuel/air charge each cylinder receives and burns.

If we were to feed nitrous oxide to the combustion chambers without a richer fuel mixture, the extremely lean mixture and corresponding temperatures would melt the pistons. This

means we have to administer greater quantities of fuel at the same time we feed nitrous into the engine. We do this with two solenoids connected to a common signal that will fire both at the same time. One electrically-fired solenoid administers the nitrous; the other administers fuel. When we punch the accelerator, we fire both solenoids. When both solenoids fire, coupled with a wide-open throttle, the engine goes wild with power we didn't know it had.

The additional power achieved through the use of nitrous (also called "squeeze") doesn't come from the nitrous itself. Power actually comes from the rapid ignition of fuel in the combustion chambers. Heat and the expansion of molecules channel the power across the piston dome, turning linear energy into rotary motion.

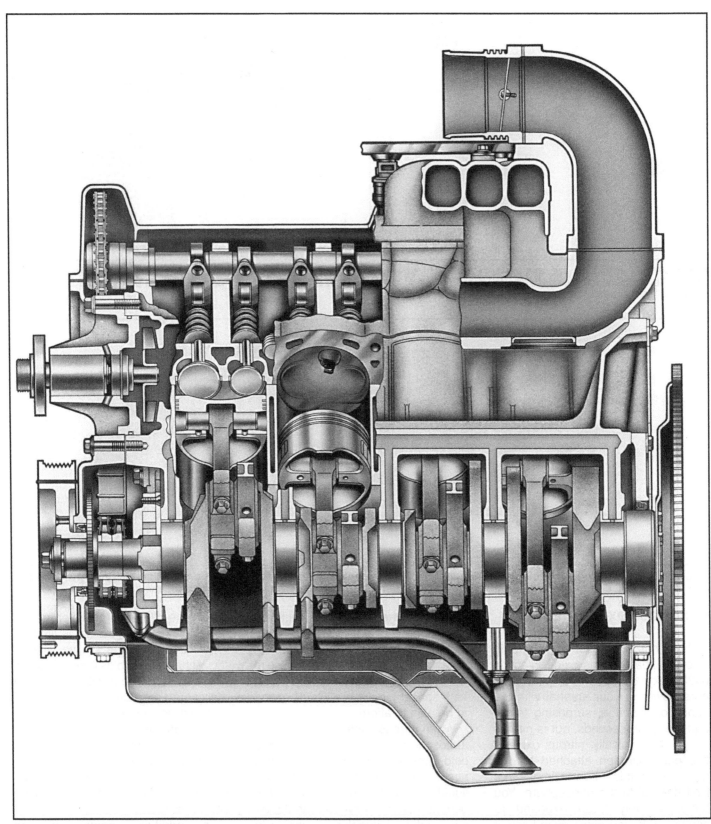

Never in the history of Ford power has proper packaging been more important than it is with electronically-controlled engines. Manifolds, throttle body, injectors, camshaft, heads, and exhaust system must all work together as a cohesive group for best results.

The addition of nitrous oxide into the mix makes the fuel crazy, so to speak. It accelerates the ignition of fuel, which makes the additional power. Instead of a smooth light-off (woof!), we get more of an explosion (boom!).

Call it a light-off with an attitude. When you consider it is good for 100 or more horsepower, attitude is an understatement.

A word of caution is in order here. Power must be managed responsibly

or the result can be disaster. Using nitrous oxide doesn't come without a price. Aside from the operating costs, you can ruin your engine if nitrous isn't used properly. Detonation or spark knock while using nitrous can permanently damage pistons. This is where proper tuning and calibration is important. Overdo it and you will lose an engine. Start low and calibrate upward in baby steps until you are comfortable with the results. If it feels like you are pushing your engine too hard, you probably are. Listen for detonation (pinging). Retard the timing and check the nitrous oxide/fuel mixture calibration if detonation exists. Repeated detonation will shorten engine life.

It has been proven through dyno testing that engines can tolerate a lot of nitrous without catastrophic results. However, let us assure you that nitrous used irresponsibly will destroy an engine. We've seen what it can do. Pistons melt when there's too much nitrous and not enough fuel. To get the fuel pressure needed to meet the intense demands of nitrous, we need an electric fuel pump that will deliver adequate pressure and volume to the nozzle. Pay close attention to the manufacturer's instructions addressing jetting and calibration. Most nitrous oxide system manufacturers offer complete kits that include the fuel pump and detailed instructions on how to set the system up.

Nearly any engine can run on nitrous and survive. It is how well you tune the engine and the nitrous system as a unit that determines if the engine lives. It bears repeating: Too much nitrous will destroy your engine. This is why we advise cautious growth. Begin the process at the combustion chamber and work back. Your engine's compression ratio should be no higher than 10.0:1 if a 200 to 300 horsepower increase is desired (not likely on your budget street engine). Even with a 100 to 200 horsepower increase (using nitrous), compression should never go above 11.0:1. Truthfully, with today's pump gasoline, you should keep it at 10.0:1 to err on the side of safety.

Exhaust valve size is important, too. Opt for the largest exhaust valve your application will handle, which will improve scavenging. For small-block Fords, for example, exhaust valve size should be around 1.60" or higher if it will fit. Port work on the exhaust

side wouldn't hurt either. Greater valve lift on the exhaust side is important too, which means you have to take another look at the camshaft you're considering.

A nitrous-oriented camshaft will have different valve timing events than conventional camshafts. The exhaust valve is programmed to open sooner with nitrous use. Exhaust valve lift is greater with a nitrous camshaft. Duration is also greater in the interest of allowing the enraged mixture to escape. Intake lift and timing events also differ with a nitrous camshaft because we don't need as much intake (lift or duration). With nitrous cams, we sacrifice power in normal driving conditions because valve timing and lift events don't favor normal driving. Both Crane and Comp Cams have a number of nitrous grinds that will work well in your budget Ford V-8, and both companies have answers on how to live with nitrous camming.

What heat range is the spark plug? If you're running a high-heat range, the risk of detonation is high. We get lucky when detonation melts the cross electrode and the plug quits firing before piston damage occurs. If our spark plug is too cold, it will foul under a very rich mixture. This is the lesser of two evils. We'd rather it were too rich than too lean. Too rich means we can come back and play again. Too lean means we may have harmed the engine beyond repair.

One suggestion with spark plugs and nitrous use is this: Opt for dual platinum-tip spark plugs for best results because they can handle a lot more punishment than conventional spark plugs. This suggestion is twofold. Platinum-tip spark plugs will handle richer or leaner mixtures better and without failure. High-energy ignition systems won't kill them either. Always ensure you have healthy ignition cables and do not cut corners here. A misfire on nitrous can permanently damage an engine and can cause a harmful backfire through the intake called a nitrous explosion. We've seen nitrous explosions blow hood scoops off race cars, which is very entertaining for spectators, but not much for the poor soul involved.

You need a very healthy ignition system whenever you're running nitrous.

Your best barometer of engine performance both on and off nitrous is the time-proven spark plug reading. When spark plugs are black and sooty, the fuel mixture is too rich. Your watering eyes and sense of smell will also indicate this at the tailpipe. When spark plugs insulators are snow white, the mixture is too lean, which can also be detected at the tailpipe. Ideally, the insulator will be a hearty tan color, which is dead normal and an indicator of perfect health.

Another important area to consider with nitrous use is ignition timing. When we're using nitrous, ignition timing must be retarded to prevent detonation. Here's where we have to achieve a critical balance of ignition timing and fuel mixture to prevent major engine damage. We have to use our ears under hard acceleration (listening for detonation or "pinging"). Then we have to read the spark plugs. Check for detonation (use your ears) and read the spark plugs, then advance the ignition timing two degrees at a time. Keep advancing the timing until a hint of pinging is heard. Check the spark plugs. A light tan is as close to white as you'll want to go. When pinging is heard, retard the timing 1-2 degrees at a time.

Also remember that atmospheric conditions affect how you tune the engine. If you drive from Memphis, Tennessee to Denver, Colorado, tuning and calibration will change dramatically. Memphis is nearly at sea level. Denver is more than 5000 feet above sea level. At a higher elevation, atmospheric pressure is lower and there's less oxygen in the air. A nitrous system must be calibrated accordingly.

When it comes to the fuel system, you need a life insurance policy there, too. Install a fuel pressure gauge between the pump and the solenoid. The kind of fuel you use is important also. Never use old fuel, and never use high-octane aviation gasoline. Use only 92 octane pump gasoline or 104 octane racing fuel. No exceptions.

Ideally, bottle pressure should be at 900 psi, which is possible with the use of a bottle heater. We heat the bottle to raise the pressure. As the heat increases, so does the bottle pressure. At this pressure, we get the best results.

Another thing to consider whenever you're running nitrous is the transmission. Torque converter stall speed is critical to performance in any automatic transmission. This is why a higher stall speed is recommended whenever you're running nitrous. Engines make more power whenever we're up on the camshaft and using nitrous. A torque converter that comes on too soon isn't beneficial when we're using nitrous. Shift points are yet another area to consider. This is why we have to look at the valve body and governor in the transmission as well whenever we're building

a nitrous engine. As with the rest of the vehicle, we have to think "package" and a cohesive setup that will work well together.

One other thing while we're on the subject of automatic transmissions: Whenever you're running nitrous, you need a heavy-duty torque converter with furnace-brazed fins. Nitrous will make hamburger out of a stock torque converter in short order. Once again, err on the side of heavy duty and sleep peacefully.

RAMP UP AND WIN!

One thing about nitrous is certain. It gives us immediate power, which is not always manageable. When nitrous makes our engine come on

strong at low revs, we get too much power to the rear wheels too quickly, making the vehicle unmanageable. Two-stage nitrous systems enable us to get power to the pavement without burning the tires off the rims. Two stage, as the name implies, gives us an initial burst of nitrous to get started. Then, as RPM increases, the system gives us greater quantities of nitrous and fuel once we're underway. This enables us to properly manage nitrous and fuel plus the resulting power. If we blow too much nitrous into an engine before we have sufficient revs to disburse the power, we can blow head gaskets and do other forms of damage to the engine. A two-stage nitrous system helps control the monster.

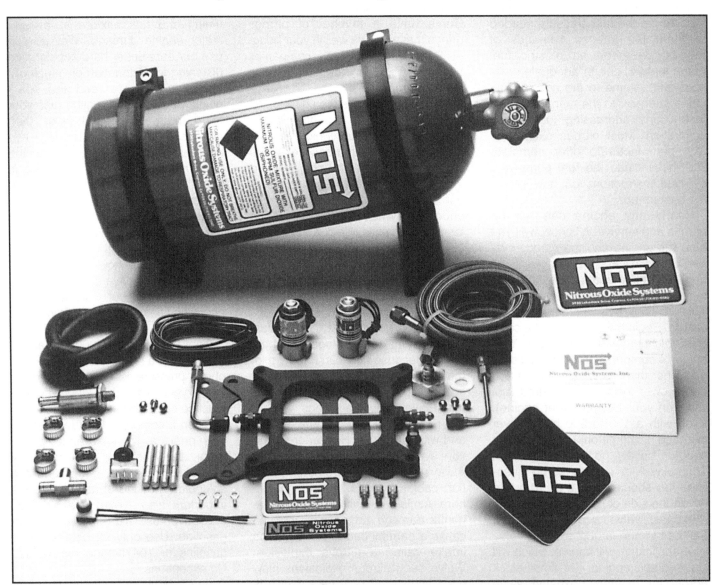

This is a nitrous oxide injection system from Nitrous Oxide Systems, a division of Holley. This kit comes with everything you need for quick, bolt-on power. The package shown is for carburetor-equipped induction systems. A system is also available for EFI (not shown).

CHAPTER 8

EXHAUST SYSTEMS

Exhaust systems have been the subject of hot debate for as long as there have been automobiles. Headers or stock manifolds? Long- or short-tube headers? What size exhaust pipes? Single or dual exhausts? What kind of muffler should I use? Must I use catalytic converters? Is louder better? Will my engine make more power with the headers uncapped?

In recent times we have been learning more about exhaust systems and their effect on power output. Contrary to what we believed for years, an engine can actually make more torque through mufflers than through open headers. In some cases, stock manifolds can even help an engine achieve better torque. Because exhaust system technology has changed considerably over the years, it's time for a refresher course in what works well today.

An exhaust system actually begins at the exhaust valve and port. Good cylinder head porting should be the beginning of a well-thought-out exhaust system. We want smooth flow from the valve face through the port into the header tubes. Although we have covered cylinder head porting elsewhere in this book, we remind you to think about port work as it pertains to your exhaust system. You would be surprised how much power you can pick up with good exhaust system scavenging. Good scavenging is what makes a power pump out of a budget engine.

Think about exhaust tuning this way. During valve overlap, we're moving unspent fuel and air into the chamber which pushes spent exhaust gasses out. If we're doing this thing the right way, we tune our valve overlap (via the right camshaft selection) to move the fuel and air in just as smoothly as we move spent exhaust gasses out. This is where our exhaust system begins. With the right valve overlap, we create a smooth flow of energy and spent gasses through the engine.

HEADERS

There are four basic types of exhaust headers for V-8 Fords: tri-Y, equal length, four-tube, and shorty. Tri-Y headers were most popular during the 1960s when it was perceived they were the best idea. As engine power and speed have become more aggressive in the years since, it has been found that tri-Ys don't perform as well in racing applications. Tri-Y headers work quite well on the street where good low- to mid-range torque is needed. Their smaller tubes and tri-Y design help maintain back pressure and separate the exhaust pulses for improved performance. Carroll Shelby's GT350 Mustangs used the tri-Y header with great success during the 1960s. These retro-headers can work very well in your street small-block application.

Four-tube headers are the system used most often today. The tubes are as close to equal length as possible, although there are some exceptions. Ideally, a manufacturer will get tube length within one to two inches, depending upon the installation. Late-model Ford small-block, equal-length headers are typically shorties to where they can be tied into a Mustang's dual-catalyst exhaust system. (You do want to be smog-legal, don't you?) Equal-length, long-tube headers also exist for early- and late-model Fords alike. If what manufacturers offer isn't sufficient to meet your specialized needs, you can fabricate your own headers via kits or simply raw materials from an exhaust shop.

Header tube size is one of the most important issues facing the engine builder who is seeking power — and a larger tube isn't always what your engine needs to make power. Smaller header tubes help an engine make better low- to mid-range torque, which is important on the street. Engine displacement and mission directly determine what tube size you are going to need. Header manufacturers have done most of the homework here already, making your job easier. Simply specify your application and intended use, and the rest is easy.

Header tubes that are too large take away the exhaust system's ability to scavenge spent gasses. When you keep header tube size smaller, you are increasing exhaust velocity (speed), which helps draw gasses out more quickly. Smaller tubes help increase back pressure, which, thanks to valve overlap, helps you get the most out of a combustion charge. When header tube size becomes too large, velocity decreases and we lose exhaust scavenging.

Tube thickness is also an important issue. Typically, header tube wall thickness ranges from 18 to 14 gauge, with the higher number being the thinner stock. For durability, you will want to opt for 16 or 14 gauge. Longevity comes from a thicker wall and durable coating. For street use, we recommend the thickest gauge, which is less likely to crack or split. Coatings range from spray-on paint that burns off to a Jet Hot coating that lasts the life of the header.

If you are building an engine for the long haul, we suggest Jet Hot Header Coatings (phone 800-432-3379). This process may cost more going in, but it means having headers that will never rust or rot through. It is the best ceramic header coating there is. Due to its very nature, it contains heat too, which keeps heat where it belongs -- inside the header for greatest efficiency. If you cannot afford Jet Hot, we suggest a super heat-resistant header paint. For the paint to set properly, you must begin with a clean surface. Clean the headers with brake cleaner, which has a high evaporation rate. Let them dry out in the sun, then apply high-temp paint in thin coats, allowing each coat to dry thoroughly before applying the next.

Another important consideration when selecting headers is smog laws in your area. Some areas do not permit the use of headers on street-legal vehicles. Some areas permit only the use of EPA or CARB-certified (California Air Resources Board) headers. Check your local motor vehicle code before spending the money. Don't kid yourself; smog checks nearly always spot the illegal beagles. If your state is big on visual inspections, running any kind of illegal header will be difficult, if not impossible. However, if you are dealing with a tail-pipe sniffer only, then opt for the best header for your application. Shorty headers are the best choice for an application where a stock appearance is important. Long-tube headers send up red flags immediately in a smog check. If you have eliminated the catalytic converter, it can get expensive in terms of fines and the installation of new converters.

Whenever you are shopping headers, always keep fitment in mind. Despite what manufacturers will tell you, not all headers fit. A good many will require some adjustment on your part. Always use high-temperature ignition wires that can withstand header heat, or install thermal boots and shields for protection. Some ignition wire manufacturers offer ceramic spark plug wire boots. If headers run close to the starter motor, heat issues apply here, too. Excessive header heat will shorten starter life. Sometimes heat disables the starter entirely. Thermal-wrapping the headers reduces underhood heat considerably. See your local speed shop for details.

Another thing to consider when you're shopping for headers is quality. Look at the flange at the head and at the collector. Examine the welding. High-quality headers have welded flanges with a solid bead for 100 percent of the seam. Those with tack welds won't last; they will leak.

Ford produced some respectable exhaust manifolds for its V-8 engines. For example, you can still buy reproduction 289 High Performance exhaust manifolds for your small-block Ford. These manifolds look like cast-iron exhaust headers and they tie nicely into virtually any exhaust system. A similar manifold to the 289 Hi-Po piece is the 1969-up 351W exhaust manifold. Like the Hi-Po manifold, these look like cast-iron headers. With some grinding and clean-up work, they look sharp and function well. These manifolds give a small-block Ford that deep, throaty sound 289 High Performance manifolds are famous for. Whenever you're shopping stock cast-iron manifolds, you want to avoid the long, straight log types which are very restrictive.

Manifold selection for 335-series engines is poor. We can't honestly recommend one. Ditto for 385-series big blocks. Manifolds in both instances are too restrictive. FE-series big blocks have wide selection. When it comes to FE-series big blocks, ideally you're building a full-sized Ford or Merc that will accommodate 390/406/427 High Performance factory exhaust headers. These awesome cast-iron bananas look terrific and sound incredible. Unfortunately, they will not fit the more compact Fairlane and Mustang. There's simply no room for them.

When it comes to late-model exhaust manifolds and headers, stock 5.0L shorty headers don't impress. They're too restrictive and the quality is poor. Opt for a nice set of quality aftermarket shorty headers, which will breathe better, last longer, and fit nicely. Among the best are JBA and Hedman headers. Late-model cast-iron exhaust manifolds are awful. Opt for aftermarket shorties or long tube headers that will go directly into the cats.

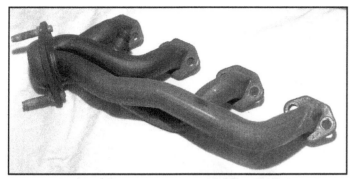

Late-model 5.0L high-output exhaust headers offer a clean design — but breathing suffers. They are just too small and restrictive.

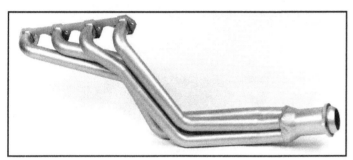

Long-tube headers offer better scavenging than shorties. The upside is improved performance; the downside is clearance and excessive heat. With late-model Fords, emission laws are an issue here.

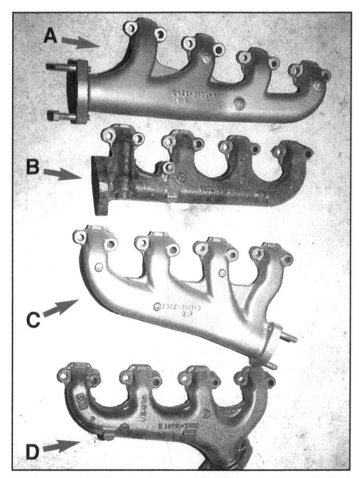

A terrific alternative to the shorty header is the 289 High Performance. The 289 High Performance exhaust manifold (A and C) is a factory cast-iron header. It offers improved breathing without clearance and heat issues. Manifolds B and D are standard 289/302 manifolds. See the differences? (Photo courtesy Dr. John Craft)

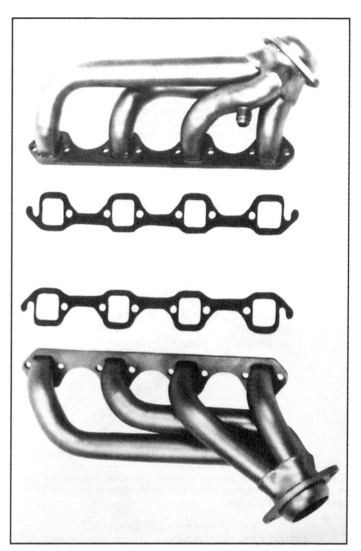

Aftermarket shorty headers are the most logical first step to performance. They offer unobstructed breathing. Check your local emission laws before installing these. Legal or illegal, they look stock and don't throw up the red flag like long-tube headers.

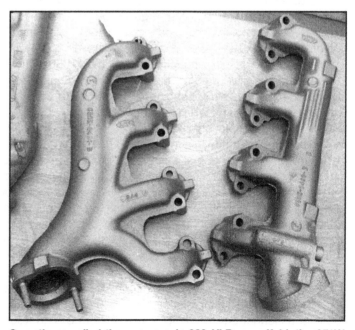

Sometimes called the poor man's 289 Hi-Po manifold, the 351W exhaust manifold is designed very much like the 289 Hi-Po. There may be some clearance issues to deal with here.

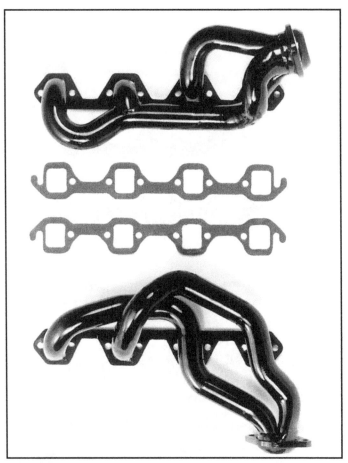

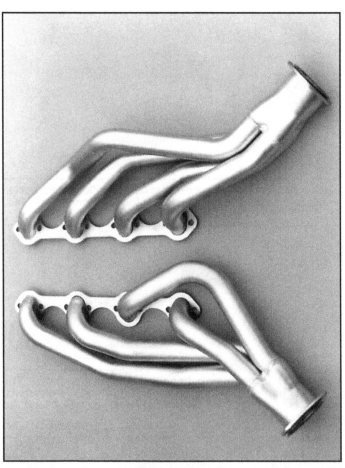

Equal-length shorty headers solve the tube harmonics challenges. They also create some new challenges in terms of fitment and spark plug access.

Another type of equal-length header is shown here for a 351W into an early Mustang. This is the Hedman #88650.

MUFFLERS AND PIPES

Like headers, there are many misconceptions about muffler design and tube size. As in header design, bigger is not always better for mufflers. Street engines need conservative pipe size for efficient exhaust scavenging. Too large and there is not enough back pressure to effectively scavenge the cylinders. Too small and the engine will struggle to breathe and will run hotter. This is why pipe sizing is so important.

Another very important issue here is catalytic converters. Federal emission standards call for the use of a catalytic converter where one was originally used on a vehicle. For cars, catalytic converters were first used in the 1975 model year. Trucks didn't see the use of factory cats until 1978. In any case, you should use them if the vehicle was so equipped — not only to conform to emission standards, but for cleaner air. Do it for a cleaner environment.

The catalytic converter's job is to clean up exhaust emissions. It does this by taking unburned hydrocarbons and carrying them through a platinum catalyst which creates simple water (H_2O). The catalyst also takes carbon monoxide (CO) and mixes it with oxygen to achieve carbon. If you don't think cats make a difference, look at the air quality in Los Angeles during the 1950s, then again at it now. Hazardous air quality isn't the problem it used to be 40 years ago. We can breathe now.

The automotive aftermarket offers quite an array of high-performance catalytic converters that allow your new engine to breathe comfortably. See your local speed shop or Summit Racing Equipment for details.

This leads us to pipe sizing and mufflers. As a rule, engine displacements and performance levels determine pipe size. Displacements between 221 and 302 call for pipe size in the 2-in. to 2 1/4-in. range. Larger displacements from 351 to 460-plus call for sizes in the 2 1/4-in. to 2 1/2-in range. Again, it's important to remember that the

larger the pipe, the more adverse the effect on torque. Too small is a bad thing; but so is too large.

Also remember to tie both sides of a dual exhaust system together via an H-pipe or X-pipe to achieve balance. Popular folklore tells us that we can achieve more power by isolating each side, but this isn't true. Both cylinder banks need to operate as a team after combustion in order to be effective. The trend now in NASCAR racing is to use the X-pipe from Pro Motorsports Engineering. Significant gains in power and engine performance have been achieved with the X-pipe. It also changes exhaust harmony significantly. At high revs, V-8s take on a buzzing European tone with the X-pipe. This is also true on the street.

When it comes to choosing a muffler, several considerations come into play. Loud can be cool, but hearing damage is not. You must seriously consider noise levels in your vehicle's cab. The steady drone of a loud exhaust system will, over a relatively short period of

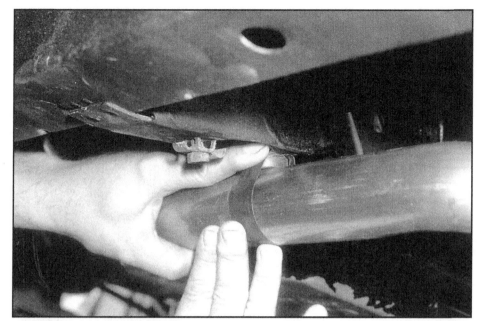

Pipe size is critical to performance. Remember, larger isn't always better. Right sizing is your best bet. When pipe size is right, you get the best torque. When pipes grow too large, torque falls or comes in at a higher RPM range.

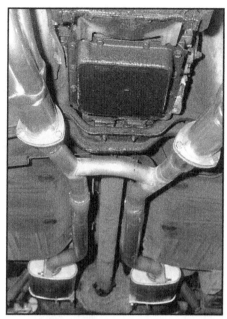

Pipe size should be uniform throughout the system. If you've got 2 1/2 in. at the headers, you should have 2 1/2 in. at the tailpipe.

time, permanently damage your hearing. It's called nerve deafness. It is disabling and it is forever.

Having a loud, obnoxious exhaust system isn't in style today. The soft burble of a throaty dual-exhaust system makes a performance statement without offending the world around us. In this author's opinion, the three-chamber Flowmaster muffler is the best street-performance muffler going because it allows an engine to breathe comfortably while yielding the best tone in the marketplace. The Flowmaster muffler gives your Ford V-8 engine that Hi-Po sound without the expense of Hi-Po parts. It makes a Windsor small block sound like a Cleveland. Flowmaster has the right muffler for your application. We suggest a three-chamber muffler for the street and a two-chamber for the race track.

One thing to bear in mind whenever you're shopping for muffler is the facts. Not all performance mufflers are what they seem. Pipe size going in and coming out isn't always what the pipe size is inside. Before you lay down hard-earned money for a pair of mufflers for your ride, ask to see a cutaway view. What does this muffler look like inside? Sometimes a 2 1/4" inlet and outlet turns into 1 1/2" to 2" inside as a means to noise suppression and back pressure. However, sometimes 1 1/2" inside can mean too much back pres-

Tailpipes at the rear bumper serve a valuable purpose: human health. Side exit exhausts and short 90-degree tailpipes right off the mufflers can damage your hearing. On the open road, they make for a miserable ride. Loud and obnoxious just isn't cool anymore. A soft, throaty, mellow tailpipe harmony is what you want to achieve. Walk softly and carry a big stick.

sure. Muffler manufacturers rarely tell you pipe size inside, only at the inlet and outlet. Can the manufacturer provide you with legitimate flow numbers? Can they show you what the muffler looks like inside? Any company proud of their product will.

Another thing you should be mindful of is muffler quality. Aluminized mufflers offer you quality and longevity depending on climate and vehicle use. Any muffler can live long in a dry climate. However, the acid test is in a humid climate with harsh road condi-

tions. It is the combination of exhaust gas deposits and condensation that kills mufflers. When moisture sits in a muffler or exhaust pipe, electrolysis happens and rust begins. Stainless-steel mufflers and pipes last virtually forever. The downside to stainless is its brittleness and inflexibility; stainless is very difficult to bend. One suggestion with any exhaust system is to drill a tiny 1/16 or 1/32" drain hole at the back of the muffler at the bottom to drain off any condensation.

Pipes that are too large hurt torque. Few budget street engines need big pipes.

Walker Super Turbo mufflers offer improved breathing and mellow sound.

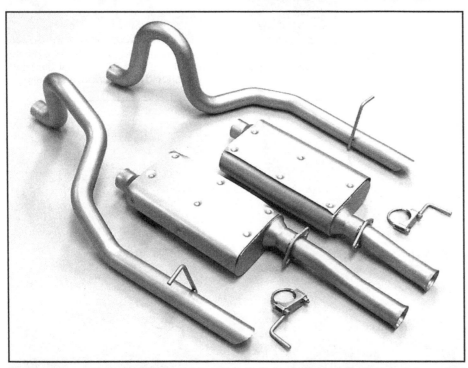

Flowmasters are undoubtedly the best sounding mufflers in the marketplace. The downside to Flowmasters are their bulky design. They don't always fit well.

Stock mufflers provide extraordinary cabin quiet while offering a soft tailpipe report. They do hinder performance, however. When you're considering larger mufflers and pipes, consider size restrictions with Mustang, Cougar, Falcon, Comet, Fairlane, Torino, and Cyclone. Pipe size limitations are in the 2 1/2 in. range.

Always tie both sides of your exhaust together as shown, with an H-pipe for more balanced operation. Separated cylinder banks give the exhaust a pop gun sound instead of a smooth burble.

CHAPTER 9

IGNITION AND CHARGING SYSTEMS

Few things about an engine build seem more mysterious and magical than the ignition system. There have been a lot of advances in ignition technology through the years. Not even 30 yeaars ago we were driving vehicles with crude point-triggered ignitions and conventional distributors. Keeping spark timing in sync with engine RPM has been a great challenge with conventional ignitions. With high-performance engines, keeping the spark alive at high revs under great combustion pressures has been asking a lot of those dated point-triggered ignitions.

Time and technology have brought us better ignition systems — even distributorless ignition, which is as precise as it gets. Because you're building a budget V-8, distributorless ignition probably isn't in the cards. So we have to concentrate on how to achieve precision ignition via the distributor. First, let's look at the basics.

POINT-TRIGGERED IGNITION

Conventional ignition systems con-sist of a primary and secondary circuit. The primary circuit consists of the battery, ignition switch, and the primary side of the ignition coil (positive terminal). The secondary circuit consists of the secondary side of the ignition coil (negative terminal), ignition harness, and spark plugs. Think of it this way: The primary circuit gets power to the ignition coil and the secondary circuit gets processed power to the spark plugs. We call it processed power because we are changing it from 12 volts to 10,000 to 30,000 volts to feed the spark plugs. A high-voltage spark is needed to bridge the spark plug gap.

To process and distribute power, we need an ignition coil, distributor, points, and condenser. Think of ignition points as a switch that is open and closed in time with the distributor. When the points are closed (switch on), the primary circuit side of the ignition coil is energized. When this happens, current flows from the ignition switch (via a resistor wire or ballast resistor) through the coil to the ignition points to ground. The points are a switch to ground. When current pass-es through the primary windings of the coil, a magnetic field builds up around these windings. As the distributor cam turns, the points open (switch off) and current stops flowing through the primary side of the coil windings. When this happens, the magnetic field collapses in the primary windings inside the coil. It then finds a path through the secondary windings inside the coil to create a very high electrical current that is routed to the spark plugs via the distributor rotor, cap, and wires. The condenser's job is to limit the amount of current passing through the points, which prevents pitting and burning.

Think of the ignition system as a voltage management-and-distribution operation. It has a tough job, and that is to keep the release of current to the spark plugs in perfect time with engine speed, load, and throttle position. At idle, the ignition system has an easy job. Contrary to what you might have been taught, fuel does not explode in the combustion chamber. It ignites in a "quick fire" just like your gas or oil burning furnace lights on a cold night. Because the fuel/air mix ignites in a quick fire, not an explosion, the spark must occur a given number of degrees of crank rotation before the piston reaches top-dead-center. Why? Because time passes from the time the spark plug fires until there is a productive mixture light-off with working heat and pressure. If we ignite the mixture with the piston at top-dead-center (TDC), we waste most of the charge because actual light-off doesn't occur in that scenario until after top-dead-center (ATDC). The engine doesn't make power in this case; it just burns and wastes fuel.

If our specifications call for static timing of six degrees before top-dead-center (BTDC), this means it is going to take six degrees of crank rotation and piston travel before the ignited mixture will work for us. When the spark plug fires at six degrees BTDC, mixture light-off happens before the piston gets to the top of the bore. By the time the piston reaches the top of the bore, light-off is well underway and we have a useful charge to drive the piston down the bore, which turns the crankshaft and makes power along with seven other cylinders on the same timed mission.

As engine RPM and power demands increase, the spark must occur earlier in the cycle. This is where two forms of spark advance come in — vacuum and mechanical. In vacuum-advance distributors, both vacuum and centrifugal advance units work together in seamless harmony for the solid application of engine torque. The vacuum advance advances the spark during engine acceleration. Leaning on the gas advances the spark via a vacuum advance diaphragm unit. This helps the engine produce torque under acceleration. The vacuum advance should smoothly give way to the centrifugal advance as RPMs increase — that is, if timing is where it should be.

Sometimes we have too much timing (too much spark advance), causing the spark to occur too early. When this happens, we have pre-ignition, or detonation, meaning the fuel ignites prematurely. The combustion shock against the piston dome creates a rapping or rattling we hear as "pinging" under acceleration. It is a popular misconception that this sound is caused by valves knocking or by rod bearing noise. It is neither. Rather, it is piston wrist pin and skirt noise caused by

the abnormal combustion shock that goes with detonation/pre-ignition.

The centrifugal advance advances the spark at a slower rate and more at higher revs. Flyweights and springs tied to the distributor shaft work together and advance the rotor position according to RPM. The more RPM we have, the more the flyweights advance the spark. Spring tension retards the spark as RPM decreases.

For cohesive spark advance operation, you need to program both the vacuum and centrifugal advances to advance the spark smoothly as the need for power comes into play. If both forms of advance are in perfect tune, the vacuum advance will hand off its duties to the centrifugal advance as engine speed increases. Too much vacuum advance too early will cause the engine to ping or misfire. Too little and the engine will fail to produce sufficient torque under acceleration. It will fall on its face. The same goes for the centrifugal advance at higher RPM. Too much spring tension and it will not advance. Too little and it will advance too early.

A distributor's advance process must be tuned in steps. First, you program the centrifugal advance to come in fully by the time an engine reaches a given RPM range. For street engines, full advance should come in around 3500 rpm. Full advance should be roughly 36-40 degrees BTDC. You dial in centrifugal advance with the right combination of flyweight weight and spring tension. As stated earlier, the greater the spring tension, the more slowly the distributor will advance. Remember, the spring's job is to retard the spark. The flyweight's job is to advance the spark. The object is to get these guys working together smoothly.

Programming the vacuum advance takes the right combination of vacuum and spring pressure inside the advance. The more spring pressure you have, the more slowly the vacuum advance will come into play. Spring pressure fights the vacuum. Vacuum fights the spring pressure. Vacuum advances the spark. Spring pressure retards the spark. You want a balance here where vacuum advances the spark smoothly while you are leaning on the throttle.

Older Autolite distributors have adjustable vacuum-advance units that use shims against spring pressure.

The more shims you add, the greater the spring pressure and the slower the advance rate. When you remove shims, you decrease spring pressure and increase the rate of advance. If your Autolite distributor is vacuum-advancing too quickly (which will cause misfire and rough operation), you need to add shims one at a time. If it doesn't advance quickly enough (resulting in sluggish performance), then you need to remove shims one at a time.

Replacement vacuum-advance units for Autolite and Motorcraft distributors are adjustable using an Allen wrench through the vacuum hose port. Turn the Allen wrench clockwise to increase spring pressure, or counterclockwise to decrease spring pressure.

This brings us to Autolite/Motorcraft dual-point performance distributors. A dual-point ignition allows for a more positive saturation of the ignition coil at high revs, which is why we have two sets of ignition points tied together in series. Prior to 1972, Ford used dual-point, mechanical-advance distributors in high-performance applications like the 390, 406, and 427 High Performance, the 289 High Performance, the Boss 302, 351, and 429 V-8s. In earlier applications like the 289, 390, 406, and 427 High Performance V-8s, the C5OZ-12127-E dual-point distributor was a mechanical-advance only for high-RPM use. Because these engines come on strong at 6000 rpm, this is where a mechanical (centrifugal) advance does its best work. Ignition timing at idle with this distributor is 12 degrees BTDC. Based on a lot of engine-tuning experience, you can push this distributor to 16 degrees BTDC at idle. The main thing to remember is not to allow total advance to go beyond 36 to 40 degrees BTDC at 3500 rpm.

Like the conventional single-point Autolite/Motorcraft distributor, the dual-point's centrifugal advance comes into play based on distributor speed, flyweight weight, and spring tension. The greater the spring tension, the later the centrifugal advance comes on-line. Likewise, the heavier the flyweights or weaker the springs, the earlier the spark advance comes into play. This is something you have to play with either in the engine with a road test or in a distributor test fixture. You know the advance is programmed right when there is a solid

The 1969-70 Boss 302 dual-point distributor had a dual-advance unit that both advanced and retarded the spark. Under acceleration, the spark was advanced. During deceleration, the spark was retarded to reduce exhaust emissions.

Ford's Autolite dual-point distributor was installed on most factory high-performance V-8s throughout the 1960s. The use of dual points spread the load over two sets of ignition points, providing a more precise spark at high revs. Most Ford dual-point distributors did not have a vacuum advance unit because these distributors did their best work at high RPM. Beginning in 1969, Ford fitted the dual-point with a dual-advance unit for improved emissions.

This is a simple single-point Autolite distributor with dual advance. The dual advance, which first saw use in 1968, both advances and retards the spark for improved emissions. Earlier Autolite distributors only advance the spark. All vacuum advances are adjustable either through shims (Ford) or with an Allen wrench (aftermarket).

application of torque as RPMs increase. If there is pinging (detonation), the advance is coming on too soon. Then it's a matter of calibration with the use of different springs primarily. To slow the rate of advance, use a stronger spring.

Beginning in 1969, Ford used a dual-point Autolite distributor with a vacuum dual-advance unit for improved emissions. The dual-point ignition allowed for better performance at high revs. The dual-advance unit was designed both to advance under acceleration and retard the spark during deceleration. Retarding the spark during deceleration reduces

hydrocarbon emissions. Vacuum switching based on engine coolant temperature is what determines whether or not you get spark advance or retard. Suffice it to say that the dual-advance unit was one of Ford's first steps toward more in-depth engine emissions management.

ELECTRONIC IGNITION

In 1974, Ford began using an electronic ignition system known as Duraspark. The Duraspark ignition system consists of a Motorcraft distributor with a magnetic pick-up and an ignition amplifier that mounts on the inner fender or firewall. The Duraspark ignition

system is simple to install and use. Since the Duraspark system has been installed in millions of vehicles since 1974, cores are plentiful from salvage yards. What's more, it is a proven ignition system with an excellent track record. You can even purchase a remanufactured Duraspark distributor and a new aftermarket ignition amplifier from your local auto parts store. Duraspark ignitions are available for all Ford V-8s except the Y-Block and MEL-series V-8s. Both of these engines were discontinued for more than a decade prior to the availability of Duraspark.

The Duraspark ignition system can be installed with the amplifier visible or invisible. Invisible, you can hide it in the fender well (shielded properly from dirt and water) or inside the firewall under the dashboard. All the amplifier needs is adequate airflow for cooling purposes.

There are three types of Duraspark ignition systems. Duraspark I is the first generation, with a very simple distributor and amplifier package common during the 1970s. Duraspark II is an advanced form of Duraspark I, more tied to engine function. Duraspark III has a crankshaft sensor that makes it more an electronic engine control system. For your budget V-8, we suggest the original Duraspark I system.

Two types of distributors were used on early 5.0L high-output V-8s. Carbureted versions were fitted with a magnetic-trigger Motorcraft Duraspark distributor from 1979-85. Those fitted with CFI or SEFI (fuel injection) were fitted with a different type of Motorcraft distributor that works on the Hall Effect concept.

Magnetic trigger is a conventional electronic ignition (Duraspark) that uses a pick-up module and an eight-point reluctor attached to the distributor shaft. The armature whirls around with the shaft in time with the engine's camshaft. The pick-up module senses a disruption in the magnetic field, which switches the ignition coil on and off, just like ignition points and condenser did in the old days. For the most part, the mag-trigger distributor is trouble-free. It works on conventional ignition principles with both a vacuum and centrifugal advance like an older Ford V-8 engine. The last year Ford used this distributor was 1985 on the 5.0L-4V HighOutput V-8.

Hall Effect distributors are computer

This is the Duraspark ignition system, which consists of the distributor and ignition amplifier. Both can be retrofitted to any carbureted Ford V-8 engine.

The Ignitor from Pertronix is the easiest ignition retrofit in the business, and it costs under $100. Just 15 minutes of your time is all it takes.

controlled, part of a complete engine-control package called EEC-IV (Electronic Engine Control, Fourth Generation). EEC-IV first saw use on the Thunderbird Turbo Coupe, Cougar XR-7 Turbo, and the Mustang SVO. It was used with Duraspark III. The 2.3L Turbo OHC four that powered these cars needed a precision system that would allow smooth, safe operation. EEC-IV did a good job of controlling spark, fuel, and boost curves for smooth operation. Ford applied EEC-IV to CFI first in 1984, then SEFI in 1986 when port fuel injection came to the V-8 arena. EEC-IV is a programmable system, in which you can adjust fuel and spark curves with a laptop computer.

The Hall Effect Motorcraft distributor is a conventional distributor fitted with a TFI (thick film integrated) module, profile ignition pickup (PIP), trigger wheel, and a Hall Effect switch. The trigger wheel rotates on the distributor shaft, interrupting a stationary magnet and a current carrying Hall Effect semi-conductor. As the trigger rotates between these two elements, it provides a signal for the EEC-IV system. It also allows for coil saturation and the release of high-voltage electricity to the spark plugs. A crankshaft sensor takes care of the rest of the EEC-IV triggering system.

The TFI module does what a vacuum and centrifugal advance used to do. It also controls coil discharge and dwell timing. This means the TFI module does the same job that points, condenser, and advance units used to do. Doing all of this work makes the TFI module run hot. It has

a reputation for failure due to heat issues. One solution is to use dielectric grease between the TFI module and the distributor during installation. One other solution is to retrofit your 5.0L HighOutput V-8 with a 1994-95 Motorcraft distributor where the TFI module has been moved out of the distributor to the inner fender for cooler operation.

We are sometimes asked which is the best aftermarket ignition system for a budget 5.0L/5.8L SEFI V-8. The truth is, the stock Motorcraft EEC-IV system provides all of the ignition power your budget V-8 will ever need. It packs a wallop at nearly 40,000 volts at the spark plugs. So save your money and invest it in what is really important inside the budget engine.

AFTERMARKET IGNITIONS

Stock Ford distributors have one major shortcoming: their shaft bushings don't receive sufficient lubrication for long life. They wear out quickly. As a result, excessive shaft-side play causes irregularities in point dwell and gap. The aftermarket offers alternatives to the stock Ford ignition system.

If you are attached to your stock Ford distributor, Pertronix has fast answers with its Ignitor and Ignitor II retrofit ignition modules. The Ignitor module installs in 15 minutes and never requires service for the life of the module. Remove the ignition points and condenser. Then fasten the Ignitor to the breaker plate and connect the leads, just like you would a set of points. Then set the air gap and

install the shutter wheel. Pop on the rotor and distributor cap, and the job is finished. The beauty of the Ignitor is its simplicity. No periodic maintenance required and no one knows it's there but you. It's perfect for the stock, original driver that you would like to keep stock in appearance. One more thing about the Ignitor. Should it fail, you can reinstall the points and condenser, which will get you back on the road in short order. The Ignitor has an excellent reputation for reliability, so failure is uncommon.

If when you install the Ignitor the engine will not start, or operation is erratic, check the ground first. There should be a ground strap between the breaker plate and the distributor housing, just like Ford did it from the factory. If the ground strip is missing, the engine likely will not start, or it will mysteriously shut down and not restart.

A solid supporter of stock Ford ignition systems is Performance Distributors in Memphis, Tennessee. Two types of Motorcraft Duraspark distributors are available from Performance Distributors. The basic Duraspark distributor offers a heavy-duty ignition module, high-energy distributor cap, and custom curving applicable to your application. The DUI (Davis Unified Ignition) coil-in-cap distributor from Performance Distributors gives you the benefits of GM's HEI ignition in a Ford-specific distributor. This custom-curved system eliminates the external ignition coil and steps up the power to your spark plugs.

In the quest for precision ignition

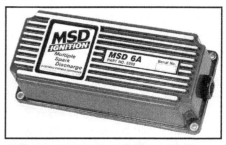

Performance Distributors offers two basic types of distributors for Ford V-8s. The basic Duraspark distributor (left) features a heavy-duty module, high-energy cap, and custom curving for your application. The deluxe DUI package (right) has a GM HEI coil-in-cap system that eliminates the external ignition coil. Both are outstanding ignitions.

MSD offers this 6A multi-spark discharge system that can be tied into nearly any type of ignition system. This system puts an intense multi-spark discharge across the spark plug gap to ignite the fuel mixture. It overcomes the adversity of fouled plugs or large gaps with a super hot spark. Ideally, you will marry this system to an MSD distributor.

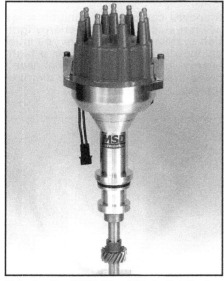

This is the MSD Pro Billet distributor. We suggest this distributor for high-performance street and racing applications. For street use, opt for an MSD distributor with a vacuum advance.

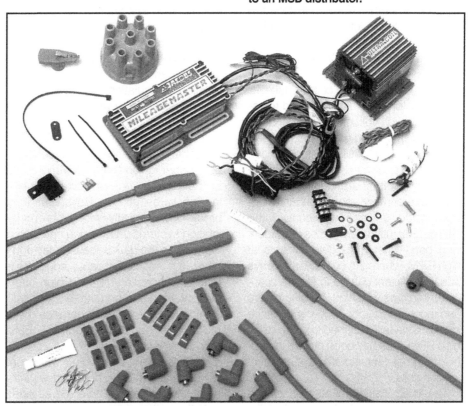

This is the Jacobs Electronic ignition system. The Ultra Coil delivers a tremendous amount of power to fire the spark plugs. We have found the Jacobs system to be touchy if it is not installed properly. Follow the directions to the letter.

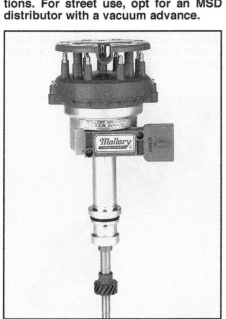

This is Mallory's drop-in replacement for 5.0L and 5.8L SEFI V-8s. It offers precision spark control in an attractive billet package.

over the years, the aftermarket has been steadily researching and developing better systems. Probably one of the most revolutionary ignition systems was Mallory's Unilite from the 1970s. It survives today pretty much in its original form because it has performed so well. The only maintenance it ever requires is the occasional dusting of the photo trigger, and replacement of the rotor and cap. Unilite is a simple, reliable ignition system that drops in place of your stock distributor.

Mallory's Unilite is just a small part of the aftermarket ignition options. MSD Ignition Systems has an outstanding

performance history in more applications than anyone else. If you opt for the complete MSD ignition package, you can be assured of terrific performance throughout the life of your engine. Street engines need an MSD distributor with a vacuum advance unit for crisp throttle response and low-end torque. The vacuum-advance unit advances the spark in rhythm with throttle pressure and acceleration, which gives you the low-end torque needed for street use.

If you are building a weekend racer, then an MSD distributor without a vacuum advance may be more to your liking. The very nature of a high-performance racing engine is higher revs, which makes the centrifugal advance more appropriate than a vacuum advance.

The Jacobs Electronics ignition isn't distributor-based, but is more a compliment to your Ford's ignition system. This system enhances stock and aftermarket distributors with a more powerful spark like we find with a lot of aftermarket ignition amplifiers. The Jacobs Ultra-Coil, for example, packs quite a punch with a spark that will withstand high compression, high-cylinder-pressure situations. This system is not tolerant of shaky installation, nor is any other aftermarket ignition system. Follow installation instructions to the letter for best results.

IGNITION COIL

The job of the ignition coil is to take 12 volts of automotive electricity and transform it into high voltage powerful enough to jump a spark plug gap. What may surprise you is how similar a stock ignition coil is to an aftermarket type. In principle and function, they are identical. Ignition coils have primary and secondary windings inside designed to contain the charge that ultimately jumps the spark plug gap. Where this gets sticky is at high RPM, where the coil doesn't always build a sufficient charge to fire the spark plugs in a timely fashion, causing misfire and poor operation. High-performance ignition coils are designed to work well at high RPM. This has been proven in actual testing between stock and aftermarket ignition coils.

The MSD Blaster coil fits in place of a stock ignition coil, which makes installation easy. On top of that, it's a faster coil that will stay alive and current at high RPM. It has proven itself better than its nearest competition without taking up additional space.

SPARK PLUGS AND WIRES

One area we tend to get careless about when building an engine is spark plug and ignition harness selection. Believe it or not, there are real differences in selection in both components. Because we tend to perceive there isn't much of a difference, we cut corners here more than anywhere else. However, when high-energy ignition systems come into play, you cannot afford to operate with anything less than a healthy ignition harness and spark plugs.

Although platinum-tip and dual-platinum-tip spark plugs are expensive, they are your only choices when running a high-energy ignition system. Standard spark plugs will operate fine for a short time with high-energy systems, but their electrodes will deteriorate quickly, causing misfire and poor performance. Go the extra mile and opt for quality Motorcraft or Autolite dual-platinum-tip spark plugs for best results. Stay conservative with the gap in the .040-in. to .060-in. range. If you have opted for a stock ignition system, .035-in. (points) to .045-in. (Duraspark) is recommended.

As with spark plugs, ignition wires will tolerate few shortcuts. You want a low-resistance conductor with high-resistance insulation. Sounds elementary, doesn't it? You would be surprised at how many people don't go the distance necessary in this area. The worst-case scenario is the dated carbon/rubber ignition wires common prior to the 1980s. You can still buy these ignition wires at Pep Boys, but they break down quickly with high-energy ignition systems. In fact, you can watch them arc in the dark because they don't have the insulation and conductive qualities necessary to keep high energy contained and on course. Stick with a high-energy ignition harness from MSD, Jacobs Electronics, Ford Racing, or Accel.

You also want spark plug wires that will withstand intense header heat without breaking down. There are all kinds out there to choose from. Jacobs Electronics, for example, has ignition wire sets with ceramic boots to withstand header heat. High-heat spark plug boot wraps are also effective in the war against heat. You can also wrap the headers with a specialized insulating tape to keep the heat where it belongs (inside the header for more complete combustion and cleaner emissions).

CHARGING SYSTEM

When you are building an engine, the charging system seems pretty lackluster. Yet nothing is more important than your Ford's charging system when it comes to keeping on keeping on. You've got to have a battery and charg-

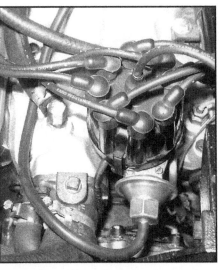

Standard carbon pack ignition wires will not stand up to high-energy ignition systems. This is where you must go the distance and opt for a high-energy ignition wire set that won't cross-fire. This includes the distributor cap.

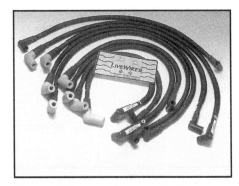

Live Wires from Performance Distributors are an outstanding value for high-energy ignition systems. These wires are heavily insulated and protected from chaffing. MSD and Jacobs Electronics also have high-quality ignition wire sets for high-energy ignitions.

If you are running a roller camshaft, you will need a bronze distributor gear, which can handle hardened roller camshafts.

Distributorless ignition systems (DIS) on late-model Fords can be adapted to your small-block Ford engine project. One example is the 1998-up Ford Explorer 5.0L HighOutput V-8, which is equipped with DIS. We're not certain if this system could be adapted to an FE-series or 385-series big block, but it's worth a look.

See your Ford dealer for this distributor cap dust and moisture boot originally installed on late- model 5.0L high-output engines. It offers outstanding protection without being too obtrusive.

ing system that will more than meet the need when it's time to hit the road.

Ford V-8 engines have used a handful of charging system types through the years. At the beginning of our subject window, 1958, Ford FE-series 332/352/361ci big blocks had a generator charging system with an external voltage regulator. If you are building a 1960 Galaxie, for example, you understand what we're talking about. Generator charging systems are terrific if you are restoring an old Ford to stock condition. Everything is available to get an old generator charging system working properly. Although rebuilt generators are not always available from AutoZone or Pep Boys, automotive electrical shops all across the country still rebuild them at a modest cost. Most of these shops will rewind, brush, and bearing your generator for under $100. With all of that

accomplished, it's as good as new.

Working hand-in-hand with the generator is the voltage regulator, which is why you should always replace the voltage regulator when you build a new generator. Voltage regulators are available from AMK Products that are exact reproductions of the original from your vintage Ford, Mercury, or Lincoln. If originality isn't important, discount houses like AutoZone and Pep Boys can order one for you.

Beginning in the Lincoln in 1963, Ford Motor Company introduced the Autolite alternator charging system with an external voltage regulator. Alternators caught on in all Ford and Mercury Division vehicles beginning in the 1965 model year. Until the 1970s, there were three basic types: 38-, 42-, and 55-amp units. During the 1970s, Ford stepped up the power to 60 amps across the board. From 1964-71, the Autolite alternator case was a rounded affair aft with a rounded mounting tab. Some had the word "Autolite" cast in the aft case. Others did not. Beginning in 1972, the same basic alternator design became a "Motorcraft" with squared nuances fore and aft. Through years of rebuilds, these cases have become decidedly mixed up with combinations of both cases which interchange.

Any time you buy a remanufactured

alternator from a discount house like AutoZone or Pep Boys, ensure that it has a lifetime warranty and that it produces 60-65 amps. If your car is equipped with a host of power accessories like stereo sound, an amp, and subwoofer, you are going to need all the help you can get in the charging department. Remember something else: No matter what any auto electric shop will tell you, you cannot get 100-plus amps out of these Autolite/Motorcraft alternators. They are designed in size to achieve a maximum of 65 amps, which works quite well with most aftermarket ignition systems and most accessories you can come up with today.

For computer-controlled Fords like the 5.0L and 5.8L SEFI V-8s, your electrical system needs 70-plus amps to keep the engine functioning properly. From 1979-85, Ford used a 60-amp alternator with a solid-state external voltage regulator in most applications. The exception is a 70-amp internally regulated unit on vehicles with a lot of accessories like rear window defrost. Beginning in 1986, Ford used 70-amp Motorcraft alternators in most SEFI applications. These alternators are internally regulated and simple to upgrade into. It is also possible to step up to a 95- or 130-amp alternator borrowed from the 1990s Ford parts bin. Ford calls it the 3G and it is just the ticket for high-demand power situations. Ford Racing has a competition alternator that is internally regulated (Part Number M-10300-A351) and produces 90 amps. This alternator is easy to install and enjoys good durability.

The rule of thumb is this: Alternators will not charge a completely dead battery even with a jump start. You should have a fully charged battery right out of the chute for best results. Even a low battery is hard on an alternator. This is why a weak battery should be trickle-charged for eight hours before use. Batteries that are quick-charged all at once will not go the distance. Trickle-charging gives a battery endurance and plenty of cranking capacity.

When you are shopping batteries, opt for the largest case you can fit into your tray. What matters most with a battery is cold cranking amps (CCA) and number of plates. The greater the number of plates, the greater the cold cranking amps. CCA is your battery's endurance level — what it will do cold and what it will do in terms of cranking capacity. In short, CCL indicates how long the battery will be able to crank your engine.

Most late-model Mustangs, for example, came from the factory with a Motorcraft battery sporting anywhere from 380 to 540 CCA. Ideally, your Ford will have a battery offering in excess of 600 CCA depending on case size limitations.

Alternators and batteries work together to keep the lights on and the engine running. The most important thing to remember is what the alternator does: It helps the battery maintain its charge. Whenever electrical demand outstrips the alternator's capacity to keep up, you lose ground and the battery slowly drains. Do this long enough and the battery dies. Always keep track of electrical demand and alternator/battery capacity.

Anytime you are servicing a Ford's electrical system — whether you are changing an alternator or swapping a switch — always disconnect the battery's negative cable first. Always protect your face and eyes when doing so. Batteries should always be disconnected before you service the EEC-IV computer system. This prevents any disturbances that might hurt the ECM. We'll take this advice a step further. Whenever you are welding on your Ford's body or chassis, always disconnect the battery first. Plus, disconnect the EEC-IV ECM while you're at it to prevent stray voltage spikes that can hurt the computer.

Another thing to remember about EEC-IV is this: Anytime you make a change in the system, from replacing a sensor to swapping a component, always disconnect the battery for at least 15 minutes to allow the EEC-IV's memory to clear. This gets you started with a clean sheet of paper, so to speak, getting your EEC-IV's adaptive technology on course. EEC-IV watches your driving patterns and adjusts spark and fuel curves accordingly. The darned thing thinks while you drive. While the battery is disconnected, the check-engine light and all fault codes become erased without the aid of your Ford dealer.

Size Does Matter...

Alternators and generators don't have a direct effect on ignition systems aside from perpetuating the current that keeps the ignition firing. However, alternator and generator pulley size matter when it comes to high-revving engines. Whenever you're going to be spinning your engine above 6000 rpm, opt for a larger alternator/generator pulley, which will bring the revolutions down, preventing an armature explosion at high RPM.

Turn it Over...

Few things are more disappointing than a fresh high-performance engine you cannot start. Vintage Ford starters don't always get the job done when it's time to turn over a new high-performance engine. This is where the compact, high-torque starter from Ford Racing Technology comes in. Not only does it provide the twist your engine needs, but it sounds terrific during the spin cycle. Those older Autolite and Motorcraft starters are period-correct for purists, but they have never been good at keeping up with high-compression engines. Compact, high-torque starters are solid answers to starting reliability today.

CHAPTER 10

ON THE DYNO...
TEN HOT ENGINE BUILD TESTS

Perhaps this is echoing what we've said in the beginning of this book, but engine projects have to follow a plan to be effective. Winging it as you go works — if you're born lucky. For most of us who build engines, having a plan and following it with discipline is where power and reliability come from. When you're on a budget like most of us are, compromises have to be made and common sense must prevail.

Like we said earlier, your engine's mission has to be established before you get started. Street engines and racing engines have completely difference missions because power management is very different. On the street, you need a broad power band that begins with good low-end torque all the way up to high RPM freeway pursuit. You need a street engine that pulls well out of the hole and will

make torque when it's time to pass. For most engines, this power band spans 2500 to 5500 rpm.

For racing, your power band should be up high in the 4500 to 6500 rpm range in a budget racer. We do this because racing engines make their power up high, which keeps the power in place and ready. When we keep an engine in its power band, we keep it ready to meet and exceed the need. In high RPM ranges, racing engines make more power than they do in the best street engines. This is what an engine's personality is all about. It is about making power and when.

Whenever you are planning an engine build-up, you want to know how much power your engine is going to make. We have compiled ten low- and medium-budget Ford V-8s and put them on the dyno to see how

much bang can be achieved for the buck. None of these tests is a guarantee that you will achieve the same results. However, given good common-sense building technique and packaging, you can achieve similar success. Perhaps you can incorporate a few speed secrets of your own.

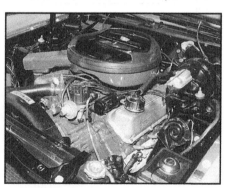

The 429/460 takes its lead from the Cleveland engine design concept. This is a powerhouse of a big-block because it offers so much performance potential.

Westech Performance shows us what can be done with a 5.0L EFI small block for under $3,500. This is a medium-budget street small block with a stock bottom end. Aside from a .030-in. overbore and dynamic balancing, the short block is relatively stock. We infused power by topping this engine with Ford Racing GT-40 heads and induction. This is a modest fuel-injected street small block you can build for approximately $3500. What you can expect from this engine is a slightly lumpy idle with crisp throttle response for good traffic light-to-traffic light performance.

Federal Mogul flattop forged-aluminum pistons give this engine 10.5:1 compression with 60cc chambers. Reconditioned C8OE connecting rods prove to us the 5.0L High Output engine is a solid mill from the factory. These rods can take extraordinary hammering again and again without failure. The Ford Racing E-303 camshaft is an aggressive hydraulic roller that gives this engine a slight lope to its idle. However, it remains a streetable mill for the daily commute. Cylinder heads and induction system are stock GT-40 pieces.

We learned on the dyno that this is a snappy mill that doesn't have a temperamental attitude. On the open road with either a T-5 five-speed or Automatic Overdrive, you can expect 20-25 mpg in a Mustang if you're using 3.55:1 gears.

On The Dyno...

RPM	Horsepower	Torque
2500	137.1	288.1
3000	167.4	293.1
3500	205.5	308.4
4000	238.5	**313.2**
4500	259.7	303.1
5000	**269.6**	283.1
5500	266.1	254.1
5600	262.0	245.7
5700	257.0	236.8
5800	252.9	229.0

Shopping List

Core:	1987-95 era 5.0L EFI Engine (Roller Tappets)
Block:	Bored to 4.030", decked .005"
Pistons:	Federal-Mogul .030" forged oversize flattops
Compression:	10.5:1
Crankshaft:	Nodular Iron, machined 010" undersize
Connecting Rods:	Stock reconditioned "C8OE" pieces with new ARP bolts
Oil Pump:	Stock, untouched
Oil Pan:	Stock (FOX body, double sump)
Camshaft:	E-303 (Ford Racing, hydraulic roller)
Lifters:	Stock
Valvetrain:	E-303 compatible springs, stock rockers, and push rods
Cylinder Heads:	Ford Racing GT-40
Induction:	GT-40 upper and lower with 70mm throttle body
Ignition:	Stock
Headers:	1 5/8" Long Tube
Parts:	$2500.00
Labor:	$ 700.00

302-4V Carbureted (455 hp)

Getting back to basics is this Westech 302-4V carbureted small block. Like the 5.0L EFI just tested above, this 302 is a .030-in. over block with a stock crankshaft. It differs with components designed to make and withstand 450 horsepower — which is the factor that drives up the price. Although this can be used as a street engine, it is more a budget racing engine with an aggressive camshaft that makes 398 lbs./ft. of torque at 5500 rpm. Peak horsepower comes in around 6000 rpm. The message with this engine is torque.

What may surprise you about this engine is its streetable demeanor. The Comp Cams Extreme Energy 282 hydraulic roller gives us plenty of camshaft without the lumpy idle you'd expect from a flat-tappet piece with the same specs. Where it gets interesting is what happens to this engine at wide open throttle. Air Flow Research aluminum heads feed those 4.030" bores via the magic of the Extreme Energy 282 roller camshaft. This is a twisty package that works well together.

The Edelbrock Victor Jr. intake manifold isn't really a street manifold but more a high-RPM racing manifold. It is a single plane design that does its best work at high RPM. This 302 makes abundant power for such a low displacement because we're feeding this beast with a Victor Jr., Demon carburetor and a healthy set of heads. For straight street use, this engine would perform better with an Edelbrock Performer RPM manifold and 650cfm carburetor.

Believe it or not, we were able to achieve 454.5 horsepower with a stock nodular-iron crankshaft, which should tell you something about durability in a stock small-block Ford bottom end. Forged Probe pistons can withstand nearly anything we can throw at them including squeeze or supercharging. Stock C8OE rods get the job done for less money here. If you're nervous about reliability from the stock rod, step up to Crower Sportsman rods for about $1000 more. However, stock rods with ARP bolts can withstand a lot of punishment. A Melling high-volume oil pump keeps moving parts amply supplied.

On The Dyno...		
RPM	**Horsepower**	**Torque**
2500	N/A	N/A
3000	186.5	326.5
3500	228.1	342.3
4000	275.9	362.3
4500	320.9	374.5
5000	368.7	387.3
5500	417.1	**398.3**
6000	448.9	392.9
6100	**454.5**	391.4

Shopping List	
Core:	1968-73 era 302-2V junk yard special
Block:	Bored to 4.030", decked .005"
Pistons:	Probe Industries .030" forged oversize flattops
Compression:	10.5:1
Crankshaft:	Nodular Iron, machined 010" undersize
Connecting Rods:	Stock C8OE rods reconditioned with ARP 3/8" bolts
Oil Pump:	Melling High-Volume out of the box
Oil Pan:	Front Sump Street Pan
Camshaft:	Comp Cams Extreme Energy 282 hydraulic roller
Lifters:	Hydraulic Rollers
Valvetrain:	Comp Cams roller rockers
Cylinder Heads:	Air Flow Research AFR-185 with 2.02/1.60" valves
Induction:	Edelbrock Victor Jr. with Speed Demon 750cfm
Ignition:	MSD
Headers:	1 5/8" Long Tube
Parts:	$6000.00
Labor:	$ 800.00

This is a budget stroker using off-the-shelf factory components like I-beam rods and a turned-down 351C or 351M crankshaft. For what it would cost to work a set of 351W heads for this engine, we found it more beneficial to spend the money on a set of Edelbrock Performer RPM heads with 2.02/1.60-in. valves with mild-pocket porting by John's Mustangs & Classics. We were able to pull better than one horsepower per cubic inch from this one.

John Da Luz is a whiz kid when it comes to squeezing hidden power from Ford V-8 engines. His insight into cylinder head port work and reducing waste elsewhere in an engine is why John's reputation for performance exists in Southern California. John focuses his energy on port work in a budget mill because that's where you'll find most of the hidden power.

This is not a cheap budget engine at more than $5000, but it shows us what can be done with a fuel-injected 347ci stroker small block. When we pump displacement into a 302ci mill to achieve 347ci, it really doesn't cost much more than building a 302. Stroker kits are labor intensive with their specially-ground crankshafts, custom rods, and pistons. There really isn't much of a cost difference when you're starting at the beginning. Where this engine gets expensive is the Ford LeMans connecting rods and other specialized features down under.

This 347 stroker from John's Mustangs & Classics is a hand-built performance mill. When you consider the Edelbrock Performer heads and John's custom build features, between $5000 and $6000 isn't much. It's a good value when you consider bang for the buck. Let John build one for you.

On The Dyno...

RPM	Horsepower	Torque
2500	108	285
3000	149	312
3500	197	345
4000	249	373
4500	291	382
5000	331	**386**
5500	361	379
6000	382	365
6500	**389**	340

Shopping List

Core:	1990 Mustang 5.0L SEFI	
Block:	Minimal machine work, .030" overbore, notching as necessary	
Pistons:	Probe custom pistons, .030" oversize, flat tops	
Compression:	9.5:1	
Crankshaft:	351C nodular-iron crank machined down for 302 block	
Connecting Rods:	5.315" 289 LeMans rods	
Oil Pump:	Melling High Volume	
Oil Pan:	Double Sump/FOX Body	
Camshaft:	John's Mustangs & Classics	
	Custom-Ground Hydraulic Roller	
	Lobe Center:	112.0
	Lift:	0.512" Intake
		0.531" Exhaust
	Duration:	282.0 Intake
		286.0 Exhaust
Lifters:	Comp Cams Hydraulic Rollers	
Valvetrain:	Comp Cams Roller Rockers	
Cylinder Heads:	Edelbrock Performer RPM	
Induction:	Edelbrock Performer RPM	
Ignition:	Stock Motorcraft	
Headers:	Hedman Long Tube	
Parts:	$4500.00	
Labor:	$650.00	

351W-4V (395 hp)

It is difficult to believe today, but the 351W engine was a no-respect mill 30 years ago. It stood in the big shadow of its corporate cousin, the 351 Cleveland. The 351C was embraced by performance buffs and racers alike thanks to its big port, canted valve heads. It made a lot of power with a modest amount of displacement because its heads breathed so well. The 351W has endured because the 351C wound up being a short-lived mill with a four-year production window. Because Ford produced the 351C for such a short time, there aren't very many cores left to build today. As a result, enthusiasts have found ways to make power with the 351W and with great results.

Here's a junkyard special 351W that has shown us nearly 400 horsepower on the dyno with a minimum amount of work. The bottom end has stock C9OE connecting rods with a nodular-iron 3M crankshaft. ARP rod bolts improve integrity. Federal Mogul forged-aluminum pistons give us 10.5:1 compression which is good for today's pump gas. We're getting 10.5:1 because the block deck has been milled .005".

Power Heads with a nice port job are what give the 351W more horsepower and torque. An aggressive flat-tappet hydraulic camshaft from Comp Cams makes the most of those Power Heads. The Edelbrock Performer RPM dual-plane intake manifold with a 750cfm Holley carburetor gives this engine terrific low-end torque. We're convinced it could use less carburetor for the daily drive in the 650cfm range. The 750cfm Holley is good for weekend racing but not much for clean emissions and good fuel economy on the street. It will make the guy's eyes behind you water from not only a fat mixture, but walking right past him with the throttle wide open.

Westech Performance managed to pull nearly 400 horsepower from a basically stock 351W platform. Here's how it stacks up.

On The Dyno...

RPM	Horsepower	Torque
2500	N/A	N/A
3000	173.9	304.4
3500	233.9	350.9
4000	285.5	374.8
4500	326.2	380.7
5000	365.3	**383.7**
5500	390.4	372.8
6000	**395.0**	345.8
6100	394.9	340.0
6200	390.7	330.9

Shopping List

Core:	1969-71 era 351W-2V junk yard special
Block:	Bored to 4.030", decked .005"
Pistons:	Federal-Mogul .030" oversize forged flattops
Compression:	10.5:1
Crankshaft:	Nodular Iron, machined 010" undersize
Connecting Rods:	C9OE 351W rods reconditioned with ARP bolts
Oil Pump:	Melling High Volume, blueprinted
Oil Pan:	Front Sump Street Pan
Camshaft:	Competition Cams, specs unknown, Aggressive hydraulic
Lifters:	Flat-tappet hydraulics
Valvetrain:	Roller-tip, stamped-steel rockers
Cylinder Heads:	Power Heads, 351W w/ port job
Induction:	Edelbrock Performer RPM w/ 750cfm Holley carburetor
Ignition:	Mallory Unilite
Headers:	1 5/8" Long Tube
Parts:	$3000.00
Labor:	$ 400.00

351W-4V (399 hp)

This is a garden-variety 351W engine with a freshening-up from Westech Performance to achieve an impressive 400 horsepower. Like the 395-horse 351W we just mentioned, this engine has a stock bottom end with C9OE rods, 3M nodular-iron crankshaft, and forged flat-top pistons. Where this engine differs from the other 351W is the Ford Explorer GT-40P iron heads. Though these heads flow a little better, they don't produce any more power than vintage 351W castings which makes this a lessen for all of us. The downside to the GT-40P heads is their odd straight plug design that doesn't accommodate aftermarket headers. These heads mandate the use of custom headers to clear the spark plugs.

Like our 395-horse 351W, this one sports a 10.5:1 compression ratio and a Comp Cams Extreme Energy 282 like we used on the 450-horse 302. The Extreme Energy 282 is an aggressive, hydraulic flat-tappet camshaft with a tolerable idle and brute torque right off idle. Torque comes from the 351W's 3.50" stroke and taller deck. Combine the stroke with the port sizing we find on GT-40P and 351W heads and you get generous sums of power. What we have here is an engine you can drive daily and take to the drag races Saturday night.

An Edelbrock Performer RPM and Demon 750cfm atomizer crown this prince with ample fuel and air for impressive torque. This is a nice combination you can live with in a budget daily driver without spending a fortune.

On The Dyno...

RPM	Horsepower	Torque
2500	N/A	N/A
3000	206.6	352.5
3500	247.9	372.0
4000	295.2	387.6
4500	337.2	**393.6**
5000	373.7	392.5
5500	395.3	377.5
6000	**398.9**	349.2

Shopping List

Core:	1969-73 era 351W-2V junk yard special
Block:	Bored to 4.030"
Pistons:	Federal-Mogul .030" forged oversize flattops
Compression:	10.5:1
Crankshaft:	Nodular Iron, machined 010" undersize
Connecting Rods:	Stock C9OE reconditioned with ARP bolts
Oil Pump:	Melling High Volume
Oil Pan:	Front Sump Street Pan
Camshaft:	Comp Cams Extreme Energy 262 Hydraulic flat tappet
Lifters:	Hydraulic flat tappets
Valvetrain:	Comp Cams roller rockers
Cylinder Heads:	Ford Explorer GT-40P heads with 1.94/1.62 valves out of box
Induction:	Edelbrock Performer RPM with Speed Demon 750cfm
Ignition:	MSD
Headers:	1 5/8" Long Tube
Parts:	$3000.00
Labor:	$ 400.00

351W (392ci) EFI Stroker (526 hp)

It is amazing what you can do with the venerable 351W given displacement. The Ford Racing crate motor block topped with Air Flow Research heads (2.02/1.64-in. valves) achieves more than 500 horsepower right out of the box! Look at the shopping list. For roughly $5,000 to $6,000, you can blast from traffic light to traffic light with a crate engine delivered to your door.

Crate engines as either short blocks or long blocks are fast becoming the quick and easy way to get into power without the unknowns of an engine you build yourself. These engines also come with a warranty and Ford's quality assurance.

This is not a budget crate engine by any means. At its core is a Scat nodular-iron stroker crankshaft, Crower Sportsman rods, forged custom pistons, and a seasoned .030" oversize 351W block. Bumping the Air Flow Research valves is yet another Comp Cams Extreme Energy 282 hydraulic-roller camshaft. This camshaft gives small-block Fords an extreme attitude when the throttle is pinned.

Shoehorning 392ci into a 351W block gives Ford's tall-deck, small block a big block persona. This engine makes nearly 500 ft./lbs. of torque, which is very impressive for a crate engine you can get from Ford Racing and drop into your ride for under $6000. Not bad for a crate engine.

On The Dyno...

RPM	Horsepower	Torque
2500	N/A	N/A
3000	244.7	428.3
3500	298.4	447.7
4000	361.8	475.0
4500	419.0	489.0
5000	473.7	**497.6**
5500	513.5	490.4
6000	**526.0**	460.5
6100	523.8	451.0
6200	517.1	438.0

Shopping List

Core:	Ford Racing 392ci Stroker Crate Engine
Block:	351W with stroke job
Pistons:	Federal-Mogul .030" oversize flattops
Compression:	10.0:1 depending on heads
Crankshaft:	Scat Nodular-Iron Stroker
Connecting Rods:	Custom I-Beam Sportsman Rod
Oil Pump:	Stock pump, blueprinted
Oil Pan:	Front Sump, stock
Camshaft:	Comp Cams Extreme Energy 282 Hydraulic Roller
Lifters:	Hydraulic Rollers
Valvetrain:	Adjustable Roller Rockers
Cylinder Heads:	Air Flow Research AFR-185s with 2.02/1.64" valves
Induction:	Edelbrock Victor Jr. with 2-inch spacer and Speed Demon 750cfm
Ignition:	MSD
Headers:	1 5/8" Long Tubes
Parts:	$5,600
Labor:	N/A

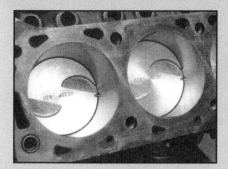  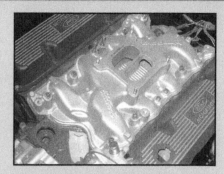

We don't hear about this one very often these days, but it remains the awesome powerhouse it was during its infancy in the 1970s. The 351 Cleveland "middle block" is a small block that acts like a big block, thanks to its large-port heads and broad-shouldered block. No one knows for sure why Ford conceived two engine families displacing 351 cubic inches, but one thing is certain: The 351C gives performance buffs a lot of bang for the buck. When you can find a good junkyard core, the 351C has a lot to offer in terms of affordable power.

John's Mustangs & Classics in San Diego, California built us a budget 351C. Despite a tight budget, we managed to squeeze 405 horsepower and 420 lbs./ft. of torque from the short-lived, super-tough Ford small block. We call it short-lived because the 351C was produced between 1970 and 1974, a very short time compared to other Ford engine families. If you are planning to build a 351C, be prepared to spend more than you would on a comparable 302/351W.

We have a difficult time suggesting a 351C if your Ford vehicle wasn't originally equipped with one. Because this engine, its parts and available cores are so few these days, building one of these from scratch doesn't come easy nor cheap. We're covering the 351C powerplants because there are a lot of vintage Ford vehicles out there that were originally equipped. We're going to show you what can be done with your 351C.

For one thing, the 351C will make a lot of power with its 4M nodular-iron crankshaft, DOOE rods, and canted valve heads. This is an engine you can hammer on all day and it will come back for more. Most of the time, the 351C will wear out the driver and the chassis first. John has built us a solid factory stocker that makes 405 horsepower and 420 ft./lbs. of torque for $4000. What's more, it makes as much power with fewer cubes than the 390 FE big block we're about to dyno next.

On The Dyno...

RPM	Horsepower	Torque
2500	142.2	373.8
3000	183.7	383.2
3500	225.6	393.8
4000	273.3	409.6
4500	319.8	418.0
5000	360.1	**420.6**
5500	391.3	410.6
6000	**405.4**	387.2

Shopping List

Core:	351C-2V customer engine
Block:	351C 2-Bolt Main bored to 4.030" for 357ci
Pistons:	Federal-Mogul forged-aluminum flat tops
Compression:	9.25:1 with 88cc chambers
Crankshaft:	Nodular-Iron turned .010" undersize
Connecting Rods:	Stock "DOOE" I-Beam reconditioned with new ARP bolts
Oil Pump:	Stock, with blueprint.
Oil Pan:	Stock with front sump
Camshaft:	John's Mustangs & Classics Custom Grind
	Hydraulic - Flat Tappet
	Lobe Center: 110.0
	Lift: 0.560" Intake
	0.585" Exhaust
	Duration: 232.0 Intake
	236.0 Exhaust
Lifters:	Hydraulic/Flat tappet
Valvetrain:	Screw-In Studs/Guide Plates/Adjustable
Cylinder Heads:	351C-2V
Induction:	Edelbrock Dual-Plane, Holley 750cfm
Ignition:	MSD
Headers:	Hedman Hedders
Parts:	$3700.00
Labor:	$ 450.00

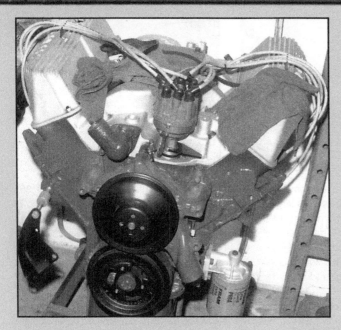

Like the 351C mentioned earlier, the FE-series big block is considered something of a dinosaur today. However, the FE engine remains the world champion powerplant that won LeMans three decades ago. Just imagine what you can do with a well-oiled 390 or 428ci big block. Because John Da Luz of John's Mustangs & Classics is a well-seasoned engine builder, we looked to him to conceive a healthy street 390 for this book.

John knew all of the right castings to use for our 390 project. Because the FE block is decidedly strong to begin with, John understood we could ring this puppy to 6000 rpm without fear of failure. He chose a garden variety C5AE-A passenger car 390 block and did the necessary preparation. He improved the oiling system and provided for better drain back. John believes engine survival is rooted in using the right fasteners and having a good oiling system.

Budget being our focus, he opted for a standard 390 2U nodular iron crankshaft and C3AE-A connecting rods beefed up with ARP bolts. On top, he did a mild port job on a set of C6OE 390-2V/4V heads. He used an Edelbrock Performer 390 for induction, sporting a 750 cfm Holley carburetor. The camshaft is an aggressive street grind hydraulic with flat tappets. John shows us how to squeeze 405 horsepower from Ford's legendary 390. Just look at what you can achieve for under $4000.

On The Dyno...

RPM	Horsepower	Torque
2500	187.4	438.8
3000	212.4	446.9
3500	259.4	452.4
4000	307.3	**460.3**
4500	350.9	459.3
5000	384.4	448.2
5500	**402.3**	423.8
6000	399.9	381.4

Shopping List

Core:	390-4V salvage special from a '66 Galaxie	
Block:	C5AE-A bored .030" oversize, decks checked okay	
Pistons:	Federal-Mogul forged-aluminum .030" over flattops	
Compression:	9.5:1	
Crankshaft:	C3AE nodular-iron turned .010" undersize	
Connecting Rods:	C3AE I-beam rods reconditioned with ARP bolts	
Oil Pump:	Stock with blueprint	
Oil Pan:	Stock 428CJ pan with windage tray	
Camshaft:	Special grind for John's Mustangs & Classics	
	Hydraulic, flat tappet	
	Lobe Center:	110.0
	Lift:	0.536" Intake
		0.560" Exhaust
	Duration:	226.0 Intake
		234.0 Exhaust
Lifters:	Hydraulic, flat tappet	
Valvetrain:	Shaft-mounted, non-adjustable FE rocker arms	
Cylinder Heads:	C3AE 390-4V heads with mild port work	
Induction:	Edelbrock Performer RPM FE with Edelbrock 750cfm carburetor	
Ignition:	Stock Autolite with Pertronix Ignitor and mild tuning	
Headers:	Hedman long tube	
Parts:	$3500.00	
Labor:	$ 350.00	

460-4V Big Block (423 hp)

This engine didn't produce the power we had hoped for from 460 cubic inches and stock heads. It is a relatively stock engine with a hot cam, forged pistons, and a modest amount of head work. However, it goes to show that you don't always achieve the results hoped for, especially when budget is calling the shots. Close attention to detail can get you better numbers than we achieved here. One hint: a better camshaft/cylinder head/induction marriage.

On The Dyno...

RPM	Horsepower	Torque
2500	N/A	N/A
3000	N/A	N/A
3500	321.4	482.3
4000	367.9	**483.0**
4500	401.9	469.0
5000	**422.6**	443.9
5500	420.9	401.9
6000	N/A	N/A

Shopping List

Core:	Stock 460-4V Lincoln engine
Block:	Bored .030" oversize with line honing and decking
Pistons:	Federal-Mogul .030" oversize forged units
Compression:	10.0:1
Crankshaft:	Nodular-iron machined .010" undersize
Connecting Rods:	Stock, reconditioned with ARP bolts
Oil Pump:	Stock, untouched
Oil Pan:	Front sump, stock
Camshaft:	Sig Erson flat-tappet hydraulic
Lifters:	Sig Erson flat-tappet hydraulic
Valvetrain:	Screw-In Rocker Arm Studs from Summit Racing
Cylinder Heads:	Stock, valve job
Induction:	Edelbrock Performer RPM with 750cfm Speed Demon
Ignition:	MSD
Headers:	Long Tube, brand unknown
Parts:	$3500.00
Labor:	$ 350.00

429ci Big Block (513 hp)

On the surface, this is a stealthy engine because it appears relatively stock. Underneath the Ford Blue paint is a powerhouse perfect for a resto-mod where a stock appearance is just as important as having power. You really can have both. This is basically the same engine shown above with Ford Racing Cobra Jet heads. You can figure roughly 100 horsepower more from better heads and a hotter camshaft. Keep in mind that you can always build a budget big block, then upgrade to better heads and cam later. Remember, invest wisely in a sound bottom end, then aim for the stars when budget permits.

This is a garden-variety Lincoln big block that has spent most of its service life pushing around a big, heavy passenger car. In stock form, it's a snoozer. Torn down to the bare block and reincarnated as a muscle engine, it's difficult to believe it was ever a stodgy luxury car mill. We punched this one out .030" oversize and fitted it with Federal Mogul forged-aluminum flattop pistons for 10.5:1 compression. This is an ideal compression ratio with the right camshaft, which enables it to run on pump gas. These pistons run a little noisy cold, then expand and fit nicely hot.

Way down under, we're running a stock nodular-iron crankshaft with D0OE rods. From the factory, this crank and these rods will withstand a lot of punishment without a hitch. This is exactly our point for a stock Ford bottom end. If you examine most of the engines we have tested here, they're fitted with nodular-iron crankshafts and stock rods with ARP bolts. None of these engines failed under the torture of a battery of dyno tests, which tends to be harder on an engine than anything else.

You can build a powerful engine from a modest budget despite what the competition says about Fords. Stick with the right combination of stock and aftermarket parts and you can't go wrong. Look at the power we squeezed from this engine. Aside from an aggressive solid-roller camshaft and Ford Racing Cobra Jet heads, this engine is virtually stock.

On The Dyno...

RPM	Horsepower	Torque
2500	N/A	N/A
3000	N/A	N/A
3500	279.1	418,8
4000	351.6	461.6
4500	400.0	466.9
5000	456.2	**479.1**
5500	496.0	473.6
6000	503.9	441.1
6100	506.8	436.4
6200	508.3	430.6
6300	512.4	427.2
6400	**512.8**	427.2

Shopping List

Core:	1968-73 era 429ci junk yard special
Block:	Bored to 4.030"
Pistons:	Federal-Mogul .030" forged oversize flattops
Compression:	10.5:1
Crankshaft:	Nodular Iron, machined 010" undersize
Connecting Rods:	Stock D0OE reconditioned with ARP bolts
Oil Pump:	Stock, untouched
Oil Pan:	Front Sump Street Pan
Camshaft:	Comp Cams 280 Solid Roller
Lifters:	Mechanical Rollers
Valvetrain:	Comp Cams Roller Rockers
Cylinder Heads:	Ford Racing Cobra Jet heads
Induction:	Ford Racing Single Plane
Ignition:	MSD
Headers:	2" Long Tube
Parts:	$5200.00
Labor:	$1300.00

CHAPTER 11

ENGINE MATH/QUICK FACTS

When you're building an engine, it's nice to be armed with the facts necessary to do it successfully. Much of engine building is about math — machining dimensions, compression and rod ratios, bore sizes, stroke, journal diameters, carburetor and port sizes, dynamic balancing, and all the rest of it. Without math, you cannot successfully build an engine. What follows are quick facts that will help you in your Ford engine building.

Cubic-Inch Displacement

Cubic-inch displacement is simply the volume displaced by the cylinders of your engine. So, if we calculate the volume of one cylinder, and multiply that figure times the number of cylinders, we have the engine's displacement.

The formula for a cylinder's volume is:

$$Pi \times r^2 \times S = \text{Volume of one cylinder.}$$

Where Pi is a mathematical constant equal to 3.14159; R is the radius of the cylinder, and S is the stroke. If you think back to your high school geometry, you'll remember that a circle's radius is half the diameter. In this case, the diameter is equal to the bore (B), so $1/2B=r$. Plug that in, and our formula becomes:

$$Pi \times (1/2B)^2 \times S = \text{Volume of one cylinder}$$

We can simplify this further by plugging in the

numerical value for Pi, then doing some basic algebra that doesn't necessarily need to be covered here — but trust us: the equation before is equal to this equation:

$$B \times B \times S \times 0.7854 = \text{Volume of one cylinder}$$

To determine the engine's displacement, factor in the number of cylinders (N):

$$B \times B \times S \times 0.7854 \times N = \text{Engine displacement}$$

So, let's use this to figure out the displacement of a Ford engine that has a 4-inch Bore and a 3-inch Stroke:

$$4.000" \times 4.000" \times 3.00" \times 0.7854 \times 8 = 301.59 \text{ ci}$$

Ford rounded 301.59 up to 302 ci, or 4.9L.

(Note: One liter is equal to about 61 cubic inches.)

Calculating Compression Ratio

An engine's compression ratio is the ratio between two volumes: The volume of the cylinder and combustion chamber when the piston is at BDC, and the volume of the combustion chamber when the piston is at TDC. But there's more to consider than just cylinder volume and head cc's. To get the

engine's TRUE compression ratio, you need to know these volumes:

- Combustion Chamber Volume (**C**)
- Compressed Head Gasket Volume (**G**)
- Piston/Deck height (**D**)
- Piston Dish Volume (**P**) or Dome Volume (**-P**)
- Cylinder Volume (**V**)

When the piston is at BDC, the total volume

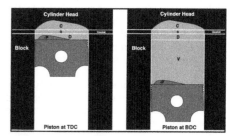

This diagram shows all the volumes you need to know to calculate an engine's true compression ratio: Cylinder volume (**V**), piston dome (**-P**) or dish volume (**P**), piston/deck height (**D**), compressed gasket volume (**G**), and the combustion chamber volume (**C**). The compression ratio is the volume of the piston and combustion chamber (**V + P + D + G +C**) when the piston is at Bottom Dead Center, compared to the volume of the combustion chamber (**P + D + G +C**) when the piston is at Top Dead Center.

is all of these volumes added together. When the piston is at TDC, the total volume is all of these EXCEPT the Cylinder Volume (V). So ... true compression ratio is this:

$$\frac{V + D + G + C + P}{D + G + C + P}$$

Combustion Chamber Volume
Combustion chamber volumes for stock heads and aftermarket heads are typically available from the manufacturer. If you cant find the info or if you've modified the combustion chambers, you'll have to measure the volumes (using a plastic deck plate, burettes, and a graduated cylinder) or have your local machine shop do it for you.

Converting cc's to ci's
Combustion chamber volume, dome volume, and dish volume are generally measured in cc's, not cubic inches. To convert cc's to cubic inches, divide the measurement in cc's by 16.4.

$$cc/16.4 = ci.$$

Compressed Head Gasket Volume
Compressed head gasket volume is simply the volume of the cylinder hole in the head gasket – think of it as a very shallow cylinder. So, its volume is computed the same way you compute cylinder volume:

$$B \times B \times Gasket\ Thickness \times 0.7854 = Compressed\ Head\ Gasket\ Volume$$

In this case, the gasket's compressed thickness is .038 inches, so ...

$$4.000" \times 4.000" \times .038" \times 0.7854 = 0.4775232\ ci$$

Piston/Deck Height Volume
Piston/Deck height volume is the small volume at the top of the cylinder that is not swept by the piston. Measure piston/deck height with a dial indicator. Bring the piston to top dead center (TDC) and measure the distance from the top of the piston to the deck of the block. This is normally somewhere between .008 and .025 inch. If the block deck has been machined, say .010 inch, then deck height will be smaller.

Once again, this volume is a shallow cylinder. Compute its volume by plugging the piston/deck height measurement (D) into the cylinder volume formula:

$$B \times B \times D \times 0.7854 = Piston/Deck\ Height\ Volume$$

In our example, this measurement was .015 in, so we plug in that value to compute piston/deck height volume in cubic inches.

$$4.000" \times 4.000" \times .015" \times 0.7854 = 0.188496\ ci$$

Piston Dome/Dish Volume
The last bit of information we need is the volume of the piston dome or dish (dish

includes valve reliefs, too). Because the dishes or domes are irregularly shaped, it's necessary to either measure the volume using burettes and graduated cylinders, or you can usually get the measurement from the piston manufacturer. If the piston is domed, the dome reduces the amount of volume in the combustion chamber, so its volume is subtracted. If the piston is dished, the dish increases the volume of the combustion chamber, so its volume is added. In this example, our 302 has flat-top pistons with valve reliefs that measure 2ccs in volume. That 2ccs increases the cylinder volume, so we give it a positive value. (If the pistons were domed, the dome would reduce the cylinder volume, so we'd give it a negative value). Either way, the volume has to be converted from cc's to ci's:

$$cc\ /\ 16.4 = ci$$
$$2cc\ /\ 16.4 = .121951\ ci$$

So, let's check the true compression ratio for that 302ci engine, assuming it has a combustion chamber volume of 63cc, a compressed head gasket thickness of .038 inch, and a piston/deck height of .015 inch. Here's what we've figured out so far:

V= Cylinder Volume: 37.6992 ci *(calculated)*
C= Combustion Chamber Volume: 63cc (3.8414634 ci) *(measured)*
G= Compressed Head Gasket Volume: 0.4775232 ci *(calculated)*
P= Piston Dome Volume: .121951 ci *(measured)*
D= Piston/Deck Height Volume: 0.188496 ci *(calculated)*

Now (finally!) we're ready to calculate our true compression ratio, using the formula we developed earlier:

$$\frac{V + D + G + C + P}{D + G + C + P}$$

Plug in the values:

$$\frac{37.6992\ ci + 0.188496\ ci + 0.4775232\ ci + 3.8414634\ ci + .121951\ ci}{0.188496\ ci + 0.4775232\ ci + 3.8414634\ ci + .121951\ ci}$$

$$\frac{42.328634}{4.629434}$$

That gives us a true compression ratio, for this engine, of 9.1:1.

Choosing The Right Carburetor Size
Seems a lot of folks specify a larger carburetor than they actually need. Here's an easy formula that will put you on target every time, as long as you're honest with yourself about where your engine's going to operate. We want to look at cubic inches and the best volumetric efficiency (VE). With street engines, volumetric efficiency is typically around 75 to 80%. Boost the performance and VE goes up to 80 to 95%. The best indicator of engine performance is an engine dynamometer. This

formula will calculate the required carb size for your engine:

$$\frac{VE\ (Volumetric\ Efficiency) \times CI \times Max\ Rpms}{3456}$$

For example, we've built a 460 that performing strong on the dyno. The dyno figures tell us 85% VE. On the street, we figure the max RPM this engine will see is 5,500 rpm. So, if we plug in the numbers, we get:

$$\frac{.85 \times 460 \times 5,500}{3456}$$

Do the math, and we end up with 622.25115. In this case, we'd opt for a 650cfm carb.

Calculating Horsepower & Torque
Horsepower and torque are words we hear a lot in the automotive realm. Which do you believe is more significant to power output? It may surprise you to learn that torque is the more significant number. Did you know horsepower and torque are the same at 5,252 rpm on any engine? That's because Horsepower is derived from torque. Here's a good formula to remember:

$$Horsepower = \frac{RPM \times Torque}{5,252\ rpm}$$

If you do a little cross-multiplying, you can also rearrange this equation to compute torque from horsepower:

$$Torque = \frac{5,252rpm \times Horsepower}{RPM}$$

Estimating Horsepower at the Drags
Your car's approximate horsepower and torque can be determined with a simple quarter-mile pass at the drag strip. Begin by weighing your vehicle — you can find scales at a farm coop (anyplace that sells grain or feed by the truckload) or truck weigh station along the interstate. Then make several quarter mile passes and calculate an average top mph. Then make the following calculation:

$$Horsepower = \frac{Weight \times 0.4 \times 1/4\text{-mile } MPH}{282}$$

Assume your car weighs 3,000 pounds, and your average quarter-mile time was 100mph. Plug in the numbers and we get...

$$\frac{3000\ lbs \times 0.4 \times 100\ mph}{282} = 425.53191\ hp$$

If you know what RPM your engine was turning as you went through the traps, you can also figure out the torque your engine generates. If we went through the traps at 6,000 rpm, we can calculate torqueis determined by doing the following formula:

$$\frac{5,252 \times 425\ hp}{6000rpm} = 372ft\text{-}lbs.\ of\ torque$$

Save yourself the cost of a dyno, do the calculations yourself and save. These calculations are approximate, but close enough to determine your engine's output.

MORE GREAT TITLES AVAILABLE FROM CARTECH®

CHEVROLET

How To Rebuild the Small-Block Chevrolet* (SA26)
Chevrolet Small-Block Parts Interchange Manual (SA55)
How To Build Max Perf Chevy Small-Blocks on a Budget (SA57)
How To Build High-Perf Chevy LS1/LS6 Engines (SA86)
How To Build Big-Inch Chevy Small-Blocks (SA87)
How to Build High-Performance Chevy Small-Block Cams/Valvetrains (SA105P)
Rebuilding the Small-Block Chevy: Step-by-Step Videobook (SA116)
High-Performance Chevy Small-Block Cylinder Heads (SA125P)
How to Rebuild the Big-Block Chevrolet* (SA142P)
How to Build Max-Performance Chevy Big Block on a Budget (SA198)
How to Restore Your Camaro 1967–1969 (SA178)
How to Build Killer Big-Block Chevy Engines (SA190)
Small-Block Chevy Performance: 1955-1996 (SA110P)
How to Build Small-Block Chevy Circle-Track Racing Engines (SA121P)
High-Performance C5 Corvette Builder's Guide (SA127P)
Chevrolet Big Block Parts Interchange Manual (SA31P)
Chevy TPI Fuel Injection Swapper's Guide (SA53P)
How to Rebuild & Modify Chevy 348/409 Engines (SA210)

FORD

High-Performance Ford Engine Parts Interchange (SA56)
How To Build Max Performance Ford V-8s on a Budget (SA69P)
How To Build Max Perf 4.6 Liter Ford Engines (SA82P)
How To Build Big-Inch Ford Small-Blocks (SA85P)
How to Rebuild the Small-Block Ford* (SA102)
How to Rebuild Big-Block Ford Engines* (SA162P)
Full-Size Fords 1955–1970 (SA176P)
How to Build Max-Performance Ford FE Engines (SA183)
How to Restore Your Mustang 1964 1/2–1973 (SA165)
How to Build Ford RestoMod Street Machines (SA101P)
Building 4.6/5.4L Ford Horsepower on the Dyno (SA115P)
How to Rebuild 4.6/5.4-Liter Ford Engines* (SA155P)
Building High-Performance Fox-Body Mustangs on a Budget (SA75P)
How to Build Supercharged & Turbocharged Small-Block Fords (SA95P)
How to Rebuild & Modify Ford C4 & C6 Automatic Transmissions (SA227)
How to Rebuild Ford Power Stroke Diesel (SA213)

GENERAL MOTORS

GM Automatic Overdrive Transmission Builder's and Swapper's Guide (SA140)
How to Rebuild GM LS-Series Engines* (SA147)
How to Swap GM LS-Series Engines Into Almost Anything (SA156)
How to Supercharge & Turbocharge GM LS-Series Engines (SA180)
How to Build Big-Inch GM LS-Series Engines (SA203)
How to Rebuild & Modify GM Turbo 400 Transmissions* (SA186)
How to Build GM Pro-Touring Street Machines (SA81P)

MOPAR

How to Rebuild the Big-Block Mopar* (SA197)
How to Rebuild the Small-Block Mopar* (SA143P)
How to Build Max-Performance Hemi Engines (SA164P)
How To Build Max-Performance Mopar Big Blocks (SA171P)
Mopar B-Body Performance Upgrades 1962-1979 (SA191)
How to Build Big-Inch Mopar Small-Blocks (SA104P)
High-Performance New Hemi Builder's Guide 2003-Present (SA132P)

OLDSMOBILE/ PONTIAC/ BUICK

How to Build Max-Performance Oldsmobile V-8s (SA172P)
How To Build Max-Perf Pontiac V-8s (SA78)
How to Rebuild Pontiac V-8s* (SA200)
How to Build Max-Performance Buick Engines (SA146P)

SPORT COMPACTS

Honda Engine Swaps (SA93P)
High-Performance Subaru Builder's Guide (SA141)
How to Build Max-Performance Mitsubishi 4G63t Engines (SA148P)
How to Rebuild Honda B-Series Engines* (SA154)
The New Mini Performance Handbook (SA182P)
High Performance Dodge Neon Builder's Handbook (SA100P)
High-Performance Honda Builder's Handbook Volume 1 (SA49P)
How to Build Cobra Kit Cars + Buying Used (SA202)

*Workbench® Series books feature step-by-step instruction with hundreds of color photos for stock rebuilds and automotive repair.

ENGINE

Engine Blueprinting (SA21)
Automotive Diagnostic Systems: Understanding OBD-I & OBD II (SA174)
Competition Engine Building (SA214)

INDUCTION & IGNITION

Super Tuning & Modifying Holley Carburetors (SA08)
Street Supercharging, A Complete Guide to (SA17)
How To Build High-Performance Ignition Systems (SA79P)
How to Build and Modify Rochester Quadrajet Carburetors (SA113)
Turbo: Real World High-Performance Turbocharger Systems (SA123)
How to Rebuild & Modify Carter/Edelbrock Carbs (SA130P)
Engine Management: Advanced Tuning (SA135)
Designing & Tuning High-Performance Fuel Injection Systems (SA161)
Demon Carburetion (SA68P)

DRIVING

How to Drift: The Art of Oversteer (SA118P)
How to Drag Race (SA136P)
How to Autocross (SA158P)
How to Hook and Launch (SA195)

HIGH-PERFORMANCE & RESTORATION HOW-TO

How To Install and Tune Nitrous Oxide Systems (SA194)
David Vizard's How to Build Horsepower (SA24)
How to Rebuild & Modify High-Performance Manual Transmissions* (SA103)
High-Performance Jeep Cherokee XJ Builder's Guide 1984–2001 (SA109P)
How to Paint Your Car on a Budget (SA117)
High Performance Brake Systems (SA126P)
High Performance Diesel Builder's Guide (SA129P)
4x4 Suspension Handbook (SA137)
Automotive Welding: A Practical Guide* (SA159)
Automotive Wiring and Electrical Systems* (SA160)
Design & Install In-Car Entertainment Systems (SA163P)
Automotive Bodywork & Rust Repair* (SA166)
High-Performance Differentials, Axles, & Drivelines (SA170)
How to Make Your Muscle Car Handle (SA175)
Rebuilding Any Automotive Engine: Step-by-Step Videobook (SA179)
Builder's Guide to Hot Rod Chassis & Suspension (SA185)
How To Rebuild & Modify GM Turbo 400 Transmissions* (SA186)
How to Build Altered Wheelbase Cars (SA189P)
How to Build Period Correct Hot Rods (SA192)
Automotive Sheet Metal Forming & Fabrication (SA196)
Performance Automotive Engine Math (SA204)
How to Design, Build & Equip Your Automotive Workshop on a Budget (SA207)
Automotive Electrical Performance Projects (SA209)
How to Port & Flow Test Cylinder Heads (SA215)
High Performance Jeep Wrangler TJ Builder's Guide: 1997-2006 (SA120P)
Dyno Testing & Tuning (SA138P)
How to Rebuild Any Automotive Engine (SA151P)
Muscle Car Interior Restoration Guide (SA167P)
How to Build Horsepower - Volume 2 (SA52P)
Advanced Automotive Welding (SA235)
How to Restore Your Corvette (SA223)
How to Restore Your Pontiac GTO (SA218)

HISTORIES & PERSONALITIES

Yenko (CT485)
Lost Hot Rods (CT487)
Lost Hot Rods II (CT506)
Grumpy's Toys (CT489)
America's Coolest Station Wagons (CT493)
Super Stock — A paperback version of a classic best seller. (CT495)
Rusty Pickups: American Workhorses Put to Pasture (CT496)
Jerry Heasley's Rare Finds — Great collection of Heasley's best finds. (CT497)
Jerry Heasley's Rare Finds: Mustangs & Fords (CT509)
Street Sleepers: The Art of the Deceptively Fast Car (CT498)
Rat Rods: Rodding's Imperfect Stepchildren (CT486)
East vs. West Showdown: Rods, Customs Rails (CT501)
Junior Stock: Stock Class Drag Racing 1964–1971 (CT505)
Definitive Shelby Mustang Guide 1965–1970, The (CT507)
Hurst Equipped (CT490)

CarTech®, Inc. 39966 Grand Ave., North Branch, MN 55056. Ph: 800-551-4754 or 651-277-1200 • Fax: 651-277-1203
Brooklands Books Ltd., PO Box 146 Cobham, Surrey KT11 1LG, England. Ph: 01932 865051 • Fax 01932 868803
Brooklands Books Aus., 3/37-39 Green Street, Banksmeadow, NSW 2019, Australia. Ph: 2 9695 7055 • Fax 2 9695 7355

Visit us online at
www.cartechbooks.com for more info!

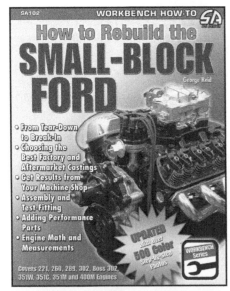

CPSIA information can be obtained at www.ICGtesting.com
Printed in the USA
LVOW020007010713

340918LV00009B/272/P